Mo

"Leigh Dundas' first book is a *tour de force*. A modern-day Joan of Arc, Leigh's masterful narration takes the reader to places most women and even men have never seen – from the back rooms of child brothels in Jihadi country ... to the board rooms of America – where she defeats tyrants who would willingly trade freedom for pecuniary gain or fictitious security. Brilliantly written, with unmatched prose and unflinching honesty, Leigh leaves us here as she does on stage: laughing, crying, rejoicing – and remembering that the fate of the planet hangs on the courage that is found within us all."

— General Michael Flynn
U.S. Army, Retired, Former Director NSA & DIA

"This book is like none other: it literally takes your breath away. I found myself laughing out loud, moved to tears, and fired up with inspiration. Human trafficking is a dark topic, and Leigh beautifully interweaves the stark realities of the children caught in these situations even as she delicately gives voice to the hope and resilience they possess. Demonstrating in clear terms how her anti-slavery work in foreign countries necessitated a 5th Generation response, Leigh details as well how those skills translated successfully into defeating unconstitutional initiatives here in America during the last 1,000 days. Equal parts humility, humor and heart-wrenching honesty, Leigh leaves the reader with the clear message that our talents and skills come second to our decision to take fearless action ... and that battles are won by those with the courage to *Just Stand Up*."

— Mel K
Host of the Mel K Show

"Leigh Dundas is on fire once again, her passion and intellect on full display in this bracing and candid narrative that reminds us all that it's never too late to take a stand for liberty – and that indeed, we must. Impossible to set down, this book is a gripping page-turner that speaks to the triumph of the human spirit ... and is a must-read for the citizens of this planet!"

— Clay Clark
Host of the Thrivetime Show
And the Re-Awaken America Tour

ISBN 978-1-933408-65-1

LBD Publishers
Anaheim, CA 92801

Telephone (323) 526-7110
Fax (323) 526-7112
www.legalbooksdistributing.com

Printed in the United States of America
April 2023

Leigh Dundas

Just Stand Up:

My Fight for Freedom

From The Brothels of Asia to the Streets of America

Author's Note

Many topics are discussed in this book, including ones relating to healthcare and federal, state and local laws. All such discussions represent solely my viewpoints. The written discussions which follow are not medical or healthcare advice, and in fact cannot constitute same, as I am not a physician. And while I am an attorney, neither do any of the discussions herein represent legal advice, nor do they constitute the formation of an attorney-client relationship with the reader.

The events in this book are all true, and based on my recollection of situations from my childhood and my professional career. In many cases, they were reconstructed from journals I kept throughout my lifetime. In all cases, they represent the best and most accurate memories I have of these time periods in my life. That said, none of us are perfect, and I apologize in advance for any inadvertent inaccuracies I may have made in the re-telling: such mistakes are solely my own.

Due to the sensitive nature of topics discussed, in certain cases I have employed pseudonyms to protect the privacy of those involved.

And a final note for any survivors of sexual abuse, sex-trafficking, child abuse – or other violence – who may be reading the words that follow. First, my apologies that you experienced what you did: *You shouldn't have.*

Second, the topics in this book may act as a trigger. Please be apprised of that fact at the outset, and give yourself the grace to go slowly, or not at all – as many chapters of this book, particularly toward the end, are devoted to my work combating the child brothel industry. Throughout, I have done my best to accurately portray both the sadness inherent in these situations, as well as the joy in seeing those who have confronted the worst things in life rise above such challenges to succeed.

Hats off to you, the incredible women and children who have survived so much. It's my honor to know you.

For you?

Are the true warriors.

For my mother, husband and child.
Collectively, you are the wind beneath my wings.
I love you bunches & oodles, to the moon & back.

And for Max and Ron.
Without whose work, my work would not be possible….
Thank you.

<u>The American Crisis</u>

These are the times that try men's souls.
The summer soldier and the sunshine patriot will, in this crisis,
shrink from the service of their country;
but he that stands by it now, deserves the love
and thanks of man and woman.

Tyranny, like hell, is not easily conquered;
yet we have this consolation with us,
that the harder the conflict,
the more glorious the triumph.

~ **Thomas Paine,**
December 19, 1776

CONTENTS

FOREWORD

In March of 2022, I stood before thousands at the San Diego Re-Awaken America Event, and asked Leigh Dundas to return to the stage to join me.

Leigh had just finished architecting four enormously powerful campaigns that had simultaneously kneecapped tyranny and helped in great measure to re-secure Freedom in our country: she engineered the Nationwide Walkout in November of 2021, and one month later took on the head of the FAA as well as the five largest domestic carriers in a quest to secure pilot safety in the wake of the vaccine mandates (which had sent the number of dangerous "in-flight" medical pilot/passenger incidents soaring). Then, in January of 2022, Leigh pursued whistleblower status for two U.S. military colonels who had discovered truly shocking information in the Department of Defense databases indicating that the rates of many diseases had skyrocketed in the months after the vaccines were mandated for service-members. And one month later, Leigh spearheaded the trans-coastal People's Convoy for Freedom.

As Leigh walked back on stage that March afternoon to the warm applause of her third standing ovation, I let the crowd know that I'd always "felt more comfortable" with her in our corner.

And then I grabbed Leigh's hand, raised it high, and told her that she was a "warrior," a "champion for this country," an "unbelievable gift from God," and nothing less than a modern-day "Joan of Arc."

My view has not changed since that day. I doubt it ever will.

And Leigh's first book is, quite simply, a *tour de force.*

As is she.

Do yourself a favor and get a copy, as I guarantee that through her passionate words, Leigh will make you believe anew that Freedom is always worth fighting for … and that – together – we can ensure that America remains the Land of the Free and the Home of the Brave.

~ General Michael Flynn
April 16, 2023

Introduction

"Mama, did she just offer to sell her child to you?"

It was 2013, and my eight-year-old daughter and I were standing in a tiny canoe in the middle of Ton Le Sap Lake, Cambodia, miles from shore. I pulled my gaze from my daughter's stricken face, as my husband gently touched my elbow, directing my attention back to the emaciated Cambodian woman and her baby who had silently rowed up next to us.

The woman looked briefly at my child, dressed head-to-toe in her favorite pink color, and then once again gestured to her baby who was standing naked at the end of her flimsy canoe, as she repeated her haunting question.

"Thousand dollar, you take?"

I heard my daughter's rapid intake of breath as she realized the answer to her own question – that indeed, this starving woman had offered to sell us her baby. It was my daughter's first glimpse into the path of slavery and impotence that entraps so many on this planet. But it was not my first brush with such topics.

Chapter 1

The year was 1975, and our family had just moved into an English Tudor-style house that had been built in 1929, in the hills above Whittier, California. My mother and I were in the kitchen when we heard a knock at the front door. Given that the house was nestled on a one acre parcel set in a little rural valley off a two-lane winding road, knocks at the front door were about as rare as solar eclipses.

We had no neighbors at all on one side of us, just a large rolling field. And on the back side of our property lay a deep ravine that could not be easily traversed, and then more steep hills leading up to a pine forest. On the other side of our house was another property that led up a different hill toward a congregational church in which my parents had been married, and which also hosted a preschool that I attended every morning. While in front of our property lay the road. A few houses were situated on the other side of the road, but the road itself was something I had never crossed, given that my parents were constantly shaking their heads in dismay at the newly-licensed teenagers who would drive way too fast around the blind corners, ending their speeding experiments in all kinds of gory car accidents.

Full of curiosity at the rather insistent knocking at our front door, my mother dried her hands on a dish towel, heading through the living room toward the other end of the house. For my part, I trailed along behind her, staring at her shoes while using her thighs as cover.

An only child with a clever imagination, who had just been thrown into living in an "old" house replete with a basement and a scary attic, I wasn't about to bet the proverbial farm on this knocking noise heralding the arrival of a friendly neighbor. For all I knew, or could dream up, we might have a ghost. But as we rounded into the tiny foyer all I saw through the glass front door was a chubby little boy with his eyes screwed up, desperately trying to see inside a darkened interior from his perch on our stoop in the blazing sun.

"Can I help you?" asked my mother, opening the heavy, lead-windowed door.

I was rather flummoxed. It was not Casper the Friendly Ghost, nor any of the other ghosts I watched on Saturday morning cartoons. And it was not a traveling salesman. It was a kid. A kid who was staring at me.

"Uh, yeah. I live in the house over there," the blond boy paused, gesturing with his left hand back up the road, "and I was wondering if you had any little boys I could play with?"

My mother laughed. "Well, not really. I do have a little girl. But she's probably a bit younger than you are. How old are you?"

"Five, I'm five," said the little boy as he held up a hand with all of his chubby fingers and thumb extended, clearly for my benefit. His blond head bounced left in an attempt to peep around my mother's thigh, which I was still using as a shield.

I raised my eyebrows in shock. Did he think I was an idiot? I knew what the number five was – and without his sign language assistance. This impromptu meeting was not off to a good start.

"Well, my child is not a boy, she's a little girl. And she's not five. She's three…" replied my mother, trailing off.

I looked up at her. Surely, she was not offering me up to this random child who thought that because I was a girl – and somewhat younger – I couldn't even count without the benefit of fingers? The kid once again leaned to the side to try and get a better look around my mother's legs, behind which I was further retreating.

My mother continued, seemingly unaware of my lack of interest in the proposition. "I'm pretty sure my daughter would like to come outside and play for a bit. How about I get you kids some crayons and coloring books, and you can sit down right over there on the front lawn and get to know each other?" my mother proffered, as she put her hand on my shoulders and guided me forward.

Now my mother is a sweet person, and all told, was a really great mom. But she had clearly never raised children possessing "y" chromosomes. And by offering up what amounted to a fine art date to a five-year-old boy – who was clearly looking to climb trees with an age peer – she had pretty much lost all interest on his part.

But not wanting to seem rude, the little boy nodded, albeit less than joyously, while my mother did her level best to disentangle my hands from their death grip on her legs. After which, she promptly marched both of us toward a shady spot on the prickly St. Augustine Grass, remaining blissfully oblivious to the fact that both of us now looked about as enthused as if we were headed toward a guillotine. Once there, she plopped us down with some broken crayons that had been living out their days in an Easter basket, which my mother had recently converted into being my "art supplies kit." (We weren't exactly wealthy – and my mom was good about re-purposing all manner of odds and ends).

Then, my mother disappeared back into the house. The year was 1975, after all.

"I'm Kevin," said the kid, as he reluctantly grabbed a crayon.

"Oh," I replied flatly.

Clearly realizing he was going to have to take the laboring oar on the conversation, he asked, "Do you have a name?"

I set my crayon down. Still quite unsure of this whole strange turn of events in my afternoon, but finally deciding I had nothing to lose by engaging, I replied, "Yeah, I'm Leigh."

He nodded once. And then we both continued coloring, most unenthusiastically, for all of about a New York second.

"Wanna do something else?" he asked.

Now I liked crayons about as much as any three-year-old little girl, but I was also nobody's fool. As an only child, I knew I had plenty of uninterrupted time to color by myself, read by myself, and play my Donny Osmond record on my new Play Skool record player… all by myself. If this unusual little boy wanted to do something more exciting, I was in.

"Yeah, let's do something else," I replied after only a moment's hesitation. Eyeballing him hard, it occurred to me that he might want to do something a bit more active. For my part, I knew I did.

"Wanna ride my Big Wheel?" I inquired.

"Heck yeah!" came the instantaneous reply.

And so began some of the best days of my childhood, growing up in the 1970's in the sleepy hills of Southern California. I forget if Kevin's parents or mine bought a second Big Wheel. All I know is that, not long after the first play date, there were soon two Big Wheels sitting side-by-side next to my garage.

Our driveway had a very steep grade down to our house, from where it branched off in the middle of a U-shaped turn on the road. And I would come home everyday after preschool to grab my red Big Wheel, watching as Kevin grabbed his matching one, after which we would run to the top of the driveway in our cowboy boots, and then fly down the hill.

Soon, Kevin and I had intentionally dismantled the blue hand brakes that one could deploy against the right rear tires – because who needed brakes?? And we'd further realized that if we didn't stop the Big Wheels where my driveway leveled off near the house, then we could proceed to make a left turn at the garage, and travel without halting to a second dirt driveway.

That dirt driveway descended down another hill toward our old barn before stopping at a steep ravine. Connecting the paved and dirt sections of the two driveways extended the length of the ride by more than double – from five seconds to about fifteen seconds – before we would dismount and run straight back up the hills to do it all over again. (Years later, when my own daughter was about three-years-old, I tried the same drill at my mother's house. Only to be shocked to discover that while, as a child, I had spent literally four hours every day running straight up very steep driveways with only 10-15 second breaks in between the sprints, the intervening decades had apparently taken a toll on my cardiac conditioning, because now even two passes running straight up the long hills had me huffing and puffing like a freight train).

After a week or so, even the wild rides down both segments of driveway had lost some of their "wow" factor. One sunny afternoon,

Kevin stood up next to his Big Wheel and gave me an inquisitive glance.

"You know, this would be a lot more fun if we had a jump. Does your dad have any wood around?"

An overripe orange dropped from the tree that overhung the driveway and rolled toward my feet. I watched its approach as I mulled over Kevin's question. I was pretty sure I'd seen some plywood from a recent barn repair on the other side of the garage.

"Yeah," I replied, "follow me. I think there's some wood over here."

Kevin took my lead, covertly sneaking with me around the garage wall to grab the wood. No discussion was needed – Kevin and I had just automatically dropped into stealth mode. We both knew my mother was pretty cool with letting us do our thing most of the time. But she also had a significant mother-hen streak that could get activated, and I wasn't sure how she would feel about us borrowing wood from my father's scrap pile to make a jump.

"This piece looks good enough – ya' got any bricks or anything like that?" Kevin whispered. Clearly, he had found what he thought we needed, and was now moving onto Part Two of his plan: figuring out how to elevate the jump.

"Umm, yeah, there's some old bricks over here, I think. And maybe a concrete block or two…." I said, as I headed over to a different pile. I proceeded to sneak some bricks back out to the driveway, where Kevin had already laid down the plywood.

"So if we prop the sheet of plywood up on the bricks, like this," Kevin noted, "and we make sure both sides are level… yeah, that looks pretty solid." Kevin paused and leaned on his creation to test its strength. "And now, Leigh, you just need to lay down on the ground, and kind of roll your body crosswise under the piece of the plywood that overhangs the brick towers supporting it, so you're tucked underneath the lip of the jump. And then I'll go up to the top of the driveway, get up some speed, and fly off the jump – and over you as well – kind of like Evil Knievel!!!"

"Wh—Whattt?? I asked in horror. Making a jump seemed kind of cool and dangerous, and I'd been totally down with the whole "building a jump" plan. But I wasn't so sure about Kevin's last phase of the plan, which appeared to involve a live human being – namely, me – hunkering down under the jump as Kevin and his Big Wheel flew over the top of me.

"I dunno…." I said, while squinting back down the driveway to make sure my mom couldn't see or hear what we were up to.

"Come on, Leigh, puh-lease??" Kevin begged.

After a few more seconds spent unsuccessfully trying to convince me to get underneath the piece of plywood overhanging the bricks, Kevin realized I was not going to budge on being the human guinea pig for his plan. Switching tactics, he suddenly proposed that I do the jump while he scooched under the wood.

This seemed to be the safer route – but I still eyeballed him suspiciously as he laid his body down crosswise, preparing to scoot underneath the lip of the jump on the asphalt driveway. My hesitation was now centered on the fact that Kevin was a bit of a chubby kid (at that point in time), and frankly, I wasn't certain he was going to fit underneath the overhanging piece of plywood. But after some concerted maneuvering, he managed to roll himself up underneath the jump, and proceeded to give me a "thumbs-up" sign.

Assuming that meant we were good to go, I grabbed my Big Wheel and high-tailed it to the top of the drive. Flipping a U-turn, I jumped aboard and began hurtling down the hill.

Unfortunately, this was at the same time that my father was returning home from work. Turning down the driveway – just in time to see me flying off the top of the jump and over my best friend who was laying under it – my father cautiously steered his car around the jump, giving us a smile and flashing his own quick "thumbs up" sign … at the same time that my mother wandered outside the house, a look of sheer horror on her face.

My mother had never been good at hiding her feelings. And one did not need to be an empath to divine that she was slightly worried to see us performing Big Wheel jumps made from stacks of wobbly bricks, a sheet of used plywood that still had some odd nails hanging off of it, and featuring live human children as extras in the act (one of whom was her only daughter). I vaguely recall her objecting somewhat loudly, only to be promptly steamrolled by my father who, in his inimitable way, just pronounced: "Let them be kids – it'll be fine…."

Generally speaking, my parents were both behaving that day true-to-type: my father was the parent always inclined to support more dangerous endeavors, and my mother invariably took the cautious route. I had learned, even by the ripe old age of three, that if I wanted to do something risky, it was best to lobby my male parent. Conversely, if I needed someone to put the kibosh on an idea because I myself was not really sold on it, then my mother was the best bet.

Most of the time, this worked well, but sometimes one of my parents would shock me by going against type.

Chapter 2

The most outstanding memory of my parents NOT playing to type was the time I decided – after watching a documentary on the Vietnam War and becoming quite enchanted with the fascinating system of tunnels the Viet Cong had made – that my bestie Kevin and I should dig a subterranean tunnel into the basement of our house.

As mentioned above, our house had been built in the earlier part of the century. And not with the drywall construction so common to newer houses, but with lath-and-plaster construction. What this meant is that when you dug a hole into a wall in our house, inside of that wall was a bunch of hard concrete sandwiched between little horizontal pieces of wood. No semi-hollow gypsum drywall in our 1929 house – nope. Instead, just a bunch of floor-to-ceiling, thick pieces of wood that were held together with concrete. Every single inch of every single wall was built like this.

As one might surmise, that kind of construction created a rock-solid house. And indeed, my childhood home proved itself to be well-built, withstanding a series of earthquakes that rocked Southern California during my childhood, and which culminated in the Whittier Quake of 1987.

During that little roller, I found myself literally heaved from my peaceful slumber and shot vertically up into the air. It was a strange feeling indeed, as one moment, I'd been peacefully slumbering in the normal horizontal position in my bed, only to find in the next moment that I'd been unceremoniously and rather violently thrown onto my feet next to myriad falling objects in my bedroom, including a desk lamp which had burst into light as it exploded by smashing onto the floor.

I should preface this little detour by noting that, just prior to the earthquake of 1987, my father had been on a bit of a religious kick, lecturing us the entire preceding week on the final verses of the Bible, and daily assuring me that if I ever woke up to "find the end of the world had come" – and that he and my mother had been "taken away by God" – that I was to "put my faith in Jesus Christ our Lord and start praying non-stop," and that then and only then I might not be "Left Behind."

Such was the backdrop to my being awakened in the early morning hours to a topsy-turvy world that felt like there was a jackhammer under my bedroom floor. Upset and frightened, I decided to frantically run through the house looking for my parents ... unfortunately, to no avail. Being a little disoriented after having been woken mid-slumber next to exploding lights, I assumed that either the planet had fallen into World War III, or it was the End Times about which my father had coincidentally been preaching all week.

Muttering feverish prayers, I flew out the side door to our house and into the backyard. I should also mention at this juncture that it had been 105-110 degrees the week prior, and that our old house had no air conditioning. So while I had started my slumber the night before clad in my usual PJs, at some point in the middle of the night – while sweating and feeling like I'd been hurled into a furnace – I had decided to shed the unnecessary clothing. Had we not been hit with a humongous earthquake the very next morning, this would not have been a problem.

But we had been hit. And here I now was, sleeping in my birthday suit which – convinced as I was that I had been Left Behind, and thus believing prayers to be more important than clothing – I had not stopped to rectify. Nor had I bothered to put on my eyeglasses.

A truly unfortunate combination, given that I was now, at age 15, stark raving naked … and streaking out the back door of my house into the yard. All the while, looking around wild-eyed in the hopes that God had not "taken all the people" while leaving only me behind.

I should also add that, normally, standing naked in my backyard would not have posed much of a problem, as our house sat on a densely wooded lot: large pine trees from earlier centuries dotted our acreage, along with a host of 100-year old avocado trees that were equally mature in stature. Most of our trees also had copious vines hanging from their branches. It was our own little forested valley, with no visible neighbors. Meaning that, on a typical day, one could have hosted a party for a dozen nudist-hippies with absolutely no problem whatsoever.

But this day was different – I just didn't know it yet.

Screaming at the top of my lungs, I stood in the back yard searching for my parents. "Mom! Dad!! Where ***ARE*** you??!"

As it turned out, my parents had not yet been taken away by their Maker. Instead, they were down by the barn, feeding the horses and other assorted animals. A fairly typical routine which, in my blind panic, I'd not stopped to consider.

Hearing my voice, my mother strolled out of the barn doors rather lackadaisically. But then – taking one incredulous look up the hill to glimpse her naked-as-a-jay-bird teenage daughter dancing around distraught in her altogether – she instantly fired back: "Leigh Combs, you GET BACK INSIDE THAT HOUSE! ***RIGHT NOW!!!"***

Quite abruptly, I quit dancing around in freak-out mode, and came to a standstill, at once relieved to find that my parents were still on this planet and that I had not been Left Behind, but simultaneously a bit confused. Only then did it begin to dawn on me that: (1) not only were we NOT in the End Times, but that (2) this was also probably NOT World War III, and that (3) this just *might* be an earthquake.

But I remained confused. Because if this was an earthquake, then why was my normally sane and cautious parent instructing me to go back inside a three-story structure that was still swaying violently from side to side?

I braved a quick look behind me to confirm the house was about to fall over. Yep, all three stories were still leaning precariously to one side – while off to my left, a giant tidal wave was coming over the edge of the swimming pool.

I promptly fired back: "Are you CRAZY, Mom?? The house is about to fall over!!"

Again came the instantaneous retort from my mother. "I said – GO BACK INSIDE – ***RIGHT NOW!!!"***

Not understanding for the life of me how my sane parent had lost her gourd, I simply yelled back: "NO!"

I could almost hear the exasperated breath leaving her lungs before she hollered back a third time, up the hill to where I was still standing, free of even a single stitch of clothing. "LEIGH COMBS, I said: GO. BACK. INSIDE. IMMEDIATELY, PLEASE!" Inhaling a quick breath, she continued: "We hired a fencing company to rebuild the horse stalls – remember??! And all the workers are down here at the barn – right now – staring at you. ***And you appear to be NAKED!!!"***

Truth be told, this little detail had completely escaped my immensely near-sighted vision. In my haste that morning, I had not only failed to take time to put any clothes on, I had also failed to retrieve my coke-bottle glasses from my nightstand before electing to streak outside the house in my altogether.

I stopped screaming and jumping around for a moment while the dawning horror spawned by my mother's words washed over me. Then, squinting my eyes nearly shut – which trick I'd found always improved my vision somewhat – I started to make out *not* just one or two male workers… but what appeared to be a small horde of about a dozen young men.

All of whom, for their part, had taken a break from their shovels. A work break which, no doubt, had first been precipitated by the unforeseen earthquake violently rolling through the Whittier Hills. But which break was now being substantially extended to take in the wholly unexpected but no doubt delightful turn of events involving the homeowner's teenage daughter streaking out of her house buck-naked while hopping frantically up and down next to the swimming pool that was about to send a tidal wave crashing over her.

Now, with the benefit of thirty-five years of reflection behind me, I'm sure it probably seemed to the workers like things were about to morph into some kind of strange real-life-meets-fiction redo of the Flash Dance scene where Jennifer Beals pulled a string and buckets of water came cascading down on the stage. That the workers weren't exactly eager to return to their allotted task of digging fence holes – and seemed instead inclined to remain glued to the next installment of whatever "the crazy naked girl might do for her next act" – is with the benefit of hindsight somewhat understandable.

While the guys probably got more than they had bargained for that Thursday morning in October of 1987, so too had I. Awakened rudely by Mother Nature, convinced we were either at war or in the End Times, only to discover too late the situation at the back of the property, I wisely chose to high-tail it back into my swaying house and ride out the rest of the earthquake hunkered down under the dining room table.

But all that was years in the future when Kevin and I decided in the late 1970's to tunnel into my mother's basement. Taking a few minutes during the warm and sunny afternoon, I elected to hat up my partner-in-crime on the Viet Cong's amazing tunnel system, and my plans to replicate them. As well, I pointed out to Kevin that – unlike the lath-and-plaster construction that beset the rest of the walls in my home – the basement was a root cellar that the previous owners had literally dug out by hand, one bucket at a time. Thus, the basement walls – unlike the regular house walls – were originally just dirt. Dirt which my mother had finally had enough of one day, and so she erected some upright posts and tacked plywood to them, after which she slathered some stucco over the top. But having helped my mother erect those walls, I also knew them to be mainly for looks and – structurally speaking – quite flimsy.

Kevin was instantly sold on the idea of digging into my basement. "So do you think," Kevin queried, as he pointed to the south wall of my home, "we should tunnel in on THIS side? It'll probably be easier because I remember you had a laundry chute on the other side. 'Member? Where we sent your Barbie dolls for a ride that one day...."

Kevin and I were a matched set when it came to our hatred of Barbie dolls. It hadn't taken us long to decide that their highest and best use was as projectiles to hurl down the laundry chute that ran from the first floor to the basement. "Barbie-Projectiles" was a favorite game for a bit, when we were not busy dismantling the Barbie's legs or arms to use as spare parts in some other action-based scheme.

(I'm frankly still kind of amazed that neither of us grew up to be serial killers: Kevin is an honest-to-goodness gainfully employed weatherman working on live TV in the Midwest these days, while I somehow made it to law school – and avoided the Ted Bundy route that most "dismantlers of Barbie Dolls" grow into being as adults).

I concurred with Kevin that our best entry point was the south end of the basement, away from the laundry chute. Nodding my assent, I added: "I don't think these plastic buckets and shovels are going to do the trick … let's go raid my Dad's shed for the post-hole diggers and some real equipment!" We snuck by the house, keeping my mother oblivious to our newest scheme. And every day thereafter, for about a week, we took turns with the post-hole diggers we had stolen from the gardening shed.

The one thing Kevin and I had in common was persistence: neither of us ever quit anything we started. And not surprisingly, given that little personality quirk we shared, we soon had a quite respectable hole dug. It was deep enough that when we jumped into it, we were well below surface level, and had now resorted to passing buckets of dirt back up the walls of the hole to the other person (because the post-hole diggers could no longer reach the bottom).

Around the time we decided that our pit was sufficiently deep to start tunneling laterally toward the house was when my mother wandered out to check on us. She didn't usually check on us when we were in "The Hole" – as we had termed our favorite dig spot. But perhaps some unique and motherly sixth-sense had caused her to leave her housework on this fine day, and come out to visit us in the un-manicured empty part of the acre that lay behind the hedgerow.

"What are you kids up to?" she called out politely as she approached.

"Uhh, just some digging," I called back, hoping she'd eyeball us from afar and retreat back to the house.

Unfortunately, she kept on coming. And as she got ever closer, her eyes got ever larger. By the time she got up to The Hole to see that it was well deeper than the height of either of us kids, her mouth started moving. Rapidly, and not so happily. "Jesus, Mary and Joseph – what on EARTH are you kids DOING???!!!" she yelled, looking briefly Heavenward after she finished, eyeballing the gaping wound in the earth that we had created with my father's best tools.

"Oh …um, well … just tunneling to the basement, mom. Kinda like the Viet Cong did during the war! And look – isn't it cool how deep our hole is?" I intoned cheerfully, jumping into the deep gash in the Earth that we had created. I was trying to play it off, but she wasn't buying any of it.

"Leigh Combs, you get out of that hole! And then: FILL. IT. IN. Quickly – before someone gets hurt!"

Kevin and I waited until she started to leave, and then made a big show of replacing my father's tools, carrying each tool slowly and somewhat theatrically back down the driveway to the tool shed. But neither of us were of a mind to fill in our awesome hole, given how much work it had taken to create it.

The next day, when Kevin and I met up at The Hole to continue our tunnel, we found that my mother had told my dad to apparently mow the lawn early that week, and to then dump the grass clippings in the hole – before there was "a collapse" that might "take out the children." For his part, this was one time where my Dad did not stay in character by rolling his eyes and saying "Let them play." Instead, he'd apparently concurred with my risk-averse mother.

While both my folks remained strangely united in their resistance to my plan to replicate the Viet Cong's tunnel system on their property, Kevin and I remained undeterred: we waited until my parents thought we had lost interest, and then stealthily resumed digging the tunnel.☺

For my part, I forged some understandings in the mid-1970's, playing with my best friend Kevin in rural southern California – which truly seemed like God's country at the time – amidst all of our crazy fort-making and tree-climbing adventures and Big Wheel races. Understandings and rules for living that, frankly, are as true today as they were then.

Firstly, while I like girls, and have many girlfriends in my posse, when it comes to hard-core playtime, it's always the boys I'm hanging with. Doesn't matter if its snow skiing, or riding my Kawasaki 650 Stand Up Jet Ski doing tricks – or hanging with former Special Forces operatives or other adrenaline junkie guys fighting the child brothel scene in third-world countries. My guy friends are my go-to crowd when I'm doing something involving risk or adrenaline. Perhaps because they rarely if ever put the brakes on things (at least, not needlessly).

The second rule I learned playing with my buddy Kevin was that imagination is key. Whatever you imagine, or dream you can build, you in fact CAN build – with enough time, and resources. So long as you persist: attitude is everything.

There were so many times as a child – when climbing trees or building forts or making tunnels or jumps – that the first try didn't work. And the second try didn't work. But this was the 1970's. And, thankfully, helicopter parents who "rescued" their children were practically unheard of. Plus, Kevin was at least as stubborn as I was.

So it was just an understood rule between us that we wouldn't stop until we "got 'er done!"

And fast-forwarding to present time, there have been many instances over the last three years of this Freedom Fight we are in where I have tried something – as I detail in later chapters – that was not successful on the first attempt. Or on the second attempt. And sometimes, it was not successful on even the third or fourth pass. But I kept going… because the neural pathways I grooved into my brain as a child taught me that most anything was possible, if one simply does not give up.

Looking back, I'm grateful to have been born in an era where parents shoo'd their kids out the door to explore and play. (Thanks, Mom!) And now, decades later, the neuroscientists are coming out of the woodwork to confirm that what our parents did in the 1970s was correct, from a learning and growth perspective.

Unstructured play, especially outdoor play, is mission critical. It's fundamentally important to socialization, to independence, to firing up the creative right halves of our brains. And not surprisingly, cultures like Norway and Sweden that let their kids engage in free-roaming play and who also allow their children to take daily naps outdoors – even in blizzard-cold conditions – create children that are more attentive, more resilient, and better able to resolve conflict than the delicate snowflake children not infrequently raised in our country in largely indoor settings, with overly abundant access to media and technology.

Indeed, one recent study shows that adding natural elements to a playground – such as grass, trees, logs and mulch – leads to more imaginative play and reduces conflicts between children, while another study found (quite logically) that running and climbing trees develops children's strength and coordination.[1] So even if you don't own a place where children can play outside, do your best to find some space, and get your children outside to play, and you too![2]

Third rule I learned: it's better to beg forgiveness than ask permission, always. 'Nuff said.

And the fourth and most important rule I learned as a child?

That adults, and many others throughout life, will tell you that you cannot do something. But they are not the arbiter of your truth, or your journey. Most importantly, though the naysayer may be an adult or a person with a college degree – or some other person who is generally deemed "knowledgeable" – these third parties are NOT the determinant of what is actually possible. You are the steward of your life, the only real judge of what is possible.

---

[1] Lee, C. (Jan. 23, 2022). *Scandinavian-Style Forest Schools Are Booming in Europe and the US– and Spreading in Asia, Too – Could Outdoor Classrooms Be The Future?* BBC – Family Tree. https://www.bbc.com/future/article/20220105-how-asia-fell-in-love-with-forest-schools. See also, Arnold, K. (Dec. 12, 2017). *What Sweden Teaches Us About Parenting and the Outdoors.* Outside. https://www.outsideonline.com/ culture/active-families/what-sweden-can-teach-us-about-outdoor-parenting/ (noting that "Scandinavian children enjoy more unstructured outdoor playtime—the average preschooler in Stockholm spends six hours outside each day in good weather and an impressive 90 minutes in winter—and a healthier balance between screen time and green time). See also, Miri, M. (Dec. 26, 2020). *Curious About Nordic Parenting? Here's What You Need to Know.* Danish Mom. https://danishmom.com/nordic-parenting/ (noting that one "'study from Finland found that babies who nap out in the cold winter air stay asleep longer than those sleeping indoors.' Again, I see this clearly with Toby, my 3-month old baby. When he sleeps outside, I have to wake him up (or else he'll sleep for 4-5 hours in a row). When he naps inside, he wakes up regularly and need his pacifier…").

[2] Bezold, C. et al. (Dec. 19, 2017). *The Association Between Natural Environments and Depressive Symptoms In Adolescents Living in the United States.* Journal of Adolescent Health. https://www.jahonline.org/article/S1054-139X(17)30505-0/fulltext (noting that surrounding "greenness, but not blue space, was associated with [11%] lower odds of high depressive symptoms in this population of more than 9,000 U.S. adolescents" and that this "association was stronger in middle school students than in high school students…"). See also, Harvard T. Chan School of Public Health, Living Near Greenery Linked With Less Depression In Teens. https://www.hsph.harvard.edu/news/hsph-in-the-news/greenery-depression-teens/. See also, Nishigaki, M. et al. (Dec. 2020). *What Types of Greenspaces Are Associated with Depression in Urban and Rural Older Adults? A Multilevel Cross-Sectional Study from JAGES,* Int J Environ Res Public Health. 2020 Dec 11;17(24):9276. doi: 10.3390/ijerph17249276. PMID: 33322467; PMCID: PMC7763952.

To quote Henry Ford: "Whether you think you can – or think you can't – you're right."
Choose wisely.

Finally, there is no better quote of which I'm aware – that summed up my existence as a free-wheeling tomboy exploring the hills in Southern California with my best buddy Kevin – than that which I discovered from Goethe when I was 12 years old. At which point, I promptly re-copied the saying in my girlish handwriting onto a blank piece of white copy paper, which I then scotch-taped to my bedroom door:

"Whatever you dream you can do, begin it. Boldness has genius, and power and magic in it."

And next to that quote, I then taped my second favorite saying (from an unknown author) that was etched onto my cherished unicorn bookmark, which to this day still encapsulates how I feel about life:

"Sometimes, things must be believed to be seen."

Believe. Not after. Believe *before.*

We must believe *now* that this country will be righted. We must believe *now* that good people will triumph. We must believe *now* that a good planet will continue to exist for our kids and our children's kids. Our beliefs are our own personal "true norths."

And with our beliefs orienting us? We will get there.

Of this, I am certain.

Chapter 3

It was Spring of 2019. I was sitting next to a duck pond in a friend's backyard, along with a small tribe of other Orange County mothers who were busily discussing Senate Bill 276. Abbreviated to the short form "SB 276," this piece of legislation would largely eradicate the ability of a medical doctor to exempt a child harmed by a vaccine from future doses of that vaccine for purposes of enrollment in school. Created by Senator Richard Pan in California, the bill was being pushed – hard – by Pharma during the legislative process, which was creating much concern among parents whose children had been harmed by a vaccine and who still wanted their children to be able to attend school (without the fear of having to inoculate their child with a substance that had already created an allergic reaction on the first pass).

For my part, I just perched quietly on my chair. It was a gorgeous day, and as I listened to the birds chirping in the trees, I kept one ear on these parent's stories.

"When my son was born, my husband had concerns about the vaccine. And while I knew nothing about them, my 'mother's intuition' was also raising a tiny alarm. And then, well, you know, I overrode my instincts and my husband's concerns. We listened to my doctor – and got my son his first set of shots. He promptly went into anaphylactic shock. My son nearly died that day…"

Looking up at the sky, I tried unsuccessfully to stop the tears I felt building. Dabbing at my mascara, I heard the next woman start to speak.

"I actually have 3 vaccine injured kids...." the woman began.

My gaze whipped over to her. Did she just say she had *three* injured kids? I tried and failed to conceive of how that was even possible. I didn't have to wait long, as she continued her explanation.

"My first son had bad reactions to them, but I didn't really connect the reactions to the vaccines. To be honest, I wasn't really focused on my son, since my husband had just been diagnosed with cancer and we were centered on trying to keep him alive. Then, I had my second child, and of course, got him vaccinated. He also had bad reactions to the vaccines: he ended up with a really high temperature, and then was constantly sick afterwards. But again – and I hate to say it – I wasn't really focused on my kids at that point. My husband was still quite ill, and all my efforts were still focused on his care. Plus, my husband's brother was a well known physician at a hospital in another state, and every time we talked to him, he just kept telling us that our kids' adverse reactions were normal. And of course, we believed him – he was the doctor."

She paused, taking a breath as a late-arriving mom sat down. We all shifted our chairs around to make room for the newcomer. As the new mother's child ran off to join the pack of other kids that were feeding ducks, the mother with three vaccine-injured children once again picked up the thread of her story.

"But then my husband, who was still sick with cancer and had just had major surgery – and who was obviously still immuno-compromised – had a nurse start trying to force a flu vaccine on him while he was still in the hospital recovering. I was totally pro-vaccine at the time, as was my husband who worked as an attorney for a large law firm. But this nurse was just really pushy, even though vaccines were clearly contra-indicated for people with active cancer who were on chemo. So that was the first time my husband and I began to feel some hesitation on the subject: when the medical establishment was pushing vaccines – ***despite*** the manufacturer's contraindications – on a patient with active cancer who was clearly NOT supposed to be getting them."

I looked at this woman shrewdly. She was a journalist, trained to dig out truth, and her husband was no different than me in terms of vocation. The lack of understanding I'd had when she first announced that she had three injured children began to recede, and in its place, I felt a dawning empathy for her situation begin to build. I picked up a carrot from a veggie dish on a nearby end table, taking a quiet bite as she concluded her story.

"It wasn't until my daughter was born, and vaccinated – and suffered such a severe reaction that she would have periods of sleep apnea where she would stop breathing – that I started to learn what was actually in the vaccines, and realize the extent of my children's reactions and the harm. My daughter could literally never be left alone, because she would just stop breathing, randomly and without warning. It was a really difficult time, but I guess it was what needed to happen for my husband and I to start putting things together...."

The sun moved lower in the sky while little birds continued to peck energetically at the grass, as mother after mother shared her child's story that day. I continued to do my best to just listen.

Reflecting on the women's stories, I could not actually say that I was surprised to hear that their children had been harmed by pharmaceutical companies, given my earlier chosen profession. By 2019, I had been a practicing lawyer in the State of California for a quarter century, and I had begun my career representing Fortune 500 companies. Through sheer dumb luck and office geography, during my first year in the law firm, the partners had placed my office immediately adjacent to our firm's only practicing environmental lawyer.

As a result, whenever this environmental attorney would go to get coffee from the kitchen in the morning, my door was the first door he passed. My door was also the first door he passed *en route* to the restroom, or when he would grab his briefcase and make for the elevators each night.

And as any lawyer in any large law firm can attest, the primary expedient by which a young attorney fills their workload is through senior attorneys passing junior attorneys' offices – and being suddenly struck by inspiration that there are other "new attorneys" who can help them complete their work. At which point, with no further adieu, said senior attorneys normally knock on the new lawyer's door, and proceed to drop off all manner of work they need done. (And when I say "all manner of work" I truly mean "all manner" – I once had a senior partner swing into my office, mentioning that he'd agreed to write a book but had then "forgotten about it," and assigned me to write the chapters… all of one week before the book was due to the publisher).

So being located right next to the one environmental attorney in my office was a virtual guarantee that I was going to be gifted some environmental law cases. And here's the thing: had I actually wanted to do environmental law work, being in such close physical proximity to the office's only such lawyer would've been a godsend. Unfortunately for me, I did ***not*** want to entertain such work: generally speaking, I rather hate math and science, both of which are assumed to be prerequisites for that kind of a specialized career. (Indeed, I'd completed my one college science requirement by banging out an Oceanography 101 class … and promptly proceeded to never take another science class again).

So for an attorney whose science midterm in college involved petting dolphins, being placed next door to Mr. Environmental Law Partner was *not* a particularly auspicious start to my legal career. That said, I'd been at the firm long enough to know that I should keep my mouth shut. And as a result, I was hit with a small tsunami of environmental law cases in my early years of practice. Worse, because we were a big firm, we did not represent clients who were trying to save the planet like Greenpeace – those non-profits regrettably did not have the funds to hire top-flight law firms.

Rather, our firm represented the chemical companies that were polluting the planet. And this unfortunate reality resulted in a rather inglorious period of years where I attempted to expiate my guilt over representing people and companies who were literally killing the planet by going home from work each night to write "hug-a-tree, save-a-whale" type poems in an attempt to mollify my conscience.

Three decades hence, I'm still not thrilled that I spent a portion of my career representing corporate polluters. But I have also learned that things typically happen for a reason, and that God has a plan.

And in this instance, while for many years I'd remained upset at having represented companies that were harming our planet, over the last three years in particular the "inside knowledge" I gained as to how such companies operate has proven amazingly helpful. Unlike many folks, who remained open-minded at the beginning of the COVID narrative to the possibility that the pharmaceutical companies were actually trying to assist the planet with the perceived crisis, I harbored no such illusions. My years spent as legal counsel to chemical manufacturers had taught me that these companies are rarely if ever doing God's work: rather, they are committed to making a profit from humans, safety studies be-darned.

And, over the decades, I'd also done a fair bit of my own side research into the crimes such companies had perpetrated. Starting with Rachel Carson's stark recap of pesticides in Silent Spring which I'd first encountered in college, I continued over the years to absorb similar works when time permitted.

Thus, thirty years of research later – and by the time COVID came on the scene – I possessed a decent working knowledge of Thalidomide,[3] DES,[4] DDT,[5] Agent Orange and Operation Ranch Hand,[6] the Radium Girls' nightmare,[7] and a host of pharmaceutical horror stories like Vioxx.[8]

---

[3] Thalidomide was a drug used to treat nausea in pregnant women in the 1950's and 1960's, which ended up creating horrible birth defects in the offspring (missing limbs and shrunken appendages). See Kim J. et al. (2011). *Thalidomide: The Tragedy Of Birth Defects And The Effective Treatment Of Disease.* Toxicol Sci. 2011 Jul;122(1):1-6. doi: 10.1093/toxsci/kfr088. Epub 2011 Apr 19. Erratum in: Toxicol Sci. 2012 Feb;125(2):613. PMID: 21507989.

[4] DES stands for a drug named Diethylstilbestrol, which was an endocrine-disrupting chemical prescribed to pregnant women for decades. DES was subsequently discovered to cause cancers of the genital tract and breast, neurodevelopmental alterations, problems associated with socio-sexual behavior, and immune, pancreatic and cardiovascular disorders in not just the pregnant women, but also their children and even grandchildren. Zamora-León P. (2021). *Are the Effects of DES Over? A Tragic Lesson from the Past.* Int J Environ Res Public Health. 2021 Sep 30;18(19):10309. doi: 10.3390/ijerph181910309. PMID: 34639609; PMCID: PMC8507770.

[5] Another endocrine disrupting chemical, DDT – short for Dichloro-diphenyl-trichloroethane – was used as a pesticide from the 1950's until the 1970's, with Madison Avenue marketers declaring in their ads that "DDT is good for me!" and urging pregnant mothers to use wallpaper soaked in DDT pesticides for their newborn children's nurseries. Unfortunately, DDT turned out to be carcinogenic, and a biologist by the name of Rachel Carson wrote a detailed and frightening book in the early '60's named Silent Spring which I highly recommend. Carson, R. et al. (1962). *Silent Spring.* Houghton-Mifflin. See also, Arnold, C. (July 1, 2021). *Consequences of DDT Exposure Could Last Generations.* Scientific American. https://www.scientificamerican.com/article/consequences-of-ddt-exposure-could-last-generations/.

[6] Agent Orange was a chemical defoliant used during the Vietnam War to lay bare the jungles and enable combat, but unfortunately was subsequently determined to be a carcinogen that created severe birth defects, cancer, miscarriages and skin diseases, affecting millions of US military service members and the Vietnamese, as well as their children. History Channel. (Sept. 20, 2017). *What Is Agent Orange?* https://www.youtube.com/watch?v=uJaJbq9aRFI

The trajectory was always the same: products with shoddy or non-existent safety studies would be released with great fanfare onto the unsuspecting masses – and welcomed into society through clever Madison Avenue advertising – only to be pulled from the market months or years later due to the "discovery" that the drug or chemical in question was carcinogenic, neuro-toxic, or otherwise exceedingly harmful to people's health.[9] So it was with an open mind – and a very clear understanding that Pharma was not exactly the planet's savior – that I approached these mothers' stories on a sunny spring day in 2019.

And these women were obviously not crazy people. They were, almost exclusively, professionals like me: journalists, lawyers, physicians, teachers, business owners (and shockingly, even former pharmaceutical company employees). But to a person, they had children who had suffered extreme adverse events, post-vaccination.

After driving home from the meeting, I went online and looked up the package inserts for the childhood vaccines. These inserts are the legal disclaimers which every company is required to put on a product, warning the would-be consumer of the potential side

---

[7] Radium was used in the 1920's by female factory workers to make watch hands glow, and the girls would lick the paint brushes bearing radium to keep the tip pointed while painting the hands of the watch. Unfortunately, radium is carcinogenic, and many of these girls died a horrible death from cancers involving the face, jaw and mouth (as well as other body parts). See Moore, K. (2017). *The Radium Girls: The Dark Story of America's Shining Women*. Highbridge Publishing.

[8] Vioxx was a painkiller released by Merck, and recalled in 2004 due to a 4 and 5-fold increase in cardiovascular and other adverse events. See a book written by Tom Nesi entitled *Poison Pills: The Untold Story of the Vioxx Drug Scandal* (Nesi. T. (2008) Thomas Dunne Books. And see also, a journal entry of the same name: Solomon, D. (March 2, 2009). *Poison Pills: The Untold Story Of The Vioxx Drug Scandal.* J Clin Invest. 2009;119(3):427-427. https://doi.org/10.1172/JCI38430.

[9] For a further verbal explanation of these incidents, as well as photographs of some of these products and their impacts, see my Rochester New York Clay Clark Re-Awaken Speech from August 13, 2022: https://rumble.com/v2hmapa-leigh-dundas-at-re-awaken-tour-in-rochester-new-york-august-13-2022.html.

effects. Not surprisingly, every one of the reactions of these mother's babies was listed.

Every. Single. One.

I can't say I was surprised to find this out. Dismayed, yes, but surprised? Not really.

Then, as luck would have it, I met Joshua Coleman. A concerned father living in my state, Joshua's son had suffered spinal cord swelling and been rendered a permanent paraplegic after his DTAP shot.[10] Spinal cord swelling and paraplegia/quadriplegia are known side effects of this triple-dose vaccine.[11] Joshua's son was one of the ones who would not qualify under the version of the bill being considered by our legislature – despite his horrific injury.

And why, when it came to folks like the Colemans, was California attempting to demonize the parents of these injured children? In 2015, California had passed Senator Pan's first bill on the subject of

---

[10] DTAP stands for the Diptheria, Tetanus, Pertussis vaccine, and carries a known side effect of vaccine-induced transverse myelitis, which is the fancy name for swelling of the spinal cord. A public Facebook entry posted by Robert Kennedy, Jr., on April 15, 2019, noted that Otto Coleman is a "courageous and charismatic 10-year-old wheelchair bound by vaccine induced transverse myelitis. Neither he nor his 6-year-old brother, Fenton, will be eligible for medical exemptions under the narrow definitions in California State Senator Pan's draconian new law. Vaccines took Otto's legs and now Senator Pan is trying to strip him of his constitutional right to an education and relegate him to second class citizenship. SB 276 will bar Otto and Fenton from attending both public and private school and daycare. Pan will also replace Otto's doctor with faceless bureaucrats who will dictate risky medical interventions for Otto — and other medically fragile children — from Sacramento without having ever met or examined him. Dr. Pan is Otto's senator…."

[11] Transverse myelitis is a neurological condition created when the insulation barrier around the nerve cells called myelin begins to break down, which can lead to spinal cord swelling, and result in paralysis. "Transverse myelitis has been associated with many different vaccines commonly administered to adults, infants, and children. Many people who experience this neurological vaccine injury received flu, measles-mumps-rubella (MMR), tetanus-diphtheria-pertussis (TDaP), or Hepatitis B vaccinations." Shannon Law Group. (Jun 28, 2017). *Vaccines Can Cause Transverse Myelitis. https://shannonlawgroup.com/vaccinations-can-cause-symptoms-of-transverse-myelitis/*

vaccines, eradicating the ability of parents to opt their children out of vaccination based on that family's religious or personal beliefs. I had been working overseas in the months leading up to the passage of that bill, fighting the child brothel trade, and watched from afar as that bill passed our state Legislature and was signed into law. I remembered being horrified that it had passed seemingly so easily, particularly given that many religions are against certain kinds of medical injections, interventions or drugs – including Christian Scientists, Jehovah's Witnesses, Seventh Day Adventists, and members of various Jewish sects. I had friends in each of these religions – and all of them could point to scriptural beliefs centered on *not* allowing the body to be contaminated with certain agents the religion believed to be unholy.

It was also not exactly a secret that an overwhelming number of Christian churches were against abortion. Given that many of the vaccines used aborted fetal tissue in their cultivation process, the fact that so many devout Christians were also opposed to vaccination did not surprise me.[12] And as an attorney raised in part by grandparents who fled communism – and who believed our Constitution was second only to the Bible – I had a firm attachment to our First Amendment and its promise that as Americans we could practice a religion of our choosing.

So the passage in California of Senate Bill 277 in 2015 had been nothing short of shocking to me – that a state like California was taking the bold step of entirely eroding millions of parents' rights to opt their children out of inoculations on religious grounds.

---

[12] The Hepatitis vaccine is cultivated in "human fibroblasts" from "aborted fetal tissue." Miller, N. Z. (2005). Vaccines: Are They Really Safe and Effective? New Atlantean Press, p. 64 (citing CDC, (1999, Oct. 1), Prevention of Hepatitis A Through Active Or Passive Immunization: Recommendations Of The Advisory Committee On Immunization Practices (ACIP), MMWR Weekly 48 (RR-7); 13-20, and further citing Winkler, D. Hepatitis A Facts. Concerned Parents for Vaccine Safety, www.access1.net/via/vaccine/hepafacts.htm.).

It was simply, to my mind, unconstitutional. And yet that had not stopped my governor from signing SB 277 into law.

Four years later, and after Senator Pan had promised on the record during the earlier legislative hearings in 2015 that his bill would only eradicate *religious* exemptions to vaccination – and that he would *not* return to later eradicate the rights of parents and doctors of vaccine-injured kids to *medically* exempt their injured children – now this senator was revealing his true colors. It would seem that Senator Pan had just flatly lied to the almost forty million people in my state during the earlier bill's legislative hearings, because he could now be found trouncing through California drumming up support for his new Senate Bill – SB 276 – that was set to do the exact thing he'd earlier promised he would ***not*** do: strip California doctors and parents of their right to medically exempt children previously harmed by their vaccinations from future doses of those inoculations.

To put it politely, I was pretty certain that Pan had lost his darned mind on the earlier 2015 bill, but now I was certain. (Actually, I knew how the game worked: I believed then and continue to believe now (though I've not confirmed my hypothesis) that the pharmaceutical industry found some very compelling reasons or promises – be they monetary, political or otherwise – to cause Pan to want to push their agenda).

The problem with the whole scene is that Senator Pan is a doctor, as well as being a politician. He'd taken an oath to "first, do no harm." He'd gone to medical school. He'd treated patients. And Pan knew – as any practicing physician does – that in medicine "one size" does not "fit all."

And on that note, and as an attorney who has represented physicians at various times throughout the years, I can attest that it is a basic concept that when a doctor gives a person a substance – and that patient proceeds to have an allergic reaction to said substance – the doctor does NOT typically then continue to give the patient successive doses of the same agent that just caused the patient harm. Simple common sense is in accord: if your doctor gives your baby a shot of penicillin, and your child then proceeds to suffer an anaphylactic reaction, trust me when I tell you that said doctor will NEVER recommend – let alone give – a second penicillin shot to that baby, lest they kill him or her.

And were the doctor to do so, it would be straight-up malpractice. Just imagine the subsequent conversation in the attorney's office – if the doctor were idiotic enough to do the above:

"So let me get this straight, Doc. You injected little Johnny with a shot of penicillin to cure his ear infection. And then he threw an anaphylactic reaction, and his throat swelled shut. And he stopped breathing and nearly died. But luckily you managed to recover him and bring him back from the brink. So now, two months after that last episode, the parents bring little Johnny back to you for *another* ear infection. And knowing full well that Little Johnny almost died the first time you administered penicillin, notwithstanding that fact you chose to hit him with a ***second*** shot of penicillin… after which he had a ***second*** allergic reaction …. ***and then died??***"

No attorney or malpractice insurance agent in their right mind would ever want to see such a conversation or cross-examination take place. And because of that – and frankly, because most physicians are not raving idiots – typically doctors do NOT give patients second shots of things the patient already had an allergic reaction to. Not unless the doctor is looking to lose his license to practice.

But, in my state, in the Spring of 2019, such inanity is exactly where we were headed with Senator Pan's new piece of legislation: if your child were to be injured by a vaccine, your doctor would no longer be able to write a note exempting your child from future shots of the inoculation which had already harmed him (unless your child had suffered a certain type of reaction). Instead, you and your doctor would have to administer a second dose to Little Johnny – and risk Johnny experiencing a serious injury or fatal reaction – assuming Little Johnny wanted to keep exercising his constitutionally-protected right to attend school.

It's hard to fathom that such is the precipice at which we'd arrived in Commie-Fornia in the Spring of 2019. But that is in fact where we stood. And there were very few exceptions listed in Senator Pan's bill. Indeed, pretty much the only exceptions were if your child had suffered anaphylaxis or encephalopathy (brain swelling). Then, your child might have a shot at obtaining a medical exemption from future doses of the inoculation which had caused him to suffer brain swelling or anaphylaxis in the first instance (although your child might not need such an exemption, given that such vaccine-induced side effects can lead to fatalities or other severe effects that are incompatible with future on-campus academic pursuits).

But for those children that had suffered one of the myriad known side effects of the vaccines that was ***not*** anaphylaxis or brain swelling – but was nonetheless still a ***very severe reaction?*** Under the new bill, that child would no longer have his physician in a position from which that physician could exercise his medical judgment to exempt the child from future shots.

So for instance, if your child went blind after the shot? Despite that being a listed side effect of many of the vaccines, according to Senator Pan's bill, such a reaction was not on the short list of anaphylaxis or encephalopathy – and thus a parent would have to risk injecting their child with a second dose of the agent that had already blinded their child (assuming they wanted to keep the kid in school).

Or perhaps your child was paralyzed by an allergic reaction involving spinal cord swelling after receiving the DTAP vaccine – like Joshua Coleman's son – and was now confined to a wheelchair for the rest of his life? You guessed it: courtesy of Senator Pan's SB 276 bill, paraplegia – although a pretty severe reaction in my humble opinion – was not one of the two recognized exceptions (like brain swelling or anaphylaxis), and thus a physician could not really use the resulting paraplegia reaction to form the basis of a medical exemption. Instead, the paralyzed child would need to undergo another dose of the same agent that had ***already paralyzed him*** if he wished to keep going to school.

To say such a set-up was problematic was an understatement. There is a reason that doctors are supposed to be the ultimate arbiters of what is good for a patient's health: they and they alone possess the schooling, the training, and the experience to make such judgments … ***after*** they have done a thorough medical exam on the patient. Pharmaceutical companies and politicians do not have any of the requisite tools to make such judgments for patient's health – nor can they be held accountable if they do a bad job. And the State of California, ironically, recognizes that corporations and entities should not be allowed to practice medicine, and further prohibits what it considers to be the "corporate practice of medicine" under various laws. Meaning only living breathing doctors can make medical judgments for patient's courses of care: not corporations or governments.[13]

[13] The California Corporate Practice of Medicine prohibition, as it is known, is derived from two sections in the Medical Practice Act, Business and Professions Code Section 2052 (requiring a medical license to practice medicine), and Section 2400 (declaring that corporations have no professional rights, privileges, or powers). To learn more, visit the California Medical Board webpage found here: https://www.mbc.ca.gov/Licensing/Physicians-and-Surgeons/Practice-

Of course, Pharma and the legislators did not appear to be giving thought to such things when they were considering passing SB 276 into law.

Information/#:~:text=BPC%2C%20section%202400%2C%20states%2C,influencing%2C%20the%20physician's%20professional%20judgment

Chapter 4

As a veteran environmental attorney, to say that I remained askance at the proposed legislation would be an understatement. And, having represented many manufacturing companies that were not dissimilar to pharmaceutical giants, I well knew the gnarly types of chemicals that could be added to their proprietary concoctions and inoculations (and which could foreseeably cause some children to experience allergic reactions or side effects).

Many people have heard that mercury is in the vaccines, and they've heard right. Mercury, by the way, is what made the mad hatter mad.[14] It's one of the most severely neuro-toxifying chemicals known to man. In children, it can damage intelligence, learning ability, language and motor skills, and can even cause permanent brain damage – while in adults, mercury can cause central nervous system damage, as well as cardiac, immune and reproductive issues (which issues are often heralded by symptoms including tremors, memory loss, and fatigue).[15] As noted by Dr. Philip J. Landrigan, professor of pediatrics and director of the Environmental and

[14] Hat-makers used mercury in their processes because mercuric nitrate was known to toughen animal fibers, which would allow the animal fibers to "matt together" to make a more firm hat. The hatters' inhalation of mercury vapors went on, over time, to cause many to develop symptoms of chronic mercury poisoning (including psychosis, excitability, and tremors), which led to the moniker "mad as a hatter." Mercury was used in hat making until 1941 in the United States. CDC. (Mar 4, 2010). *NIOSH Backgrounder: Alice's Mad Hatter & Work Related Illness,* https://www.cdc.gov/niosh/updates/upd-03-04-10.html#:~:text=This%20presumably%20reflects%20the%20character's,a%20process%20called%20%E2%80%9Ccarroting.%E2%80%9D. See also Healthline. (May 19, 2021). *What is Mad Hatter Disease (Erethism)?* https://www.healthline.com/health/mad-hatter-disease#in-history.

[15] Kay, J. (Nov. 23, 2003). *Toxic Fish Alert – Survey Finds Mercury in 4 Species At Markets in Bay Area. SF Gate.* https://www.sfgate.com/health/article/TOXIC-FISH-ALERT-Survey-finds-mercury-in-4-2511346.php.

Occupational Medicine Division at the Mount Sinai School of Medicine:

> Mercury is a big public health concern that has not yet received the attention that it deserves.[16]

Ironically, and notwithstanding all the foregoing, for many years, ethyl-mercury was added to childhood vaccines. And, in fact, is today still added to certain vaccines as a preservative. According to the FDA's website as of February 2023 (emphasis mine):

> Thimerosal, ***which is approximately 50% mercury by weight,*** has been one of the most widely used preservatives in vaccines.... Depending on the vaccine formulations used and the weight of the infant, some infants could have been exposed to cumulative levels of mercury during the first six months of life that exceeded Environmental Protection Agency (EPA) recommended guidelines for safe intake....[17]

Less widely known is the fact that, in addition to being added to certain vaccines, mercury is also added to silver dental fillings. Indeed, most people's "silver fillings" – despite the misleading moniker – are not actually made of silver at all, but rather a mercury amalgam. As the LA Times noted some twenty years ago:

> Amalgam fillings are made up of 50% mercury, a neurotoxin and hazardous waste. Each filling has as much mercury as a fever thermometer....[18]

---

[16] Id.

[17] FDA. (2018, Feb 1). *Thimerosal and Vaccines*, https://www.fda.gov/vaccines-blood-biologics/safety-availability-biologics/thimerosal-and-vaccines.

[18] L.A. Times (Oct. 28, 2003). *Dental Offices Cited as a Source of Bay's Mercury.* https://www.latimes.com/archives/la-xpm-2003-oct-28-me-sbriefs28.2-story.html

Unfortunately, mercury is a rather soft metal, and it tends to release tiny bits of itself into people's saliva when they chew.[19] Then, after the tiny particles of mercury are liberated, they float around in folks' bodies, and get ported off into our bones and organs, and worst of all, our brains.

Those who guffaw at the notion that their little "silver fillings" could be remotely toxic might want to research the following.

Just after the turn of the most recent century, the San Francisco Bay was found to be mercury toxic – and according to the San Francisco Environmental Commission, dental amalgam disposal was responsible for 65% of the mercury contamination in San Francisco Bay.[20] The city's environmental services department did testing, and further confirmed that the "largest controllable source of mercury entering the San Jose/Santa Clara Water Pollution Control Plant" was a result of "amalgam fillings from dental offices."[21]

---

[19] Both Poison Control and the FDA agree that individuals with dental amalgam fillings have "measurable amounts of mercury in their blood and urine" because the "mercury from the filling evaporates, is inhaled, and then absorbed into the blood stream" and further because "increased, but still small, amounts of mercury are released when people grind their teeth or chew…." See Soloway, R. *Do Fillings Cause Mercury Poisoning?* https://www.poison.org/articles/do-fillings-cause-mercury-poisoning. See also U.S. Food and Drug Administration. (Sept. 24, 2020). *Information for Patients About Dental Amalgam Fillings.* https://www.fda.gov/medical-devices/dental-amalgam-fillings/information-patients-about-dental-amalgam-fillings#:~:text=Dental%20amalgam%20fillings%20may%20release,tooth%20grinding%20and%20gum%20chewing

[20] *From Mad Hatters to Dental Amalgams: Heavy Metals, Toxicity and Testing.* (2014). The Free Library. (Retrieved Apr 10, 2023). https://www.thefreelibrary.com/From+mad+hatters+to+dental+amalgams%3a+heavy+metals%3a+toxicity+ and...-a0173519166 From Mad Hatters to Dental Amalgams: Heavy Metals, Toxicity and Testing (citing San Francisco Public Utilities Commission Website. (2003, Sept. 2). http://sfwater.org/detail.cfm/MC_ID/14/MSC_ID/118/MTO_ID/22/C_ID/1620.

[21] Woolfolk, J. (Sept. 5, 2008). *San Jose Requires Dentists to Keep Mercury-Alloy From Fillings Out of Bay.* The Mercury News. https://www.mercurynews.com/%202008/09/05/20san-jose-requires-dentists-to-keep-mercury-alloy-from-fillings-out-of-bay/

After this charming discovery, various regulatory agencies ordered nearby dentists to stop letting their patients spit their mercury-toxic saliva into the spittoons that drained into the Bay, and to instead install "amalgam separators" in their offices that would hopefully remove the vast majority of mercury-toxic substances prior to the waste hitting the bay.

The dentists, of course, maintained they were not to blame – as the San Jose Mercury News noted in the opening paragraph of its article on the topic (see FN 21 citation):

> Dentists insist the silvery amalgam fillings they have used for generations to plug holes in teeth are perfectly safe, but state authorities fear they may be polluting San Francisco Bay with toxic mercury.

While dentists like Kathleen Cooper, executive director of the local dental society, continued to hew to the notion that they did "not believe that amalgam from our dental offices is causing any type of mercury problems," the environmental agencies meant business – and threatened to "fine any dentists who failed to comply with their new rules as being in violation of hazardous waste laws."[22] Accordingly, and despite their lack of willingness, the dentists complied with the directive, installing the amalgam separators which then captured the mercury which the EPA considered to be a "hazardous waste" due to the "mercury and silver content of the amalgam."[23]

---

[22] Id.

[23] US E.P.A., Office of Water. *FAQ on the Dental Office Category Rule* (Nov. 2017). https://www.epa.gov/sites/default/files/2017-12/documents/dental-office-category_frequent-questions_nov-2017.pdf

And lo and behold, the mercury pollution levels in the San Francisco Bay proceeded to drop by a jaw-dropping 75% – after which the EPA decided to attempt to promulgate the same rule for dental offices nationwide:

> Bay Area communities already require dentists to use amalgam capture devices and have seen their mercury pollution levels drop nearly 75 percent. Now the rest of California and the nation will see these same benefits [due to this] … proposed rule [which] would cut mercury and toxic metal discharges to public wastewater systems by at least 8.8 tons a year nationwide.[24]

Put simply, mercury is not your friend: whether it is located in the fillings in your mouth, or your broken thermometer, or your vaccine, or your nearby lake. And new studies are now attesting to the fact that the development of neurodegenerative diseases like Alzheimer's are often affected by mercury toxicity and how lucky a person was – or was not – in the gene distribution lottery.

To wit, certain genes have been discovered to either increase or decrease the likelihood of developing dementia, specifically, the apolipoprotein E gene (hereafter, referred to as "APOE gene"). As a backdrop for the conversation that follows: one can have various

---

[24] *U.S. EPA Proposes to Eliminate Mercury Pollution from Dentist Offices Nationwide.* (Sept. 26, 2014). Lake County News. https://www.lakeconews.com/index.php?option=com_content&view=article&id=38545:us-epa-proposes-to-eliminate-mercury-pollution-from-dentist-offices-nationwide&catid=1:latest&Itemid=197 (quoting Jared Blumenfeld, EPA's regional administrator for the Pacific Southwest). For more information, a review of the Mercury Source Analysis that was prepared for San Francisco Public Utilities Commission in 2004 would be indicated, which review estimated that nearly half the mercury pollution in the Bay was coming from dental offices without amalgam separator units (which units work to decrease the discharge of mercury into the environment). Barron, T. (2005, July 30). *Mercury Source Analysis for 2004 (Prepared For San Francisco PUC),* See also, US Environmental Protection Agency. (2014, Sept. 14). See also, *U.S. EPA Proposes to Eliminate Mercury Pollution from Dentist Offices Nationwide, https://www.epa.gov/archive/epapages/newsroom_20archive/news%20releases/ad0a21871142e70285257d5e006f3b83.html.*

arrangements of either the APOE2, APOE3 or APOE4 gene. The good news is that the most common expression of the gene is APOE3 – and this is not believed to affect Alzheimer's risk one way or the other. [25] And for the lucky few of us – approximately five to ten percent – who possess the APOE2 gene, having even one copy of this gene is believed to ***reduce*** Alzheimer's risk by up to 40% … or minimally stave off onset of dementia until later in life.[26]

The problem is seen with the folks who carry the APOE4 gene. The APOE4 gene has been directly linked to Alzheimer's. And an estimated 25% of the population – or one in four people – are believed to carry at least one copy of that gene (while 2-3% of the population unfortunately carries two such copies of the APOE4 gene). Possessing one copy of the dreaded APOE4 gene increases risk of Alzheimer's by 2-3 times (especially if you are female), while having two copies of the unlucky gene increases the risk by 12%.[27] On a related note, mutations in amyloid precursor protein and

---

[25] National Institute of Health, National Institute on Aging, Alzheimer's Disease Genetics Fact Sheet (March 1, 2023), https://www.nia.nih.gov/health/alzheimers-disease-genetics-fact-sheet#:~:text=APOE%20%CE%B53%2C%20the%20most%20common,disease%20onset%20in%20certain%20populations (noting that "APOE3, the most common allele, is believed to have a neutral effect on the disease — neither decreasing nor increasing risk of Alzheimer's").

[26] Wu L. et al. (2016). *Apoe2 And Alzheimer's Disease: Time To Take A Closer Look.* Neural Regen Res. 2016 Mar;11(3):412-3. doi: 10.4103/1673-5374.179044. PMID: 27127474; PMCID: PMC4829000 (noting that it "is estimated that individuals who carry two ApoE2 alleles or one ApoE2 allele and one ApoE3 allele are 40% less likely to develop AD than those who carry two ApoE3 alleles…."); National Institute of Health, National Institute on Aging, Alzheimer's Disease Genetics Fact Sheet (March 1, 2023), https://www.nia.nih.gov/health/alzheimers-disease-genetics-fact-sheet#:~:text=APOE%20%CE%B53%2C%20the%20most%20common,disease%20onset%20in%20certain%20populations (noting "APOE ε2 may provide some protection against the disease" and that if "Alzheimer's occurs in a person with this allele, it usually develops later in life than it would in someone with the APOE ε4 gene….").

[27] Dacks, P. (Nov. 16, 2016). *What APOE Means For Your Health.* Cognitive Vitality. https://www.alzdiscovery.org/cognitive-vitality/blog/what-apoe-means-for-your-health#:~:text=APOE3%20is%20the%20most%20common,lowers%20the%20age%20of%20onset.

presenilin 1 genes are associated not just with Alzheimer's Disease, but with early onset Alzheimer's.[28]

With all that said – and now that we all know APOE4 genes are NOT the genes we want to have – even more bad news follows for the APOE4 crowd: studies have shown that exposure to mercury "produces more severe outcomes in people with the APOE-4 gene…."[29] Moreover, researchers believe that the "interaction between genetic predisposition and environmental factors may cause cognitive decline to become even more serious and accelerated" in those possessing the APOE4 gene:

> [M]ethyl mercury (MeHg) have all been found to act as toxins that can interrupt cognitive function, induce neurological problems, and accelerate the risk of A[lzheimer's D[isease]….[30]

Echoing the above findings is another study that found that mercury exposure was associated with numerous Central Nervous System "disorders that frequently trigger Alzheimer's disease (AD)…."[31] And for those who believe their family history predisposes them to

---

[28] Campion D, et al. (Sep 1999). *Early-Onset Autosomal Dominant Alzheimer Disease: Prevalence, Genetic Heterogeneity, and Mutation Spectrum.* Am J Hum Genet. 1999 Sep;65(3):664-70. doi: 10.1086/302553. PMID: 10441572; PMCID: PMC1377972 (noting that these "results show that PSEN1 and APP mutations account for 71% of ADEOAD families….").

[29] Berntsson E, et al. (Aug. 12, 2022). *Mercury Ion Binding to Apolipoprotein E Variants ApoE2, ApoE3, and ApoE4: Similar Binding Affinities but Different Structure Induction Effects.* ACS Omega. 2022 Aug 12;7(33):28924-28931. doi: 10.1021/acsomega.2c02254. PMID: 36033665; PMCID: PMC9404194.

[30] Gasmi A, et al. (Feb. 28, 2022). *Toxic Metals Exposure and APOE4 Gene Variant in Cognitive Decline Disorders.* Arch Razi Inst. 2022 Feb 28;77(1):1-10. doi: 10.22092/ARI.2021.356078.1771. PMID: 35891722; PMCID: PMC9288612.

[31] Paduraru E, et al. (2022). *Comprehensive Review Regarding Mercury Poisoning and Its Complex Involvement in Alzheimer's Disease.* International Journal of Molecular Sciences. 2022; 23(4):1992. https://doi.org/10.3390/ijms23041992.

developing not simply the garden-variety Alzheimer's – but the rather-more dreaded *early-onset* Alzheimer's Disease (EOAD) – one should take note of a study that compared mercury levels in the blood of early-onset Alzheimer's patients against two control groups (one group had depression, and the other group had non-psychiatric disorders), and concluded that the ***blood levels of mercury in the early onset Alzheimer's group were "three-fold higher than the control" groups***. The study further noted, quite chillingly, that "typical brain damage" in Alzheimer's disease "commences 20 to 50 years before symptoms manifest...."[32]

Given the foregoing, and for those mindful of this issue, the logical next steps would seem to be: (1) to procure genetic testing to see if one has one or more copies of the APOE4 gene, and (2) to consider removing any and all mercury amalgam fillings from one's mouth by a dental office using the Huggins-Grube technique (because otherwise, a dentist removing such mercury amalgam fillings could unwittingly make the patient's body even more mercury-toxic).[33] (This constitutes neither legal nor medical advice, just common sense takeaways from the recent studies).

---

[32] Siblerud R. et al (2019). *A Hypothesis and Evidence That Mercury May be an Etiological Factor in Alzheimer's Disease.* International Journal of Environmental Research and Public Health. 2019; 16(24):5152. https://doi.org/10.3390/ijerph16245152.

[33] For more information on APOE and similar genetic testing, one can visit: https://dnaconnexions.com/apoe-genotype-test/. To learn more about the removal of mercury amalgam fillings in the safest manner possible, visit: https://hgdcoffice.com/about/.

Chapter 5

As can be seen by the foregoing discussion, mercury is our enemy, be it located in our inoculations, in our teeth, or in our water. Of course, there are other harmful substances in childhood vaccines that do not catch as many headlines as mercury, and about which many folks are unaware. These harmful substances are generally added to the vaccines as preservatives.

In terms of how I feel about these other additives, I'm against their use. But when it comes to the general idea that backstops the promise of vaccines that motivated Jenner's work (who discovered vaccines), I can see how the idea initially appealed to the masses.

The notion that one could take a tiny little germ, and expose the human body to that germ in order to engender an immune response that creates antibodies to that particular bug – so that when the person is re-exposed to the disease in the future their body proceeds to activate those previously-created antibodies to fight off the virus – and thereby ensure the person never contracts a full-blown case of the disease…?? That idea definitely is intriguing.

The challenge lies in the fact that the vaccine manufacturer must keep the "tiny germ" preserved in such a way that it doesn't grow in an out-of-control manner in the vial, and cause the person injected to receive a full-blown case of the disease. Because then, what would be the point of the inoculation – if everyone who got the shot contracted the disease? On the other hand, the manufacturer must also ensure that the "little tiny germ" doesn't become so inactivated or "dead" that it is then entirely ignored by the recipient's body – such that no antibodies are created.

While I'm describing the basics of vaccine science in kindergarten terms to keep the discussion simple – terms which would no doubt horrify all of my brilliant doctor friends like Judy Mikovits and others who are experts in the subject – the bottom line is that in order to keep the "little tiny germ" in the perfect state and stored in a stable fashion over time, the vaccine makers must add all sorts of chemicals to the mix, including preservatives and adjuvants (defined as ingredients added to the vaccine to make the person's immune response stronger).[34]

One of the chemicals added to vaccines is acetone.[35] Acetone is the active ingredient in paint thinner: it will take the paint off your walls, and remove the nail polish from a woman's fingernails.[36]

---

[34] For a more thorough discussion of childhood vaccines, see: Mikovits, J. et al. (2021). *Ending Plague: A Scholar's Obligation in an Age of Corruption.* Skyhorse.

Regarding adjuvants, see Centers for Disease Control and Prevention & National Center for Emerging and Zoonotic Infectious Diseases (NCEZID), Division of Healthcare Quality Promotion (DHQP). (2022, Sept. 27). *Adjuvants and Vaccines,* https://www.cdc.gov/vaccinesafety/concerns/adjuvants.html#:~:text=An%20adjuvant%20is%20an%20ingredient,adjuvants%20help%20vaccines%20work%20better. (noting that an "adjuvant is an ingredient used in some vaccines that helps create a stronger immune response in people receiving the vaccine….").

Regarding preservatives including mercury used in vaccines, see Health & Human Services & Office of Infectious Disease and HIV/AIDS Policy (OIDP). (2021, Apr. 29). *Vaccine Ingredient,* https://www.hhs.gov/immunization/basics/vaccine-ingredients/index.html#:~:text=Preservatives%20%2C%20like%20thimerosal%2C%20protect%20the,harmful%20germs%20to%20get%20inside, (noting that the purpose of "preservatives, like thimerosal, [is to] protect the vaccine from outside bacteria or fungus….").

[35] Acetone in pertussis vaccine: "Acetone-Treated Pertussis Vaccine—A Potent And Safer New Pertussis Vaccine," Journal of Biological Standardization, Volume 13, Issue 4, October 1985, pp. 315-320. Acetone in typhoid vaccine: "Typhoid Vaccine WHO International Standard," Medicines & Healthcare Products Regulatory Agency: Confidence in Biological Medicines, https://www.nibsc.org/products/brm_product_catalogue/detail_page.aspx?catid=TYVK. Acetone in adenovirus vaccine: U.S. CDC (recapitulated at: https://en.wikipedia.org/wiki/List_of_vaccine_excipients).

[36] Medical News Today, *What is Acetone, and Does it Have Risks?* https://www.medicalnewstoday.com/articles/what-is-acetone (stating that acetone "is a liquid solvent that can break down and dissolve other substances" and that companies "include acetone in products such as nail polish remover, paint remover,

The vaccine manufacturers also add ethylene glycol-type compounds to their shots. Most people know ethylene glycol by its street name: antifreeze. It's the bright green liquid that keeps your cabin's pipes from freezing in the winter, and which is also added to car engines for the same reason.[37]

Formaldehyde is also added to the inoculations. Of course, formaldehyde is a known and recognized Group 1 Carcinogen, whose primary use is embalming dead people – and for which exposure funeral home workers are required by OSHA (the Occupational Safety & Health Administration) standards to wear full body protective equipment.[38]

The flu shot is one vaccine that contains many of the aforementioned chemicals. For those not aware, the shot is made by taking chick embryos and inoculating them with the influenza virus. After which, the mixture is "cultivated" for several weeks, before it is laced with

---

and varnish remover. Some also use acetone to manufacture plastics, lacquers, and textiles....")

[37] American Chemistry Council, *Ethylene Glycols*, (stating that "ethylene glycol is a chemical commonly used in many commercial and industrial applications including antifreeze and coolant" and further noting that "ethylene glycol helps keep your car's engine from freezing in the winter and acts as a coolant to reduce overheating in the summer"), https://www.americanchemistry.com/industry-groups/ethylene-glycols#:~:text=Ethylene%20glycol%20is%20a%20chemical,reduce%20overheating%20in%20the%20summer

[38] "The International Agency for Research on Cancer (IARC) classified formaldehyde as a Group 1 carcinogen for humans in 2004, based on toxicological data and epidemiological evidence obtained in workplaces, all published before that year." Protano, C. et al. (2022) *The Carcinogenic Effects of Formaldehyde Occupational Exposure: A Systematic Review,* Cancers 2022, 14, 165. https://doi.org/10.3390/cancers14010165 *The Carcinogenic Effects of Formaldehyde Occupational Exposure: A Systematic Review.* https://mdpi-res.com/d_attachment/ cancers/cancers-14-00165/article_deploy/cancers-14-00165-v3.pdf?version= 1640913556. See also US Department of Labor, Occupational Safety and Health Administration. (July 8, 2005). *Formaldehyde Exposure and Ergonomic Hazards in the Embalming/Funeral Home Industry.* https://www.osha.gov/laws-regs/standard interpretations/2005-07-08.

"formaldehyde and preserved with thimerosal, a mercury derivative" as well as ethylene glycol.[39]

A little known datum – that is perhaps mere coincidence – involves the fact that, after the practice of giving flu shots to pregnant women in the United States became commonplace, fetal deaths skyrocketed by 4,250%.[40]

Another little known fact about the flu vaccine – aside from the unprecedented hike in fetal deaths which occurred after pregnant women were urged to take it – is that if a person had "five consecutive flu shots between 1970 and 1980, the chances of Alzheimer's was 10 times greater than for those getting ... no shots," according to leading immunogeneticist and medical doctor, Hugh Fudenberg (who has published more than 850 peer-reviewed papers).[41]

Pharmaceutical entities will also add aluminum to the shots, another neurotoxin which can unfortunately have an augmented effect when

---

[39] Miller, N. Z. (2005), *Vaccines: Are They Really Safe and Effective?* New Atlantean Press, p. 83 (citing Connaught Laboratories, (1993, Feb. 24), *The Making of a Flu Vaccine.* Los Angeles Times (reprinted in the Kansas City Stajr) and citing Physicians Desk Reference (PDR), (1999), (53rd Edition), Medical Economics: Montvale, NJ., pp. 2324 & 3315. O'Shea, T. *Vaccination Is Not Immunization*, 4th Ed., pp. 117.

Polyethylene glycol is also thought to be the driving chemical behind the cases of anaphylaxis seen in the recent roll-outs of the COVID vaccine. See, Priya Sellaturay, et al. (2021), *Polyethylene Glycol (PEG) Is A Cause Of Anaphylaxis To The Pfizer/BioNTech mRNA COVID-19 Vaccine*, NIH National Library of Medicine, Wiley Public Health Emergency Collection, https://www.ncbi.nlm.nih.gov/pmc/articles/PMC8251011/.

[40] Goldman G. (2012, Sept). *Comparison of VAERS Fetal-Loss Reports During Three Consecutive Influenza Seasons.* Journal of Human Environmental Toxicology. het.sagepub.com/content/early/2012/09/12/0960327112455067.abstract.

[41] Hugh Fudenberg, MD, is Founder and Director of Research, Neuro-Immuno Therapeutic Research Foundation. (See Dr. Fudenberg's speech at the NVIC International Vaccine Conference, Arlington, VA September, 1997); see also, O'Shea, T. *Vaccination Is Not Immunization*, 4th Ed., p. 119 (citing Fudenberg, H. (2000). *Hazards of Vaccines.* Journal of Clinical Investigation. Vol 4, pp. 97-105).

in the presence of mercury, particularly when injected into male children. In terms of the mechanism for how such heavy metals may cause harm: many of us have read about or researched the blood-brain barrier. This barrier is meant to keep the brain from being exposed to harmful molecules in the blood that might damage the brain.

Some of the items which are particularly damaging to the brain are classed as neuro-excitotoxins, and they include formaldehyde, mercury, aluminum, and MSG – the same list which is found to varying degrees in various inoculations.[42] Unfortunately, the body's defense system of the blood brain barrier is entirely missing in childhood – babies are not born with it. In point of fact, the barrier does not begin to develop until adolescence, and the human body does not complete the work of erecting that barrier until the physical body is mature. Which means that the above list of additives that are found in the childhood vaccines have free reign when it comes to arriving at – and wreaking havoc on – the brain…because the barrier that would normally halt their progress does not exist at the time the children are injected with such neuro-toxic agents.[43]

Another vaccine that contains a neuro-toxin is the pertussis vaccine: it contains aluminum. As a baseline for discussion of this vaccine, it should be noted that pertussis is a disease which is rarely fatal. What

---

[42] In addition to the flu vaccine and the pertussis vaccine, the Hepatitis A vaccine also contains many of these ingredients – it is made from human connective tissue cells that were infected with Hepatitis, and are then cultivated in "human fibroblasts" from "aborted fetal tissue," while the end-result further contains aluminum hydroxide, formalin, neomycin, and 2-phenoxyethanol, a toxic chemical comparable to antifreeze. O'Shea, T. *Vaccination Is Not Immunization*, 4th Ed., pp. 123. Miller, N. Z. (2005). *Vaccines: Are They Really Safe and Effective?* New Atlantean Press, p. 64 (citing CDC, (1999, Oct. 1), *Prevention of Hepatitis A Through Active Or Passive Immunization: Recommendations Of The Advisory Committee On Immunization Practices* (ACIP), MMWR Weekly 48 (RR-7); 13-20, and further citing Winkler, D. *Hepatitis A Facts. Concerned Parents for Vaccine Safety*, www.access1.net/via/vaccine/hepafacts.htm.).

[43] O'Shea, T. *Vaccination Is Not Immunization*, 4th Ed., pp. 154 (citing Blaylock, R. (1997). *Excitotoxins: The Taste that Kills Health.* Health Press).

should further be known is that the vaccine for the disease is not particularly effective – at most, it is 40-45% effective.[44] That said, inoculation for pertussis is often "combined" with other vaccines for diphtheria and tetanus, and the "[c]omponents of this triple shot… are then 'stabilized' using formaldehyde – a known carcinogen" and the doses further contain "thimerosal – a derivative or mercury – and aluminum potassium sulfate" both of which agents are "toxic to humans."[45]

Many have argued that the mercury compound of thimerosal was removed from this vaccine. But it should be noted that at the time of this writing, the CDC was *still* stating that the pertussis "vaccine contains a trace amount of thimerosal … from the manufacturing process …."[46]

Perhaps because of the fact that this vaccine contains three particularly toxic agents including aluminum, mercury and formaldehyde, it is known among physicians to have a high rate of adverse events related to breathing: on the mild end of the spectrum is the fact that a JAMA study showed that children diagnosed with asthma were more than five times more likely to have received the pertussis inoculation, while on the more concerning end of the spectrum lies the fact that there has been an "extraordinary increase in episodes where breathing either nearly ceased or stopped completely" after pertussis inoculation – and, as well, an alarming study that examined more than 100 children who

---

[44] Miller, N. Z. (2005). *Vaccines: Are They Really Safe and Effective?* New Atlantean Press, pp. 40-43 (citing Moskowitz, R. (1984, Spring). *Immunizations: The Other Side*, Mothering, p. 36); Halperin, et al. (1989, Nov.), and also citing *Persistence of Pertussis in an Immunized Population: Results of the Nova Scotia Enhanced Pertussis Surveillance Program*, Journal of Pediatrics, pp. 686-693).

[45] Id.

[46] Centers for Disease Control & Prevention. (2022, Sept. 6). *About Diptheria, Tetanus, and Pertussis Vaccines.*

died of SIDS and concluded that **more than two-thirds had been vaccinated with Pertussis in the days just leading up to the "SIDS" death**.[47]

As a result of the high rates of injury – including inexplicable rates of SIDS deaths occurring in the hours just after DTAP or DPT vaccination – many countries have discontinued it, including Sweden, Japan, Germany, Britain and other European countries – and notably, not one country has begun re-using it since its discontinuation.[48]

In a similarly frightening vein to the discovery of high rates of SIDS deaths in the hours just after DTP/DTAP inoculation was the discovery in the 1980's that "about 50 percent of all African green monkeys – the primate of choice for making polio vaccines – were infected with simian immunodeficiency virus (SIV), a virus closely related to human immunodeficiency virus (HIV)," which HIV virus, of course, is the infectious agent that precedes AIDS.[49]

---

[47] Miller, N. Z. (2005). *Vaccines: Are They Really Safe and Effective?* New Atlantean Press (citing Odent M. et al. (1994, Aug 24). *Pertussis Vaccination and Asthma: Is There a Link?* Journal of the American Medical Association, pp. 592-593, and citing Scheibnerova, V. (1990, Oct.). *Cot Death as Due to Exposure to Non-Specific Stress and General Adaption Syndrome: Its Mechanisms and Prevention,* (New South Wales, Australia: Association for Prevention of Cot Death, and citing Scheibnerova, V. and Karlsson, L. (1991, May 27-29). *Association Between Non-Specific Stress Syndrome, DPT Injections, and Cot Death,* Second Immunization Conference, Canberra, Australia: Association for prevention of Cot Death, and citing Scheibner, Viera. (1993). *Vaccination: 100 Years of Orthodox Research Shows That Vaccines Represent a Medical Assault on the Immune System.* Blackheath, NSW, Australia: Scheibner Publications, pp. 59-70 and 225-235).

[48] O'Shea, T. *Vaccination Is Not Immunization,* 4th Ed., pp. 103 (citing Trollfors, B. (1981, Sep 12). *Whooping Cough in Adults.* British Medical Journal, Vol. 283, p. 696).

[49] Essex, M. et al., *The Origin of the AIDS Virus.* Scientific American. 1988; 259:64-71. See also, Karpas, A., *Origin and Spread of AIDS,* Nature, 1990; 348:578. See also, Kyle, W., *Simian Retroviruses, Poliovaccines and the Origin of AIDS.* Lancet, 1992; 339:600-601. See also, Elswood, B. et al. *Polio Vaccines and the Origin of AIDS,* Medical Hypothesis, vol. 42, 1994, pp. 347-354.

Harvard Medical School professor Ronald Desrosier said:

> The practice of growing polio vaccines in monkey kidneys is a "ticking time bomb" [due to the fact that] … some viruses produced by monkeys may be transferred to humans in the vaccine, with very bad health consequences.[50]

This discovery, in turn, caused many infectious disease experts to wonder if the introduction of HIV to the human population may have been a result of the fact that 50% of the monkeys used to culture polio vaccines tested positive for the precursor to what was essentially Monkey AIDS – particularly since Robert Gallo, an expert on the AIDS virus, noted that some versions of the SIV monkey virus are virtually indistinguishable from some human variants of HIV:

> "The monkey virus *IS* the human virus…."[51]

Nothing like the precursor to monkey AIDS being in the chemical cocktail for the polio vaccine: Really – what could go wrong??

---

[50] Rock, A., (1996, Dec.), *The Lethal Dangers of the Billion Dollar Vaccine Business.* Money, p. 159.

[51] Curtis, T. (1992, March 19), *The Origin of AIDS: A Startling New Theory Attempts to Answer the Question 'Was It an Act of God or an Act of Man?* Rolling Stone, pp. 57, 106+.

Chapter 6

As an attorney who has spent much time in court over the years, I've always been partial to using analogies and metaphors to explain topics. With that said, let's assume I were to hand the reader a shot glass full of the above-discussed agents – mercury, formaldehyde, aluminum, and Simian Immuno-Deficiency Virus – while we were at a holiday party, and I then encouraged you to consume the cocktail. Let's further assume that, after you ingested the concoction, you then became injured or died. It does not take a rocket scientist to extrapolate that I would not be able to leave the party without law enforcement's finest cuffing me, perp-walking me out of the front door, and then charging me with murder (or minimally, manslaughter).

Rightly so.

And yet, we take trace amounts of all these same neuro-toxic and carcinogenic substances and shove them into a vial, along with some viruses cultured on monkey kidneys that not infrequently test positive for the SIV virus which we now know is virtually indistinguishable from the human HIV virus, and – so long as an MD in a white lab coat with the right credentials is the one injecting the infant with the aforesaid substances – not only will that doctor never be arrested for that baby's death or injury, neither will the parent of the harmed child be able to sue the doctor in civil court to hold the doctor accountable (courtesy of a federal law passed in 1986 that exempts pharmaceutical makers from liability).[52]

---

[52] Pantokoek, K. (2022). *Can I Sue Vaccine Manufacturers?* Findlaw (asking "if you believe that your child has been injured as a result of vaccination, can you sue the

And here's the real kicker: said doctor can frequently then also garner a few hundred thousand dollar bonus at the end of the calendar year from the health insurance companies, if the pediatrician can convince a certain percentage of his or her pediatric patients to take all the vaccines.[53] And as regards bonuses for the COVID-19 vaccine, Anthem Blue Cross Blue Shield of Kentucky was initially bonusing physicians $20 per Anthem member if 30% of a doctor's Anthem patients were vaccinated before September 1, 2021, $45 per person if 40% were juiced, $70 per person for doctors that could get half their Anthem patients to take the COVID vax, $100 per patient if the doctor exceeded the 60% threshold, and a whopping $125 per patient vaccinated if the medico could get 3 our of every 4 of his Anthem patients inoculated against COVID-19 – while a final incentive payment would be further given for patients newly vaccinated during the last quarter of 2021 which ranged from $100 per patient to $250 per patient – in lock-step increments with the tiered model above.[54]

And while a discussion of the COVID vaccine is beyond what I'd originally wanted to touch on in this book, particularly given that

---

manufacturer of the vaccine for damages?" and noting that the "short answer is, no, you likely cannot sue the vaccine manufacturer… [due to] The National Childhood Vaccine Injury Act of 1986"), https://www.findlaw.com/healthcare/patient-rights/can-i-sue-vaccine-manufacturers-.html

[53] We. (June 20, 2016). *How Much Money Do Pediatricians Really Make From Vaccines*. Wellness And Equality, https://wellnessandequality.com/2016/06/20/how-much-money-do-pediatricians-really-make-from-vaccines/ (noting that as the "table above explains, Blue Cross Blue Shield pays pediatricians $400 per fully vaccinated child. If your pediatrician has just 100 fully-vaccinated patients turning 2 this year, that's $40,000. **Yes, Blue Cross Blue Shield pays your doctor a $40,000 bonus for fully vaccinating 100 patients under the age of 2. If your doctor manages to fully vaccinate 200 patients, that bonus jumps to $80,000.** But here's the catch: **Under Blue Cross Blue Shield's rules, pediatricians lose the whole bonus unless at least 63% of patients are fully vaccinated, and that includes the flu vaccine. So it's not just $400 on your child's head – it could be the whole bonus….")** (emphasis in original).

[54] https://providers.anthem.com/docs/gpp/KY_CAID_PU_COVID19VaccineProviderIncentiveProgram.pdf?v=202201202223

there are so many other books on the market which are dedicated in their entirety to the topic and which provide amazing coverage of the issue, for those readers who may not have reviewed the other treatises, I'd ask you to consider – in addition to reviewing the hefty monetary inducements being handed out by companies like Anthem to ensure doctors are performing massive numbers of vaccinations – the following data concerning the COVID inoculation:

1. After mass rollout of the COVID vaccine in early 2021, death rates in the United States for those between the ages of eighteen and sixty-four jumped by 40%, according to the Scott Davison, CEO of OneAmerica – a $100 billion life insurance company founded in 1877:

> We're seeing right now the highest death rates we've ever seen in the history of this business. The data is consistent across every player in the business.
>
> Just to give you an idea of how bad that is, a three sigma or 200-year catastrophe would be a 10 percent increase .... So, 40 percent is just unheard of.[55]

2. Pfizer wanted to wait 75 years – until we were all dead – to release its documents regarding safety trials on the COVID vaccine, but thankfully was instead ordered by a judge to start releasing 55,000 pages per month. Why would any company that had nothing to hide seek to wait ¾ of a century to release its data – if its data truly supported the fact that this was, e.g., "a great vaccine that reduced transmission and had few to no side effects?"[56]

---

[55] Beane, P. (Jan. 3, 2022), *Insurance Executive Says Death Rates Among Working-Age People up 40 Percent*, NPR, https://www.wfyi.org/news/articles/insurance-death-rates-working-age-people-up-40-percent.

[56] Wolf, N. (May 29, 2022), *Dear Friends, Sorry to Announce a Genocide – It's Really True: They Know They Are Killing the Babies*, Substack, https://naomiwolf.substack.com/p/dear-friends-sorry-to-announce-a?s=r

3. Female test subjects were ordered by Pfizer to NOT become pregnant, and yet 270 of them did. Pfizer then allegedly "lost track" of 230 of those women – which is unethical, unlawful, and something I – as an environmental attorney – have never heard of occurring, in any clinical trial, anywhere. Yet more horrifying than Pfizer "losing track" of 85% of its pregnant women, of the 36 pregnant women that Pfizer did manage to keep tabs on, fully 28 of them lost their babies. **You read that right: more than ¾ of the babies of pregnant moms inoculated with the Pfizer COVID vaccine died.**[57]

4. In highly vaccinated Scotland, almost twice the number of babies died the year after vaccine rollout (2021) as died in previous years, while in Ontario, Canada, 86 babies died in 2021 versus a normal baseline number of 4-5 deaths (which represents a 1,700% increase over prior years) – and this is just the tip of the iceberg: these statistics on infant deaths and declining birth rates are unfortunately being mirrored in the U.S. and other European countries (which is not surprising given that the ingredients of the Covid vaccine leave the injection site, travel through all bodily membranes, and then appear to accumulate in disproportionate amounts in the female ovaries).[58]

There is much more information like this – which could fill endless 500-page books – and has. Many of these facts are being trumpeted by incredibly well-educated liberals like Dr. Naomi Wolf, a Rhodes Scholar who holds a PHD from Oxford University and a degree from Yale, and who has been an out-spoken feminist for many years, and who was a lead consultant for Democrat Al Gore's campaign for the presidency in 2000. (To find her written work, just do an internet

---

[57] Id.

[58] Id. (citing: https://www.heraldscotland.com/news/19726487.investigation-launched-abnormal-spike-newborn-baby-deaths-scotland/ and also citing: https://nonvenipacem.com/2021/12/10/explosive-rise-in-ontario-stillbirths-triggers-parliamentary-questions/).

search of her name: the results will return her Substack articles which contain in-depth analyses of these issues, as well as a list of books she's published over the last few decades). Additionally, Robert Kennedy, Jr. wrote a fantastic book on the subject entitled "The Real Anthony Fauci" which was published in 2021 that I highly recommend. And for those interested in the simple math and actuarial tables showing evidence of increasing harm across the board since vaccine roll-out, I would research Ed Dowd, a former Blackrock portfolio manager who controlled a $14 billion growth equity portfolio for 10+ years, and who – by his own admission – spent the vast majority of his professional career analyzing mathematical trends in order to project future potentials and return the best results for his employer and clients. His book, "Cause Unknown" (Skyhorse Publishing, December, 2022) takes a very thorough, statistical walk through the data that has come out since the vaccine rollout.

Setting aside the COVID vaccine issues detailed above in order to return to the topic of the shots recommended in the childhood vaccine schedule: I find all of this to be rather unholy. The fact that parents cannot sue the companies that cause harm. The fact that I've never heard of a single doctor giving true, informed consent to the parent prior to injecting their baby with these childhood vaccines. The fact that a doctor who kills a child by administering a childhood vaccination with no true informed consent will never be brought up on criminal charges for manslaughter (which is the typical charge when one accidentally causes another's death, even if it's not intentional). The fact that – as a mother – if I allowed my child to ingest these chemicals, I would be arrested, but that the pharmaceutical industry and medical doctors can put these chemicals into my child, and then get a free pass for any harm or death that ensues.

That said, what truly pushed society into the Twilight Zone was when my state, in 2019, began to flirt with passing a bill that said that a child who was already injured by these chemical cocktails could no longer go to school – and their pediatrician could not write an exemption to future shots after the first inoculation caused injury (unless that child's earlier injury fell into two very narrow allergic/adverse reactions) – all because a morally bankrupt sellout state senator named Richard Pan deemed all other "allergic reactions" to vaccines to be unworthy of consideration as the basis for a medical exemption.

Having sat in the Spring of 2019 for hours in my neighbor's garden – trying not to cry while I listened to one story of severe vaccine injury after another – I decided on the spot to help these women fight Senator Pan's awful piece of legislation. And throughout the remainder of that spring and summer, I did my part: I visited senators in the Capitol. I educated folks. I did grassroots work. And I found that many of the senators who were sympathetic to the issue believed we should write editorials in newspapers like the Sacramento Bee or the Los Angeles Times.

And thus? We wrote the editorials. But we could not get them printed, because the press was biased against the parents' stories and position.

This was all rather shocking to me. Typically, if a newspaper is going to cover an issue, they will run one editorial on behalf of the one position, and a second editorial covering the opposing side. And even when newspapers are heavily biased against one position, they will still generally let the less-favored side buy advertising space and convert it for purposes of running the editorial. (Put differently, the favored position gets free press, while the less-favored side has to pay for coverage).

But the newspapers in California in 2019 were categorically unwilling to let anyone opposing SB 276 have editorial space: they'd been bought – either literally or figuratively – by Big Pharma's money and weight. And after consecutive months of being shut-out, I'd had it. I had worked for many years for clients that paid top dollar. As attorneys working for the biggest companies in the world, we weren't paid to lose, nor give up when we hit road blocks. We were paid – when we hit a barrier – to find a way around it.

With that ethos still running strongly in my veins in 2019 – and fed up to the gills with the newspapers' shut-out and the fact that "free press" appeared non-existent in California during that season – I woke up one morning determined to find a work-around. I knew the print journalistic outlets were biased against us, but what about television?

Deciding to find out their stance, I called a friend who worked in advertising. She promised to check into things, and get back to me. A few hours later, we hit pay dirt: the answer came back that the TV stations would in fact allow "our side" to advertise.

I put the word out, and waited for other organizations to make a television ad. Someone like Del Bigtree or Bobby Kennedy's group. But as time passed, I came to understand that they were busy with other important projects.

As I was continuing to unsuccessfully hunt for someone to produce a TV ad, one morning I had a bright idea for a 30-second TV spot on the vaccine topic. I was in the shower (of course!) when inspiration hit. Not wanting to forget my idea, I hopped out of the shower, threw on a towel, and ran to my desk to scribble the idea on the back of an envelope. Filled with inspiration, but lacking a recording studio, I then ran into my husband's closet and – using his business suits as a sound buffer from external noises (including my daughter's

Chihuahua that liked to bark her head off at every passing mailman and butterfly) – I then recorded my 30-second script as an audio file onto my cell phone.

Running back to my desk, I opened a browser, and cruised through companies that rented out stock video clips. Identifying some imagery that I thought could work as the video track for my little TV ad, I made a "script" of what image should play during which part of the audio file I'd recorded, and then I handed the whole kit and caboodle to my husband who had some basic video editing skills.

And voila, a few days later, we had made a TV commercial!

Who knew it was so easy?

I should probably issue a tiny warning at this juncture, for those who might be inclined to try this at home: if you are going to employ your husband as your video editor, and video editing is not his normal day job – and you happen to be a high-strung and very-OCD-inclined-Type-A lawyer – you might want to be prepared for him to threaten to divorce you late one night… after you ask him to, e.g., "make the sound file crescendo 3/100ths of a second earlier." And another warning to accompany the first: it takes a LONGGG time to make a 30- second TV ad.

Indeed, the first time my husband and I made a sex-trafficking awareness video, it took us about a week to make a simple five minute clip. And my daughter – ever the astute one – wandered over to my hubby's desk at the ripe old age of ten, and said: "So, lemme get this straight. Y'all have been working all day, every day, all week long. To make a five minute video. So if I'm doing the math right, basically it took you guys AN ENTIRE DAY to produce ONE MINUTE of video?!?!?!!!"

And my husband and I – who up until that moment, had been so dang proud that we'd finally called it a wrap without killing each other in the process – were rendered speechless with the dawning realization that it had, indeed, taken a week out of both of our lives to produce one tiny, five-minute video segment.

I share the above saga by way of noting that anyone can make a TV commercial (although you might need some couple's counseling afterward – if you use your spouse as the editor). But in all seriousness, it's really not that hard: you do not need to rent out a Hollywood studio or beg a favor from Del Bigtree. And frankly, we should all be doing this.

Because we are at war right now. And one of the first rules of war is that you do NOT lose your comms channels – again, you do NOT give up ANY OPEN MICROPHONE or any open channel by which you can communicate.

So while the newspapers were not willing to tell the story of the families of vaccine-injured children in California in 2019, and while social media was heavily censoring the topic as well, TV stations were letting us run commercials.

Which begs one very important question: Why are we not making more use of this medium, when it's still available to use and is successful at changing hearts and minds? I don't know the answer to that question. All I know is that we must change our existing operating basis if we want the truth to be known.

The final installment of the saga involving my little creation of a TV ad concerning SB 276 is that I not only made a TV ad, but that we further managed to fundraise the money necessary to run the ads on mainstream television channels. And I am proud to say that within twenty minutes of that TV commercial hitting the airwaves around Sacramento, the newspapers started calling us.

That's right: the newspapers – which for months had been stonewalling us and refusing to take our calls and refusing to take our money to run editorials – were now calling us.

"Who are you – and what's the name of your organization?" asked the Sacramento Bee reporter, as I answered my cell phone the afternoon of our first day of running the ad. And before I could even answer the first volley of questions, more came my way: "Why are you running this ad? How long do you plan on airing it? Is it only running in the Sacramento market – or do you plan on running it across the entire state?"

I smiled, tasting the first victory I had experienced during the many months of battling the press on this issue. And however long I had originally planned to run the TV ads, this much I now knew: we were going to be running them a WHOLE LOT LONGER than I'd initially anticipated – because the press would not be hounding us ... unless those ads were taking a pound of flesh off their intended targets.

All told, there was so much work done, by so many here in California, which went into opposing SB 276. My group ended up producing more than a half-dozen TV ads, and fundraising like our lives depended on it, in order to get them aired around Sacramento. And doctors, lawyers, parents of severely injured kids – so many citizens across this great state took time out of their lives to march into the Capitol and voice their opposition over the long weeks and months of the legislative season. I was but one droplet in a sea of water moving toward justice.

And I watched. I watched as SB 276 continued to make its way through the legislative process. I watched as senators we had elected openly mocked the parents of vaccine-injured kids.

Indeed, I watched a particularly pathetic excuse for a human being named Senator Lorena Gonzalez tell these parents "We don't play" and continually cut their mic and scorn them during the legislative hearing she was in charge of. Mind you: many – not some, but many – of these parents had two-year-olds who were perfectly normal, happy, healthy, walking and talking … before the MMR vaccine had caused their children's brains to swell, creating lifelong debilitating injuries that meant these same parents could never leave their children's bedsides. I now knew scores of parents from all walks of life who had been placed in a hell I could not begin to fathom: having to watch their dreams for their children circle the drain. Having to sit at the side of the beds of their adult-babies some twenty years later … because their children's brains were still on fire and inflamed, forever stuck in infantilized states that often resulted in incessant crying and screaming intermixed with violent bouts of self-injury that in some cases were so violent the child would chew their own tongue in half.

"We don't play?" ***"WE DON'T PLAY???!!!"***

On what planet was I living that elected representatives were allowed to so inhumanely devalue these parents' existences – and the parent's right to speak about their children's harm in an attempt to prevent future suffering??

I watched thousands of parents take days out of their lives, time away from their jobs, to repeatedly make the trip to Sacramento and wait seven hours in the heat outside our Capitol for their 30 seconds at the microphone to voice their opposition to the bill. And I watched as these same self-sacrificing parents were contemptuously derided and dismissed out-of-hand over and over again with the label of "Anti-Vaxxers" – the scornful label spewed out venomously by legislators, doctors and members of the lay public alike.

And for what? The fact that their child had an allergic reaction to a cocktail of chemicals – any one of which chemicals plenty of Americans are allergic to?

How many folks reading this passage are allergic to antibiotics? To MSG? To formaldehyde? Is it really that shocking that little babies with livers the size of almonds cannot process some of these chemicals to which even adults are allergic?

Yes, I watched. Immensely saddened by the scorn and derision evinced by politicians like Richard Pan and Lorena Gonzalez and Anthony Portantino. Since when, as a society, did we become okay with the concept of dehumanizing people over their individual adverse reactions to an allergen?

Heck, half the people I know are allergic to natural substances, like cat hair or peanuts, or flowers. But I do not call them "Anti-catters" and scorn them because they sneeze when Fluffy Kitten walks out of my kitchen to trigger their asthma attack. And I certainly don't laugh at the 10% of the population that is allergic to Penicillin, or the 3% of people who are allergic to peanuts – nor do I label them "anti-peanutters" or "anti-Penicillin-ers" and override their doctors' judgment – making rules that say they cannot go to school or work unless they agree to get more exposures to the very thing to which they are so deathly allergic.

No one is kicking these allergy-besotted individuals out of our houses or stores or schools – or making fun of them for the fact that their particular unique body doesn't like a certain substance. So why

– pray tell, why – were we doing exactly that to the parents of vaccine-injured children?

And let me stop here, to state the obvious fact so oft-ignored by those who choose to loudly or evenly silently ridicule these families: the parents of vax-injured kids were NEVER anti-vaxxers.

They were pro-vaccine.

They got their kids a shot ***because they believed*** what Pharma and their pediatrician told them. And it was only after these parents believed Pharma's lies, and after the point in time where Pharma betrayed these parents by sacrificing their babies' health – and in some instances, their babies' very lives – on Pharma's Altar of the Almighty Dollar ... it was then and only then that these parent's become "anti-vax."

Who are we to judge? Because the ugly reality is that, if you were in their shoes, you would also quite likely be "anti-vax" – or more accurately, "pro-medical freedom."

And after all this work in California, by all of these amazing families, our elected officials still bowed to Pharma's incredible pull – despite the fact that on some of these committees, I watched a third of the senators or legislators speak of their own experiences where their child or a relative had suffered vaccine damage.

But at the end of the day, none of it was enough to counter Pharma's influence. California became the first state to add insult to injury by telling these families that unless their kids had suffered a very narrow type of allergic reaction (anaphylaxis or encephalopathy), their vaccine-injured kids would now be essentially deprived of their constitutional right to attend school because such children would likely never be able to procure a medical exemption.[59]

Put simply: my "golden" state is now a modern-day witchhunter. Demonizing kids whose only crime is that their little bodies were allergic – not to peanuts or cats – but to the formaldehyde or acetone or other preservatives in their vaccines. We now deprive many, if not most, of these children of their right to go to school in my state, and further allow the Medical Board to professionally eviscerate the doctors who would stand up for these kids, targeting the licenses of the only physicians who actually upheld their oath by refusing to inject a child harmed by a vaccine with another round of that same agent.

All because Pharma is making a killing off these families, literally and figuratively – and is willing to pay ungodly amounts of money to Madison Avenue and corrupt politicians – in their quest to dehumanize the victims, and remove any and all people who would stand in the way of their unholy greed.[60]

To put a very fine point on it: The pharmaceutical industry is raping America – and the politicians are enabling it by holding their bags. Shame on us, as a society. For not standing up for these parents, regardless of our personal beliefs which may differ. For not insisting the pharmaceutical industry be held accountable. For allowing

---

[59] Even before SB 276 passed, the vast majority of doctors in California were unwilling to write any medical exemptions, which point was well made in this TV ad that PERK and the political non profit I co-founded, Advocates for Physicians' Rights, aired in 2019: https://rumble.com/v2hmehs-tv-ad-sb-276-kills-medical-exemption-aired-in-2019-in-sacramento.html.

[60] Pharmaceutical companies spent $6.88 billion in 2021 on consumer ads. Pharma DTC ad spend in the U.S. 2012-2021 - Statista, https://www.statista.com/statistics/686906/pharma-ad-spend-usa/#:~:text=The%20pharmaceutical%20industry%20in%20the,to%2Dconsumer%20advertising%20in%202021.

pHARMa to advertise on TV – when so many more-evolved nations do not.[61]

And I do believe we will reap what we sow. Children are our future, the ones we are charged with protecting. But instead of protecting them as we are meant to do, at a societal level we are allowing them to be sacrificed to industry whores on the altar of the almighty dollar. As a citizenry, we have blood on our hands – as surely as did the Germans who turned a blind eye to the cattlecars headed to Auschwitz.

Albert Schweitzer once said, "Man has lost the capacity to foresee and to forestall; he will end by destroying the world."

While I'm generally an optimist, I do believe if we continue to eradicate the constitutional right of citizens to opt out of medical treatments like vaccines that do not comport with their body's unique composition or with the individual's religious views – and moreover, if we continue to mandate such vaccines and predicate people's ability to work and receive schooling on their willingness to bow down to such vaccine mandates – we will soon prove Schweitzer's point. That said, I also believe that while history gives ample testimony to human beings' capacity for destruction, it also provides fair evidence of our ability to rise after watching evil take root, and say: "No more – not on our watch."

It's how the Holocaust ended.

---

[61] In 2020, 75% of TV ad spend came from Pharmaceutical companies. U.S. pharma TV ad spend 2020 – Statista. https://www.statista.com/statistics/953104/pharma-industry-tv-ad-spend-us/#:~:text=In%202020%2C%20the%20pharmaceutical%20industry,of%20the%20total%20ad%20spend..

It is how so many other injustices ended.

And, quite simply, it is our duty to ensure that today's injustices end similarly, with good people rising up and saying: "No more."

Chapter 7

We were sitting on the floor of our new house in the hills. The morning sun was slanting through the windows, casting a golden glow over the spot in which I'd chosen to plunk down cross-legged. Opposite me, my mother knelt, sweeping her dark hair back from her face as she set down her scissors and big felt-tipped marker that she called her "Cato Pen." She started cutting the sheets of copy paper into smaller pieces, and then looked up at me conspiratorially as she finished with the scissors and proceeded to uncap her favorite marker.

"I think you already know these, but it never hurts to be sure," she teased, slowly drawing large, capital letters onto the home-made flash cards.

I jiggled my foot and bounced slightly in my seated position, too excited at my favorite game to sit still. Although, truth be told, sitting still was never my strong suit. Looking out the lead-paned windows that courtesy of the imperfections embedded in the glass made the trees outside look wavy, I spied a little hummingbird flitting around a giant Bird of Paradise plant. I'd always liked the normal-sized Bird of Paradise plants which had dotted the yards of the neighbors' houses on the suburban street on which our last home had sat.

My thoughts drifted back to our previous home in the city of Whittier. It had been a small, two-bedroom, suburban tract house on a flat and well-kept tiny plot. But earlier in the year, my grandparents had initiated conversations with my parents about swapping their one-acre parcel in the hills for my parents' tinier tract home in the city, believing that a smaller house with a nice flat yard would be easier for them to maintain as they got on in years. My parents, full of enthusiasm if not money, jumped at the chance to swap houses and move their young child to a property zoned for horses.

When we had first moved into the much larger parcel that was full of elevation changes off of a rural two lane road – with no city sidewalks and relatively non-existent neighbors – I'd been surprised to wake up each morning to the sound of complete silence, punctuated by bird calls. I'd been equally surprised at the wealth of flora and fauna, particularly the enormous Bird of Paradise plants lining the side of the house on which the bedroom windows sat. These Giant Bird of Paradise plants were 40 feet tall, if not more, and their colorful blooms measured one-to-two feet long and were quite heavy. Equally fascinating was the fact that, on the chimney-side of the house, stood a tree that had blooms on it that were identical to the bright red bottle brush cleaners that sat on my mother's kitchen sink. I'm sure it had a formal name, but around our new house – and even now nearly fifty years later – it is still fondly known as the "Bottle Brush Tree."

"Okay Leigh," my mother said, drawing my attention away from the various trees, "what word is this one?"

I barely glanced at the letters before realizing that the word was, indeed, an easy one that I knew.

"Is!" I yelled loudly.

My mother cracked a huge smile, confirming my answer.

"That's right – the verb we use all the time!!" she replied, just as excitedly.

I loved playing games with my mom. Despite her penchant for being cautious when it came to risky adventures, the rest of the time, my mother was definitely the "most fun parent."

"Next card honey – what's this one?"

"Are!" I screamed again.

"Yep! And this next one is…?"

"Am!" I trilled back.

"Indeed, my love! It looks like you've got these verbs down pat!"

My mother smiled. Uncapping her marker once again, she drew more letters on new blank sheets of paper, and we continued to while away the early morning hours after breakfast: she, making new words, and me, calling out the various nouns she'd chosen, which included "dog," "cat," and "kid."

Some time later, I exhaled loudly, and my mother stopped the game, giving me an appraising stare.

"Well," she intoned, "I'm going to have to make this more challenging, so you don't get antsy."

She knew so well how I rolled. Excitable, talkative, and generally quick-minded … but easily bored. I inhaled the lovely marking-pen-smell that had pervaded the room, and began looking around again to see if I could make out where the hummingbird had gotten to, when it suddenly occurred to me that she'd been writing on the new card for a bit longer than normal.

"This word has four letters, and you're gonna want to sound it out...." my mother began.

I eagerly turned my gaze back to the card she held in front of her chest. There were indeed four letters printed on it, and it was a bit overwhelming. But I dutifully sounded it out phonetically as she'd taught me. Or at least, I tried to.

"I…" my voice petered out, and I gave it another whirl. "I…"

"Umm-hmm, that's right," my mother encouraged, "you've got the first syllable!" My mother never talked down to me, or used little words. She assumed I could keep up, and I usually did, And on the times where I didn't know a word, she would always stop to explain it to me. I took another deep breath, committed to figuring out this four-letter conundrum.

"I. RON..." I pronounced, as if I were referring to myself, and then calling out my male cousin's name.

My mother smiled really big, and I knew I'd slaughtered it. But there was no scorn or derision in her face or her tone. Just joy – that I'd almost gotten it right. In fact, there never was any condescension with my mother when we were together and playing games or learning, which was an altogether different experience than being with my father, who was prone to giving voice to his opinions in loud, angry, mocking tones.

My mom waited for a long moment, before starting to speak. "You're so close… I'll give you a little hint. It's something I use in the house, on your clothes." And then she gently started to sound out the word she'd written on the note card, but with the inflection in the right spot.

At about the same time, I finally realized what the word actually was, which culminated in me shouting "IRON!!!" as I fell giggling into her lap, and we rolled around together on the floor, celebrating my "win" in learning this big, new word.

My mom was always my safe place, my "go to" buddy when I had a question or concern or heartbreak. She was the one I could share anything with, my eternal cheerleader. In her mind, her only child was the best, the brightest, the kindest.

I'm not sure that I entered this world like that, but in hindsight, I know it matters not. For now, having lived 50 years, I've come to believe that, in many ways, we grow into the expectations others have for us.

Some years after that flash-card reading session, when I was in college, I learned about an experiment where they'd told school teachers, before class started for the year, that certain of the students were "smart" and others were just average. Labels which bore no reflection on reality, as those deemed "smart" were not actually smarter than their peers. And yet, by year's end, the children labeled as bright were handily and significantly outperforming the "average" students on various metrics.[62]

Expectations matter. They matter even when they are never enunciated.

And so, while I've no actual idea what my IQ measured upon arriving to this planet, or whether I was remotely gifted in any way, this much I do know – a full forty-seven years after that morning reading session.

---

[62] Rosenthal R. et al. (1968). *Pygmalion in the Classroom: Teacher Expectation and Pupil's Intellectual Development*. Holt, Rinehart & Winston, Inc. https://gwern.net/doc/statistics/bias/1968-rosenthal-pygmalionintheclassroom.pdf

My mother believed I was smart and able. And in retrospect?

Her belief was all that ever mattered.

My mother made learning fun. She was my first teacher. And, hands down and to this day, having graduated college and law school, my mother remains my best teacher. Not because she'd gone to school for it, nor because she'd studied early childhood development (in fact, she had not – she'd only graduated high school).

My mother was my best teacher for the simple reason that she believed. In me. Strongly and certainly. Without reservation or doubt. And she loved just as strongly, and just as certainly. She was always free with her praise and her smile for any job well done, for any goal met, for any win attained.

I had no idea I was learning so many important things throughout all those early years at my mother's side, before kindergarten even started. In my mind, I was just having fun each day, with a person who loved me and who made life entertaining and enjoyable, and who always – but always – had my back.

It's a lesson.

And without doubt, the most significant one I ever learned:

Belief – and a focus on the positive – will get you far.

So very, very far.

Chapter 8

It was some weeks later, and I was no longer sitting on my mother's bedroom floor, wriggling enthusiastically. I was ensconced on the couch, with blankets piled on top of me, and a wet, cold rag on my forehead. My mother came to lay her palm on my face.

"You're burning up, sweetheart. Have you kept the rag on your forehead like I said?"

I nodded dumbly, my feverish eyes glazed over, my mouth hanging open so I could breathe. My sinuses were entirely blocked, and I was pretty sure I would be easy to kill if someone were to, Heaven forbid, cover my mouth... which at the time, represented my sole method of getting oxygen into my system. Yep – I closed my mouth briefly to test my hypothesis – suffocation would indeed rapidly ensue.

I'd always had a good imagination. I was mulling over the notion of relaying this little factoid to my mom, but the effort to enunciate words seemed too great.

Her voice cut into my imaginings. "I'm gonna go find the thermometer, cuz your forehead is on fire."

Nodding mutely, I closed my eyes. It seemed only seconds before she re-appeared, holding the dreaded thermometer and briefly squinting at it, before shoving it into my mouth.

"Now leave it there for a couple of minutes, and try and close your mouth while it's in there."

The earlier specter of my immediate demise and suffocation bounded back to the forefront of my brain. "But bommm..." Pronouncing "m's" was difficult at best, particularly with the thermometer in my mouth.

"Shh, honey, I know you can't really keep your mouth closed, but maybe try every *other* breath or so. Hopefully that way I can get a somewhat accurate read."

I nodded again, somewhat mollified at the notion that I would not expire during the temperature-taking rodeo if I could leave my mouth open every other breath. She left the room again, and returned not long after, sliding the thermometer out of my mouth as I started to sneeze.

"Well, that's awfully high. It says 106, even though I know you couldn't keep your mouth shut. Goodness knows how high it actually is – I've never heard of a kid running a fever higher than this. I think we should take you to the hospital."

That seemed like an absolutely awful idea to me, who was still feeling a bit chilly even with three blankets piled atop my body. I begged her to not make me leave my nice cozy perch on the couch. Eventually, she relented.

"Okay, well then, for now I'm going to go find the Triaminic bottle so I can give you another dose, and then we'll have you take a nap."

Ugh. While I hated the yellow teaspoonful of Triaminic, I consoled myself with the fact that at least she wasn't going to drag me off the couch to see a medical professional. Although the notion of a nap was not exciting: I detested naps more than anything. And I had yet to be convinced that they did me any good, despite my mother dutifully putting me down for a two-hour nap every day at 1:00 p.m., and – when I was sick – putting me down for a nap every couple of hours (or so it seemed).

She left the room, no doubt on the hunt for the Triaminic. I sneezed once more, my right hand grabbing for the Kleenex box she'd left perched on the arm of the sofa. It was a big brown box – and, despite feeling like death warmed over – I had become bored. Thus, I decided to start reading the sides of the Kleenex box. It seemed like uninspiring information. So I turned the box over to the back side, where I found a picture.

The sketch looked like an olden-times picture, of a man with a big white scarf around his neck, and funny looking hair. I tried to sound out the words above his picture. "PAT-RICK… HEN-RY." Hadn't heard of him. I dragged my fevered gaze lower, and spied the words in quotes below his name. I figured out most of them, but wasn't sure about the one spelled "L-i-b-e-r-t-y."

My mother returned, holding a spoon so full of the yellow cough syrup that it was about to spill over the spoon's edges. She popped it into my mouth before I could utter a word. I swallowed, and – pointing to the Kleenex box – asked her what the word that started with the letter "L" was.

She tilted the bottom of the Kleenex box toward her. "Oh! That word is 'liberty' – and that's a picture of Patrick Henry! He was one of the founders of this country when we split off from England. He was a great orator, which means speaker, and one of his most famous sayings is the one they printed here: 'Give me Liberty, or give me Death!' And the word 'liberty' in this context, sweetie, just means 'Freedom.'"

I took a second to mull over all the info, and then my eyes widened. "So he's saying he wants to be free, and if he can't, then he'd rather die?"

My mother inclined her head. "Yep, that's about the size of it."

Eyes widening further, I contemplated the heavy thought that death would be preferable to any other living condition. I tried as well to think about *not* being free, and how bad that would feel. But some combination of cough syrup and the virus was making my eyelids droop.

My mother continued. "And you probably don't know this, but on your daddy's side, you're related to this man. I think it was his great, great, great, great, great – well, I'm not sure exactly how many 'greats' – but it was your dad's great grandpa, back up there on the family tree. That's why your Grandma – your dad's mom's – well her middle name is 'Henrietta.' They kept the family name 'Henry" as the middle name all the way down the ancestral line."

I was halfway to the dreaded nap that I'd sworn I didn't want, when my brain popped back into awake mode, shocked at the notion that I could be somehow related to this strange man pictured on the Kleenex box named "Patrick Henry."

"Are you related to him too, mom?"

My mother threw back her head, laughing aloud. "Heavens, no! I'm Hungarian and Romanian, remember? Descended from gypsies. My family didn't settle the country," she continued, still chuckling. "They were fleeing from Communists in Europe, earlier this century. Far from settling this country, they high-tailed it over here looking for safe harbor. My dad was one of thirteen kids! I think I've mentioned that before, but two of his older sisters died in childhood, and your

Grandpa's oldest brother got left behind in Europe when your great-grandparents fled to the US."

"Why were the communists bad? And are you, like, related to real gypsies –?" I stopped to snag a quick breath – "And what happened to Grandpa's brother who got left behind? And what is 'safe harbor'?" Even with a 106 degree fever, my questions came out rapid-fire.

My mom laid her hand on my head and patiently began to answer my questions. "'Safe harbor' comes from olden times when ships were out in a storm, and they needed to lay up for a bit, and so they went looking for a 'safe harbor.' It means they can rest, and not be in danger from storms or other things. And yes, I believe there are some real gypsies back there in my family line – that's why I've got these big lips and such a darker skin tone than you," she teased, raising one eyebrow humorously.

I analyzed my mother, with her black hair, and dark brown eyes. And her olive skin – so different from my white, almost-albino pallor – which was topped off by my reddish hair that would sometimes turn blond if I'd been in chlorinated water or the sun. I flashed back to all the times we'd gone shopping at JC Penney's or the Savon Drugstore down the hill in our local mall, where well-meaning little old ladies would invariably stop my mother to ask if I'd been adopted. It bothered me no end, this assumption that I was not related to my own mother, whom I absolutely adored.

I would always pipe up, yelling in my tiny indignant way: "No! I am NOT adopted! I have her smile –" at which point, I would stop to rather violently point at my mother's face – "can't you see??!!" And then, full of self-righteous upset at age three, I'd proceed to smile even wider while continuing to vehemently gesture at my mother's smile and then my own.

Being pissed, I'm sure my grin probably more resembled the bared-teeth grimace of a rabid dog than an actual genuine smile. A suspicion underscored by the fact that the most common response was for the little old lady to take a giant step back, shocked I'm sure at the lack of timidity that is generally present in most toddlers, and as well confounded by the occasional further paragraphs of vitriol that would often exit my lips.

Looking back, I cannot in hindsight really remember a time when my toddler tirade did not end with anything other than the motherly old hen slowly retreating whilst muttering about "how cute and extremely verbal" I was … as they dutifully bobbed their head up and down to acknowledge that they could, indeed, now see the resemblance between our smiles that I'd been thoroughly (if a bit ferociously) pointing out.

Continuing to gaze at my mother from my fevered state on the couch, I had to acknowledge that – while I didn't know a lot about gypsies or these Hungarians and Romanians – I'd seen a couple of pictures, and my mother definitely fit the mold.

Certainly more so than little albino me.

My mother patted my head gently. "Now you take that nap we've been talking about. And we'll talk about your other questions when you wake up."

Luckily, that day, my fever broke. And we avoided the dreaded hospital trip that capped so many other illnesses from my childhood. As I mentioned in the earlier chapter, I hadn't really put together the fact that I was vaccine-injured until 2019, when I spoke to parents of injured children in California and recognized that their child's story was often so similar to mine.

When I'd had my measles shot at some point in the middle of the 1970's, my arm had swelled up bigger than my torso, and I ran a very high fever. After which, my family doctor had looked at my mom from the comfort of his simple exam room in his old-town Whittier office – after my mother had rushed back to show the doctor her grotesquely swollen child mere hours after my ill-fated measles injection – and simply said:

"Well now – it looks like your little lady was allergic to something in that shot! AND, she appears to be breaking out in a measles rash to boot – sorry about that! You keep icing that arm, mom – and for my part, we won't be giving her any more shots! Because I like my license and don't want to risk her arm falling off – or worse!" And with a final chuckle from the good doctor, that was the end of it.

A doctor's judgment – in the 1970's in California – was akin to Biblical pronouncement. My mother proceeded, in the years after that visit, to just tell the preschool (followed by the elementary and junior high schools), that I'd had most all of my childhood vaccines, but had turned on an allergic reaction to the last inoculation, and that thereafter our family doctor had said "no more."

And, for their part, the schools never gave her any guff. My mother wasn't called an "anti-vaxxer," nor was she humiliated by other parents at PTA meetings because her child happened to be allergic to one of the Measles Vaccine ingredients. And no one disbelieved her when she would tell the story of my arm swelling up so badly that it was nearly the same size as my torso.

Most importantly, I was never discriminated against or kicked off of campus. And in my considered legal opinion from my vantage point in 2023, that is ***still*** the way it should be – ***in all states***. Government should never have the ability to override a doctor's judgment and force a person or child to get a repeat dose of something that hurt them or nearly killed them.

But with the benefit of forty years of hindsight and education, that measles shot had done much more than make my arm swell up and give me a high fever. It ushered in endless recurrent bouts of severe illnesses. Prior to my measles shot, I'd never really been sick at all. (And yes, I'm sure about that: my mother was nothing if not a mini-historian, documenting every first word spoken, first tooth, and also every injury and illness in my little pink, cloth-covered baby book). But after the measles shot, about every three or four weeks like clockwork, I would "catch another cold."

My colds, however, were never simple runny noses that went away on their own. And unlike my friends, I was never able to "go to school" with my cold. My colds were awful affairs. Sinus infections for weeks, with both nasal passages completely blocked. Sore throats that turned to Strep. Relentless ear infections and coughs that made me sound like I had tuberculosis and not just bronchitis. And often, all of these symptoms occurred at once.

Moreover, I could not ever kick a cold without an antibiotic. I also don't think I ever ran a "normal" fever of 99 or 100 degrees. If I had a fever, it was a minimum of 104 degrees, and would usually creep up past 106. It if didn't break, my mother and father would eventually bundle me up into the car, and drive down the road to the hospital that was at the end of our street, carrying me into the Emergency Room in the middle of the night.

There, the nurses would proceed to strip me down to my undies and T-shirt, as I sat violently shivering on the exam table – pulling my arms to my chest and crossing my legs in a futile attempt to conserve body heat in a room whose temperature was typically on par with Antarctica. And wondering, for my part, why being forced to be "cold" when I felt like I was dying was supposedly so "good" for my fever. This ignominy was typically followed by the nurses finding a tub, and adding me and a bunch of ice into the tub, or just attempting to pack me in ice while still on the exam table. Protocols which I remained convinced were designed to kill me.[63]

The ER rodeo was usually capped off by an upset battle-axe nurse arriving back on the scene, ripping the thermometer out of my mouth after chastising me for the fact that my mouth wasn't firmly closed – did they not understand I had to breathe?? – and then loudly pronouncing to all in the neighboring vicinity that the thermometer "must be broken" as it was "still showing 106 degrees" and that they were going to go "find a better thermometer!"

I never knew another child in the 1970's who was as sick as I routinely was. But in 2019, I met a cadre of parents whose children were vaccine-injured, and many of those children were much sicker than I had ever been. But all of that was still far in the future on the day in 1975 when I discovered that one of my ancestors was Patrick Henry.

---

[63] An interesting aside, which I learned many years later as an adult, is that fevers actually have a role to play in illness. And ironically, by artificially lowering a body's fever, we may actually be hamstringing our ability to fight off whatever infection we have. Put simply, fevers put the immune system into overdrive, and stoke the "fighting components" of our immune system which are necessary for our bodies to combat most bacterial or viral infections: "The action begins when … bacteria, viruses … stimulate … tumor necrosis factor (TNF), and interferon (IFN) to alter the hypothalamic set point … and raise the core body temperature … [which TNF and interferon, in turn,] … also act to trigger an immune and inflammatory response [including] … leukocytosis, T cell activation, B cell proliferation, NK cell killing, and increased white blood cell adhesion…." Balli S. et al. (2022). *Physiology, Fever.* StatPearls Publishing, https://www.ncbi.nlm.nih.gov/books/NBK562334/ (quoting Conti B.. *Prostaglandin E2 That Triggers Fever Is Synthesized Through An Endocannabinoid-Dependent Pathway.* Temperature. Austin, 2016 Jan-Mar;3(1):25-7).

I now view the reflexive rush by most parents to drown their kids in Advil and Tylenol in order to "lower a fever" (which fever often is nowhere near the dangerous range for inducing seizures) to be yet another example of the Pharmaceutical industry's successful brainwashing. In my house, we no longer artificially lower non-life-threatening fevers. (And, given that I survived many days of fevers in excess of 105 as a child, with no seizing and no brain damage, I also have a very different view than most of what constitutes a "truly high" fever).

I took the nap my mother had been recommending, and when I awoke, I felt better. And so my mother and I picked up with our chat. We talked about communism. We talked about a place called Europe. We talked about Hungary and Romania.

For her part, though my mother had never been to college, she was an innately talented teacher. She knew that we were hard-wired to learn through stories. She knew that it was better to show, not tell. And so, later that day, she grabbed from our den's shelf the big, orange encyclopedia that was a good seven inches in height and width.

And muscling it over to the couch, she then plopped down and turned the pages to show me where these countries were located. She read to me about the revolutions in Europe. But more importantly, she told me what her father's family had faced.

"When the communists came, they had tanks. Look honey, here's a picture of a tank," my mother said while pointing at a grainy little image of an early-era military tank. "But the poor farmers did not have tanks. They had nothing, really. And so it was never a fair fight. You will never win by fighting tanks with pitchforks and farm equipment. And yet, that's all our people had to fight back with – that and the rocks in their fields."

I thought back to the tools in our horse barn. I knew what a pitchfork was. While I was too young to do much with it other than lift it horizontally, which always felt so heavy in my hands, I also knew that compared to the big metal tanks in the pictures I was seeing in the family encyclopedia, the pitchfork would certainly be no match.

My mother continued: "So in the early 1900s, there was a time in Hungary known as 'Red Terror.' It was a period of horrific violence. The communists had taken over the country and had risen to positions of power in the cities. But in the countryside – where the farmers were – the people were against communism. And the communist government did not like the difference of opinion held by the farmers, and so the government deemed farmers like our ancestors to be 'enemies of the state.'"

I lay on the couch, wide-eyed and engrossed as she relayed what had happened to her father's family. My mother turned to more pages in the Encyclopedia, explaining how people "hated those who dared to disagree with the communist government" – and had begun to hunt them down, and kill them for their different beliefs.

"Look here, honey," my mother pointed, "it says that Tibor Szamuely wrote in the pages of the Vörös Újság (Red News)":

> Everywhere counter-revolutionaries run about and swagger; beat them down! Beat their heads where you find them! If counter-revolutionaries were to gain the upper hand for even a single hour, there will be no mercy on any ... [of us].... [So before] they stifle the revolution, suffocate them in their own blood!

My mother's voice quoting the above paragraph was still ringing in my ears as she went on to explain that the above passage was representative of the vitriolic hatred shown to the farmers and countrymen who did not agree with the quickly-rising communist government. Laying her hand on my forehead to check my temperature, she carried on further with her impromptu history lesson.

"Honey, hatred and fear can be bad things. And it was this very high level of unreasonable hatred – and fear of their fellow countrymen who thought differently – that led those in power to establishing checkpoints in cities ... where people whose only crime was NOT believing in communism would be stopped. And then arrested. For basically nothing, or on trumped up charges. And then they would be taken away and tortured with burning cigars, or with nails like they put in Jesus. Or sometimes, they'd be made to drink massive amounts of water ... that would cause their stomachs to expand until they died."

I listened quietly. I had no idea that people in modern times had been tortured like Jesus. Or that one could die from being forced to drink too much water.

My mother began to wrap up the sad story. "Often, the hostages would be made to dig their own graves before being killed. And again – their only crime? The fact that they did not support the 'Communist Revolution.' And often, even this was just an excuse, because the communists were a poor movement – and needed to steal grain from the peasants and farmers to survive."

"And my family –" she whispered, placing her hand once more on my warm forehead, "most of us were just peasants and poor farmers. So my grandma and grandpa left, because they did not want to have these things I've been telling you about happen to them. And they came to America to raise my dad – who is, of course, your grandpa – in this great country."

She stopped briefly, looking directly into my eyes, her tone as serious as it had ever been. "It's an honor to be born here, Leigh. The United States is based on freedom – for everyone. This country is grounded on the fact that simple citizens cannot not be stopped in the street for no reason, nor tortured for their beliefs. The founding fathers – like Patrick Henry who is on your Kleenex Box – they made sure of that."

I nodded, tears in my eyes, as she continued. "We have the right to what is called Freedom of Speech and Freedom of Religion – that's what the First Amendment is all about. And Freedom to Bear Arms, which are weapons – that's the Second Amendment. And these freedoms protect, most importantly, those who are in the minority. Because when you are in the majority – and lots of people agree with your position? Well then, you don't really need protection. It's the differing voice, the little guy who doesn't agree with the masses – *that* is the guy who needs protection – and that guy is protected in America. And that? Well, America's view is fairly unique, as countries go. And what is also very unique is our right to bear weapons. My dad will tell you – just ask Grandpa sometime when you're over at his house – that an unarmed people is a people in danger. Because it is only when the citizens have the right to real weapons – not pitchforks – that those who would oppress others are kept in check."

I lay on the couch, awestruck. My mother could definitely tell a riveting, impassioned story when given the chance.

"What is 'oppress?'" I inquired.

"It means to hold others down, or to do unjust things to them. And 'in check' – the way I just used it – means that the other person will NOT do that, or will minimally think twice before doing something."

I stared at the wall for a second, reviewing, in my mind's eye, the juxtaposition of the two main arteries of my family tree. On the one side, a guy named Patrick Henry who helped start this country I was living in, and argued for the protections my mother had just talked about. And on my mom's side, a people who grew up in a place without such protections, who were hunted down like animals and left to fight against the government with nothing but their bare hands and farm tools. And who escaped being made to dig their own graves by immigrating to America.

It was heavy weather for a child.

But my mother never shied away from hard questions. She never shied away from using stories about history as learning tools – knowing intuitively that people would remember the story much better than a bunch of random figures and paragraphs in a dusty history book.

And both my mother and father, despite being of widely divergent views on many things – and indeed often found to be rather violently disagreeing with each other on virtually every topic imaginable during protracted hours-long arguments – remained united on the essential points:

We lived in a great country, founded on Freedom.

A freedom that was worth fleeing to, fighting for, and dying for.

And reflecting back now on such conversations, from a vantage point many decades later? I can say with certainty that those tutorials stuck.

And for that, I remain grateful.

And never have such lessons seemed more important than they do right now, in 2023.

Chapter 9

It was the 1990's. I was staring down a senior partner in my law firm.

"Let me get this straight. The partners are buying themselves a bunch of new computers. But they are not going to buy the secretaries new computers? Most of you guys don't know how to use a computer. In fact, three of you don't even know how to turn them on. I'm not being hyperbolic. Chris, and Gary, and Joe literally ... DO. NOT. KNOW. WHERE. THE. POWER. BUTTON. IS!"

I paused to take a breath in the middle of my tirade. "While the secretaries are working on archaic dinosaur-style computers from more than a decade ago ... with monitors so bad they need coke bottle glasses just to decipher what's on the screen –"

"Now Leigh..." one of the partners interrupted, "you have to understand –"

"No, I don't. What I understand right now is really all that I 'need to understand.' You guys are allocating law firm money to new items that sure will look pretty in your offices, but for all your understanding of how they work, will be rendered useless paperweights on your desks. While the girls in the hall who actually need the new equipment to help you get your work done – and on which equipment they work eight or sometimes fifteen hours a day if you count their overtime? Yeah, they are getting the proverbial shaft because the firm has decided to just let them go cross-eyed for lack of new computer equipment. It's not right."

I turned on my heel and left. The secretaries were my friends, and on their behalf, I was pissed.

At the time of the little mid-1990's contretemps with the computers in my law firm, I was still actually a fair bit younger than most of the secretaries and indeed all of the junior attorneys, many of whom were in their later twenties or thirties and had children and husbands. But in style, and in age, and in dress and demeanor, the secretaries were much closer to who I was at the time than the curmudgeonly old fossil-ish partners. And I related to the secretaries much more easily than I did our law firm's male partners – about half of whom were older than my grandfather.

This age anomaly – with me being younger than virtually all of the lawyers and secretaries at my law firm – had come about due to the fact that I'd basically skipped high school. To be clear, I had not set out to skip high school. In fact, I was just plugging along through the public schools of Whittier, California my whole educational life, expecting I would graduate La Serna High in 1990, with all of my friends.

But then, in 1987, around the end of my eighth grade year in Middle School, my mother had received a letter in our mailbox. It reviewed her only child's standardized test scores for the preceding years, noting that I'd always scored in the 99th+ percentile. The letter went on to explain that a local university had a new program, much like the novel program at Johns Hopkins University, that allowed young children who were academically outstanding to visit their campus and take a college entrance exam. If the child scored well on that exam, the child would then be invited to start college, either part or full-time, depending on the test scores.

My mother showed me the letter the day it came in our mailbox, and asked me for my thoughts.

"Well, it looks interesting," I replied, "but I've never really considered college. I mean, Mr. Johns in Career Ed last year said we had 'many moons' before we needed to decide what we wanted our majors in college to be…."

My mother laughed in reply. "Fair enough. Well, how about this. Why don't we start by going to the orientation at this college, and getting a little more info on the program?"

And that is how my family came to find ourselves in a giant 500-person lecture hall one evening a short time later. I was intimidated, and I'm pretty sure my parents were as well. Neither of them had attended university – in fact, no one on either side of my extended family had attended college after high school. We were a solidly working class family where, for much of my youth, money was in short supply. My father worked in auto body shops for a living, and my mother was a homemaker.

Although a couple of years earlier, my father, along with his buddy, had decided to take the unprecedented step of no longer "working for the man." They'd left their respective jobs to join forces, and open their own auto body repair shop with some money my dad had won during a trip to Las Vegas.

After the new shop opened, my mother had started helping with the paperwork. But neither of my parents had ever stepped foot in the hallowed halls of a university prior to this evening's orientation.

Shortly after we sat down for the program, a young Asian girl took the microphone.

"Hi! I'm Joan, and I'm 11 years old and will soon graduate college. I'm part of this program – we call it 'EEP' – and it stands for Early Entrance Program. I'm on the college debate team, and I play the piano. And I'm part of the collegiate vocal chorale, and my majors are ...." She continued on at a rapid pace, and had my undivided attention.

I took stock of her. Hair in a ponytail, wearing a sweater dress just like mine, she was bright, and bubbly, and obviously whip-smart. She talked about how kids who were young and intelligent were allowed to start "a real university" and attend courses with actual college students. Her program was not one that simply taught college material to a group of segregated high-school kids – rather, young children were placed directly into regular university courses full of other normal-aged co-eds. Joan wrapped up her presentation, and was followed at the podium by a second preteen.

The second girl was blond, short – and not quite as bubbly or outgoing as the first – but obviously whip-smart too: she was triple-majoring and about to head off to med school. And she was even younger than Joan.

By this point in the presentation, I knew I'd finally found my tribe. From the time I'd started kindergarten, I had loved school. But I'd always been working way above my grade level. Even now, at the ripe old age of 50, I can still keenly remember coming home from my kindergarten and first grade classes, complaining that the other kids still "couldn't read" – and that the only books on the shelves in our classrooms were "Dick and Jane."

I would lament to my mother about how being forced to read over and over about "Dick and Jane's dog Spot" was not exactly holding my attention, as I'd been reading those primers at age three. By the point of kindergarten, I was cutting my teeth on real books, and also lustily eyeing the whole set of blue Nancy Drew books and golden-colored Trixie Belden stories that my mother had sitting along our den bookshelves. Books which she herself had read as a child, and which she had saved to pass onto her children.

My mother, understanding my frustration in the early years of elementary school, had approached my teachers to explain the issue. For their part, my teachers were usually quite accommodating. They would typically just let me go into the classrooms of the grade levels above my own, and "work ahead" on the upper grades' class work. But by the time I'd hit middle school in sixth grade, I had been reading at a collegiate level for awhile, and it had become ever more challenging for me to "work ahead" – since working ahead now meant I needed text books that were not physically located in any classroom of our junior high school.

Unlike some kids who were smart, I possessed decent social skills, so I'd always had friends in my grade level. And they were real friends: we bonded over ponies, and playing outdoors, and French-braiding our hair, and cartoons, and Girl Scouts. But we rarely if ever bonded over academics, because what I was studying academically was so often years ahead of whatever they were studying.

So it was with shock, and not a small amount of longing, that I eyeballed these girls who taken the lectern in this massive university lecture hall. Girls that were younger than me, and already in college.

They were my tribe. And I knew it, as surely as I knew my own name.

I leaned over to my mother and whispered, "I'll take that college entrance test whenever it's offered."

She whispered back *sotto voce*, "I'm not surprised," and then gave me a knowing smile.

Unfortunately, when the day came for me to take the test, I was sick as a dog. Luckily for me, the university kindly let me come in and take the test by myself about 10 days after the originally-scheduled test date, once I had recovered.

The exam included verbal comprehension questions, as well as math sections. But it was an SAT-equivalent college entrance exam and – given that I was all of 13 years old – I'd been taught virtually none of the math that appeared on the test. In sixth grade, I'd had a pre-algebra class, followed by two successive years of algebra – but by the end of eighth grade I'd still not taken Geometry, Trig, or Calculus – and yet there were some of all these topics on this college-level test.

The exam also had these horrible little sections of "Spatial Aptitude" and "Logical Reasoning." I soon came to learn that these portions specialized in asking truly awful hypotheticals about, e.g., "five little girls in red hats being on a train, but none are sitting next to boys…" at which point my eyes would begin to droop.

It is a chilling memory to recall even now. I was all alone in this cold, concrete brick testing room at a big college, with a noisy and visible analog clock on the wall. And somewhere in the midst of the hellacious word problems about little girls in red hats, and trains leaving opposite coasts at different times and going different speeds, I happened to glance up at the noise-making timepiece to discover I had only five minutes left before the end of that test section.

I looked back down at my test booklet, realizing anew that I was only about halfway through the math questions. Worse, a lot of the completed questions I had marked with little question marks in the margin, which was my personal shorthand for the fact that I didn't really know the answer but had guessed at it … and should double back to re-work the problem, time permitting.

I looked at the clock again. Four minutes. Not only was I now certain that I was *not* going to complete the test with time to review the answers about which I was uncertain, I was also now certain that I was not going to complete the math test at all… as there were a good 30 or 40 questions I'd yet to even look at.

My stomach dropped.

I'd never, in my life, not known answers. Not to this degree. Nor had I ever run out of time on any test, or even come close. And I'd certainly never had to resort to that horrible option I'd heard students discussing, where they would just "bubble in" the same letter answer, playing the odds and hoping they would get some questions correct through simple probabilities. I looked at my new nemesis, the ugly clock affixed to concrete blocks in the room, and knew there was nothing for it: I picked the letter "c" and started rapidly bubbling in the same "letter c" answer for the remaining dozens of questions.

Walking out of the building, I saw my mother in her car, cruising over to the curb to pick me up. "How'd it go?" she twittered brightly. She was probably not expecting what was to come, since test taking was a skill that had always come easily for me.

"Uhh, not so good. Pretty awful in fact." I struggled to hold back tears, feeling the memory of the tribe of smart girls from the orientation evening floating away. "I'd never seen some of this math, mom. Like, at all!! Like, it was so bad I couldn't even narrow down what I thought might be a right answer, or even rule out an obviously wrong answer. It was an absolute catastrophe – I've never been so clueless in my life!" At that point, I lost the struggle to maintain my cool, and just started openly sobbing.

"Oh! Sweetie – well – I'm sure it wasn't that bad! I mean, it's a college entrance exam, so of course you hadn't seen some of the material, because you haven't even gone to high school yet!" While my mother's words rang true, it was small solace.

She turned the key in the ignition and we began the drive home. And from there, the day somehow went from bad to worse as my mother made the unfortunate decision to make a quick stop at a store *en route* back to our house, where we walked smack into my classmate from junior high school, Bobby, and his mom.

As luck would have it, Bobby was the only other person I knew who'd gotten an invitation to take the same college entrance test. I did my best to tune things out as my mother and his mom started conversing.

Of course, two minutes into the mothers' little chat, Bobby piped up that he thought he'd "aced the test."

By this point, I'd barely gotten my emotions in check, and Bobby's little pronouncement – delivered as it was with a chipper tone and all the bravado attending most pre-teen boy's swagger moments – ushered in a whole new mini-meltdown on my part. Seeing my lip start to tremble, my mother wisely brought the conversation to a quick close. And while she did her level best to cheer me up, it was an exercise in futility: I knew I'd bombed that test … just as surely as I'd always known when I'd aced a test.

So it was with no small amount of shock when, some weeks later, my mother opened a letter that said her child had performed well enough on the exam that said child was now "permitted to enroll in college part or full time the following semester."

I snatched the letter out of her hands faster than a duck swallowing a June Bug – scanning it in disbelief.

"So, wow! Really?? I can start college?? But how??"

I kept reading. It seemed I had aced the vocabulary and verbal comprehension portions of the test. And, as I'd expected, I'd bombed the math sections, literally pulling in 50th and 60th percentile scores. But what I hadn't known is that the administrators of the program did not care one lick about the math sections.

In fact, if a child presented as only a "math genius" – acing all the mathematics but yielding only an average test score on the Reading Comprehension sections of the test – then the child would *not* be accepted into the program. Apparently, the thinking was that all college courses – at least the General Education courses – required the student to be good at reading, writing and comprehension. But – luckily for me – the reverse was not true: a kid could ace the English language sections and absolutely suck at the math components – as I'd done – and still be extended an invitation ... courtesy of the fact that a lack of math skills was not going to hamper one's progression through college courses (assuming one was not a Math major).

Because words were my jam, I'd somehow quite luckily – by the skin on my proverbial chin – made the cut. I sat down, still in surprise at my dream being revived.

Looking at my mother with tears in my eyes, I said simply: "I'll go."

At that point, I was just starting my first year of high school, and my decision to bail on said high school was underscored by the fact that my high school had promised I would not have to take a fourth year of algebra (since I'd already taken three years of it in Middle School) – and then reneged.

At the outset, my mother and I had both lobbied the school, and they had stated that if I could pass the Algebra One Final Exam with an "A," they would in turn allow me to take Geometry in my freshman year. Then, when I'd aced the test (I wasn't bad in all math – just math I'd not yet studied), my high school had reneged and stated I could take a fourth year of Algebra while also simultaneously taking Geometry in lieu of my elective.

I was pissed at the bait and switch and outright lies – and further upset that I was being made to study the same subject for a fourth year in a row, which subject I'd just demonstrably proven I well knew by acing their Final.

So with the math debacle still acting as a burr under my saddle, the notion of bailing on high school for the comparative freedom of college was a no-brainer. And that is how, at the age of 14, I decided to start college, after which I never looked back.

As a result of the above fast-track detour, I was a good half-decade younger than my attorney-peers when I graduated law school and started working full time at my law firm – although I was no less verbally talented than they were despite my youth. And – still offended that my law firm partners had decided to purchase for themselves what amounted to toys for their desks while leaving the secretaries without new computer equipment – I'd had no problem despite my youth in unleashing my verbal skills in an attempt to right the little injustice.

The equipment issue was near and dear to my heart, given that I had taken a year off between college and law school to work as a legal secretary in downtown Los Angeles using truly antiquated equipment (a reel-to-reel transcription unit, and a manual typewriter). Thus, more than most of the attorneys in my firm, I understood what a hardship it was to be forced to use ancient equipment when impatient partners were wanting their dictated documents transcribed at the speed of light.

Shortly after spouting off at the partner about the unfairness of the computer situation, a different partner was tapped to come into my office and "have a chat" with me. The partnership, it turned out, had taken a new vote – and decided everyone in the office would now be getting new computers – including the secretarial pool.

I smiled.

Until the partner launched into a short monologue about how I needed to learn to "be more tactful" and to not "fight every battle." These points were followed by some version of how the law firm owners "knew best" and the fact that "social capital is not infinite."

It was not my first such lecture. And it definitely would not be my last. But I was as convinced then as I am now that the partnership was, in the main, incorrect.

Martin Luther King, Jr. once said, "Injustice everywhere is a threat to justice everywhere." And though nearly thirty years have passed since that conversation with the partners – and while I've indeed chosen to not fight every battle because it's just not always possible – I *have chosen* to fight a goodly number. Particularly when it comes to something that is inherently wrong, or manifestly unfair. Or where the little guy is getting the proverbial shaft because he's not on the "power" side of the equation.

In fact, that last category of battles? Those I typically stop to fight, no matter how seemingly trivial. Because while injustice is always bad, there's something extra wrong about people who start manifestly unfair fights by picking on the littlest guy which – to this day – makes me want to finish whatever the other bully started.

I firmly believe that we, as humans on this planet, have a duty to fight injustice. When instead we choose to turn a blind eye, what that teaches the evildoer – for that is what one is, if one is perpetrating even tiny injustices – is that doing evil is okay. And thus emboldened, such evildoers, in my experience, grow in to committing even greater injustices.

Perhaps worse, by remaining silent in such situations, we model to our own minds and those of our children – as well as all others who may be watching – that injustice is fine, if only on a minor scale. But just like the fact that injustices – once committed – embolden those perpetrating them to take greater liberties and commit worse crimes, a similar phenomenon occurs on the flip side of the scale: we become accustomed to being apathetic in the face of injustice, and so we don't take note and rise up when successively greater injustices come our way.

While the 1990's may not seem that long ago, the reality is that in my law firm – in that era – it was still to some degree an "old boy's club." All the partners in my Newport Beach firm were men, save for one woman who was tougher by far than almost all of the guys combined.

My male partners were rich, smart, and powerful – and working for the largest companies in the world, while procuring great results for those companies. This resulted in the partners and the firm getting paid top dollar.

And put simply: these men were not accustomed to serious pushback from within their ranks, or to hearing the word "no" from their underlings. And they did not always take kindly to it. But their response, and their unending attempts to mold me over the years – into a "quieter and more accepting person" – thankfully never took root. As comedian Ron White coyly quipped, after he was ejected in an inebriated state from a bar and then ironically arrested for being drunk in public: "I may have had the right to remain silent… but I lacked the ability."

Such is the story of my life: I'm sure I've always had the right to keep quiet. But Heaven knows, I've lacked the ability. And it can definitely be a double-edged sword.

But for the last three years?

I'm convinced that – far from being a personality defect – it's been a saving grace. Because Edmund Burke was onto something when he noted that "only thing necessary for the triumph of evil is for good men to do nothing."

And thus my own personal rules for living have become less a quiet agenda on my part, and now something I boldly own – and encourage others to try on for size.

When in doubt, show up.

Stand up.

Speak up.

Because injustice is not a self-correcting state, and conditions do not get better in the face of your silence. In point of fact, unjust situations typically just get worse. And I've learned it's far better to fight when the situation is embryonic than to wait and later attempt to right an unjust ship that is headed for the sea floor with many aboard. Injustice, like anything in life, has a "tipping point." And it's much harder to fight and win when the odds have tipped too far in the wrong direction.

I see this in communist countries in Asia where I work. I hear it from immigrants who narrowly escaped genocides.

Do not wait.

Carpe diem, my friends, *carpe diem*. There is no better time than now to seize the day – to stand and peacefully correct injustices in your life, both big and small.

You can do it.

All the heroes we admire? They are simply men and women, just like us, who upon seeing a wrong, decided they could make it right. And who then took action to do so.

And that innate sense of right and wrong – and desire to better things? It lives within us all, as surely as we draw breath.

All we have to do is set it free.

Chapter 10

I stared with fascination at Professor Urquidi's Dry Erase board in King Hall. It was the late 1980's, and I was taking a Political Science class to meet one of my General Education requirements. Having heard Urquidi was a great teacher, I'd signed up.

By my second year of college, I'd already discovered an important rule that I still follow to this day: A good teacher makes or breaks a topic. I am convinced one could, e.g., take "Basket-Weaving 101" from a great teacher and still learn amazing and life-changing things. The reverse is, unfortunately, also true: I've personally sat in a class on my most favorite topic that was being taught by a horrible teacher who managed to somehow entirely ruin the subject for me.

And as important as it is to avoid bad teachers on any topic, the same is particularly true when we, as parents, are guiding our children through their educational years: it is a bad idea to leave children in the room of a person who is dumb or mean, or who mumbles hopelessly, or who is otherwise incompetent. We cannot risk losing our future leaders because they were taught by poor educators. Instead, I believe it is a primary duty to endeavor to put children in classes with truly great teachers, for that is how they will come to love learning. And that is a gift which is priceless.

So there I sat, with my new favorite professor as I began my collegiate career. It was an exciting time in the world. The Cold War had ended and now the Berlin Wall was coming down. There was much to discuss. But on this day, I was a bit curious – as we weren't talking about politics or current events at all (or so I thought).

Instead, my professor seemed to be off on a tangent, speaking to us about some guy named Milgram.

"So Stanley Milgram was this Yale Profesor in the 1960's. And he wanted to figure out if the Holocaust was – perhaps – the result of something other than Hitler. Because Hitler was only one guy. So this Yale teacher thought: 'Maybe the Holocaust had something to do with us – as human beings – maybe we are obedient to a dangerous degree. Even when we shouldn't be.'"

Professor Urquidi turned back to the white board, and wrote the name "Milgram" in bright red letters with his marker. As he capped the pen, I saw his tanned arms fly outward from his body, gesturing to us.

"So Milgram ran some adverts – offered people near the university the chance to come in and be part of a 'memory experiment.' Of course, it wasn't actually an experiment on 'memory.' It was an experiment on obedience. But he didn't tell the participants that."

Urquidi paused for a moment while looking out at us before resuming. "And when folks came in off the street in response to his ad, Milgram would then pair the people up, in groups of two, and then hand them little sheets of paper that had arbitrary word pairs listed on the paper. And the folks were told to 'memorize the word pairs.' Then, Milgram would split the two people up, once they were done memorizing." Urquidi stopped for a moment, turning to draw two squares on the white board before resuming. "And he would place the two people into two little, separate rooms. The rooms had solid walls, so the first guy could not see his buddy in the next room. But there was an intercom – so they could hear each other, and talk to one another."

Someone sneezed in class, and Urquidi turned back to face us. Having concluded his drawing of the two stick-figure men in their respective rooms to demonstrate his point, Urquidi then proceeded to recap the story:

"So the first guy in the experiment would say a word from the list, and his buddy – the second guy – was then supposed to give him the correct answer to the word pair. So maybe the word pairing they'd studied had been 'dog-cat.' But when the buddy, instead of responding with the correct answer of 'cat' gave an incorrect answer of 'camel' to the prompt –" Urquidi stopped briefly, for emphasis – "well, that's when it became interesting."

Urquidi paused again, a tiny frown taking over his countenance.

"It got interesting because the first dude had been told to deliver an electric shock to his neighbor – whenever his neighbor gave him an incorrect answer to one of the questions. And the first guy had seen his buddy being wired – with these electrode patches being placed all over his forearms. And the first guy – who was giving the prompts – had been told to throw a switch on a panel that looked like a Circuit Board, for every wrong answer his buddy gave him."

I hazarded a look around. Our class seemed, to a person, shocked. In fact, it had gotten really quiet. But my professor kept going, gathering speed.

"And for each wrong answer received, the first guy was supposed to throw successively higher switches – that delivered successively higher-voltage shocks to his buddy – every time some new 'wrong answer' was uttered. In order to negatively reinforce his buddy's wrong answers."

By this point, no one was talking, or sneezing. We were all glued to Professor Urquidi's recounting of this strange psychology test that some Yale professor named Milgram had thought up 25 years earlier.

"So unbeknownst to the first guy, who was delivering the shocks, his friend was actually NOT in the room next door. Nor was the friend being shocked whenever the first guy flipped a switch. Instead, the first guy was hearing pre-recorded wrong and right answers to his questions on the word pairings, as well as pre-recorded sounds of pain as the experiment progressed. So while first guy *believed* his buddy was being shocked – because of the sounds coming back over the intercom – there was no actual harm occurring. And, in the beginning, when the shock voltages were still fairly low, the first guy might just hear a grunt in response from his buddy, or perhaps a loud exhalation of air or a slight moan."

Urquidi stopped to have a sip of his coffee.

"But as the voltages increased steadily, the first guy would begin to hear the second guy start screaming in pain and begging for mercy. Which, as you might imagine, would cause no small amount of emotional distress to the first guy … who'd been told to deliver the shocks that were causing such pain to his buddy."

At this point, Urquidi drew a switch box on the white board. Underneath the first little switch he wrote: "15 volts." Then he drew a bunch of little switches with higher voltages listed beneath them. Finally, Urquidi told us the last switches in Milgram's experiment showed 450 volts with "XXX" listed underneath.

He turned back to us. "Who knows what a 450 volt shock does to a person?"

I craned my head around, remaining quiet. Neither math nor science were my strong suits.

Into the silence, a guy with a beard from the back of the class called out: "It'll kill 'ya."

Our professor nodded. "Yep. That's right: a 450 volt shock is an electric chair voltage. It's fatal."

The class remained quiet, horrified at where this was headed.

Urquidi continued: "So, as the first guy is having to flip higher and higher switches with higher and higher doses of electricity for every wrong answer given, he's hearing piped-in screaming and begging from the guy he's allegedly delivering shocks to (because remember, no one was actually being hurt, although the guy in the experiment does not know that). And so the first guy begins to hear abject begging and pleading, statements like: 'Man, you gotta stop – the shocks are causing my heart to skip beats, I'm gonna have a heart attack if you continue!'"

A student raised his hand to interrupt our professor. "Dude, is this for real? The guy in the experiment is supposed to just keep shocking his buddy – even though the buddy is begging him to stop?"

Urquidi nodded. "Yes, my friend. And your astute perception is where the rubber started to meet the proverbial road. Because THAT is what was actually being studied: the first guy's obedience level to authority. So typically, at some point during the experiment, when the sounds of pain from the buddy's room escalate – typically the first guy turns around and says to the doctor in charge of the experiment: 'Do I have to keep doing this? Because I'm not comfortable continuing – given that every time I flip a switch now, my buddy in the other room is screaming from the pain of the electric shocks … and I don't want to accidentally kill him or anything….'"

Urquidi shrugged his shoulders. And then posed a rhetorical question to the class.

"Right? I mean, what would you have done? Maybe the same: ask the experimenter for permission to stop??"

I look around the room, which is still quiet as a church. Urquidi has everyone's attention. No shuffling. No bored gazing into the distance. Everyone is staring at my professor who, for his part, turns back to the white board, uncaps a new blue marker, and draws a little picture of a doctor with a stethoscope.

"Now the guy in charge of the experiment was a doctor, dressed in a very nice white lab coat complete with stethoscope and clipboard. The whole nine yards. And for his part – now understand this doctor is really just a confederate of Milgram's who was told to 'play a part' and look like a 'stern and authoritative doctor' – the 'doctor' has been informed that he should respond to any questions or hesitations from study participants by simply stating: 'You must continue.' Which is what he does – the doctor plays his part well."

I hear a loud sigh from the guy behind me in the classroom – it sounds like the same guy who answered the professor's question about voltages – and then the student begins to speak again.

"Man, that's messed up. How many of these dudes actually continued nuking their buddy with shocks – after they said they didn't want to continue – just because some 'authoritative doctor' said they had to keep going?"

Urquidi looks shrewdly at the guy with the beard who'd asked the question.

"Well, Jon, you raise an interesting question: How many Americans in this study were obedient to a doctor in a lab coat – a doctor telling them to do something that was morally reprehensible? Asking them to cause pain to another person, or even death – so the study participants thought – by continuing to flip the switches all the way up to 450 volts ... despite their buddy's screams?"

Urquidi walked closer to the first row of his students. "In fact, Jon, you've asked the exact question that Stanley Milgram wanted answered: 'What percentage of law-abiding citizens would put their friend to death, over a wrong answer on a memory test, just because a person in position of authority said they must?"

Urquidi gazed out at his students. Crickets.

"Whatdya' think, class? Was it 5%? Was it 10% of the people who continued to flip the switches? Or do you think that everyone in the study just told the doctor to 'screw off' and walked out – because they knew that torturing people was wrong?"

The class remained silent: still dumbstruck by this sudden left-turn from politics into psychology. No one wanted to hazard a guess.

Into the uncomfortable silence, I offered quietly: "Well, I hope everyone just walked out. I mean, that would have been the appropriate thing – the right thing – to do."

Urquidi smiled. Not his normal smile, but a sad one. I was quite young, and even more of an optimist at the time than I am today.

Urquidi, I would later find out, was about seventy years old. And in the coming semesters, I ended up taking every course that man offered, including independent 400-level research courses where he tasked me with re-writing his books about politics and media – and the sly tools which journalists employ in their allegedly "factual" columns that end up being little more than fancy opinion pieces.

But on that late afternoon, all that was months in the future. Urquidi pulled his gaze from mine, looked out at the rest of the class, and with a deathly quiet tone I'd never heard him employ before, resumed the final installment of his lesson that day.

"It was 65%, my friends." He paused, his voice gravelly, before he resumed. "Fully two out of every three God-fearing, honest, sane, law-abiding Americans in the early 1960's would shock their new friend – all the way to the end of the line – to death. They did this KNOWING it was wrong. They did this KNOWING it would kill their new buddy. They did this KNOWING it was a certain death."

Urquidi had started pacing back and forth, his voice rising dramatically. But then, just as suddenly, he stopped moving, and with deadly flat eyes, concluded chillingly:

"Simply – SIMPLY – because some damn person in a position of authority over them *told them to....*"

I felt whipsawed. Looking subtly over my shoulders at my fellow classmates' faces, I could tell they felt the same. Everyone was fighting tears, shocked at the realization that the capacity for such inhumanity apparently lived within us all.

Despite the pall-like presence in the room, Urquidi did not stop.

"I want you to listen to this next. And listen well. You, and me – we – are all hardwired to be obedient. Obedience is built into our DNA. Even when something is not the best option. Even when it's not the right thing to do. "

He paused before continuing.

"You need – as you go out and live your lives from this point forward – you need to be very, very careful *who* you are listening to. You must always evaluate *what* is being asked of you. You must examine it scrupulously. Hold it up to your own moral codes. Give it no quarter; be harsh in your assessments. Do not believe anyone simply because of who they are. Do not believe me, simply because I'm your teacher. Do not believe your doctor, your friend, your boss or your government – just because of who they are. The participants in Milgram's little experiment were not 'evil men.'"

Urquidi raised an index finger, and then swept it across the class like a scythe moving through a field of wheat.

"The men in his experiment? They were *you*. They were *me*. And don't you ever forget it."

Giving us a final look, Urquidi walked over to the door, opened it, and quietly left.

But his lesson? Never left me.

I can still remember the moment as if it were yesterday. In hindsight, I feel almost like it was God speaking to me that day, through the medium of a professor I loved. I believe now, thirty-five long years later, that that single day in 1987 – that singular message – may have been the sole reason the variables in my universe aligned in a way that permitted me to skip high school and take the path that I did.

I needed to hear that message.

In that place. And at that time.

Ever the lone wolf – and even then being one of the people least inclined to follow – I still needed to hear what humanity was capable of.

And it was a message that – indeed – I've never forgotten.

A subject that – were someone to ask me right now to identify the most important lesson we could hope to adopt, or leave instilled in our children – would always make the cut.

And while I've never forgotten the message, the years have certainly refined my ability to apply it.

Chapter 11

A few years later found me in the middle of law school. Heading into summer break, I'd elected to take an internship with a firm in Orange County.

There was exactly one female partner in the law firm's Newport Beach office. She prided herself on being tough as nails and intimidated everyone. I was no exception. I'd just walked to her office to turn in my first completed project – a written memo. It seemed only a matter of minutes before she stormed down the hall and into my office.

"This is bad. Unacceptable." She tossed the memo onto my desk, and then abruptly turned to leave.

Looking back, I still cannot believe I had the temerity to interrupt her mini-hurricane of an attempted departure.

"Uh, Jacqui," I stammered, quite ineloquently, "could you give me some pointers as to how I could, umm, maybe fix it?"

Partner Jacqueline turned back to look at me. Her small brown eyes drilled into mine, much like I'd seen hawks do before dropping out of the sky to grab their prey.

"No, Leigh. It's bad. It's so, so—" she interrupted her own sentence to more fully contemplate the weight of my inadequacy – "it's just *so bad* I don't even know what to tell you to do to make it better." She hastily finished her sentence, her words raining down on my shoulders like a hailstorm of rocks.

And with each word, I could feel the prospect of landing a long-term job at this firm becoming progressively more unlikely. Motivated by the sheer terror of a career opening drying up before my eyes – in an already-tough job market that had been hit by the severe recession that exploded in the early 1990's – I interrupted her second attempted departure from my office.

"Jacqueline, could you maybe just … tell me how you would re-write the first two sentences?"

She turned back to me, clearly stunned that I would not let the issue drop. For my part, I was also stunned at what had exited my lips – I felt that I might be having an out-of-body experience.

Perhaps due to her simple surprise at being twice halted – by a little upstart of a gal who'd been all of 19 years old during my first interview a few months prior – Jacqueline took pity on me.

"Yeah, I would say…." and she then proceeded to dictate to me the first couple of sentences, showing me through her choice of words how she would re-write the memo.

Meanwhile, I was taking frantic notes on the margins of the original memo that she'd hurled toward my head – veritably shaking with the fear of not being able to write quickly enough to capture her thoughts. I knew without asking there was no likelihood of her slowing down or repeating what she was saying. While I was still busy transcribing Jaqueline's rapid-fire thoughts, she exhaled loudly, abruptly turned, and stalked regally out of my office.

I did not delay, but turned back to my computer. Switching it on, I did not think. I did not outline. I did not sketch out my thoughts… nor do any of the other things that my law school professor had taught us to do in our "pre-writing preparatory phase."

Instead, I put my fingers on the keyboard, typed out the two sentences she had given me, and then, with Jacqui's voice still echoing in my ears – for she had dictated the sentences without adornment, in a manner similar to her conversational patter – I proceeded to keep her tenor and style as I re-drafted the memo from start to end in her voice.

Thus finished, I did not pause to re-read the memo, or proof it. Or wonder how I could make it better. Or do any of the other post-writing analyses that as a young writer I liked to indulge in.

With nothing to lose – because I knew I was as good as fired if I did not correct Jacqueline's impression of me – I grabbed the papers off my printer, marched down to her office, and handed them over to her. Then, not brave enough to wait for an acknowledgment, I silently returned to my office. Where I tried not to cry, and sat contemplating what might happen next.

I did not have to wonder long. Jacqueline returned almost on my heels, slamming her way through my office door. Her eyes were wide open.

"I don't – I don't – I don't know what to say! This is great! How'd you do it?"

Prone to being a bit manic, Jacqueline was at least as lavish with her compliments as with her criticisms. I didn't know if her question was rhetorical, so I wisely decided to remain silent. Especially since I had no real answer to her query – other than the fact that I'd re-written the memo in her voice.

"Leigh, it's like a whole different person wrote it! No changes – it's brilliant. Whatever you just did – just keep doing that."

And, for the second time that day, she threw open my office door and retreated as quickly as she'd arrived.

I sat quivering, knowing I'd narrowly dodged a bullet to my professional career. And reflecting on the important lesson I'd just learned that has held me in good stead every day since.

People like to be heard, and as well have their aspirations and thoughts duplicated. And, to the extent possible, they really like to be acknowledged in wording and inflections that mimic their own. It's as if they hear you better, and like you more, when you speak to them in their tongue.

Over the years that ensued at that law firm, I continued on, working with many different partners. But from that day forward, I would start each written project by closing my eyes, and "hearing" that partner's voice in my head. Once I had a good grasp of how they spoke and saw things, then – and only then – would I pick up my pen to begin writing.

Some might call this disingenuous. I see it more as knowing your audience. Even today, when speaking, I will use different tones and different words depending on who is in front of me. Because when you match other people's reality, they understand you just that much better. And words? Well, they are an easy way to start things off on the proverbial "same page."

So while I'd learned an important lesson from working with that female partner early on, I cannot say she was my favorite person by any means, and I tended to give her a wide berth.

Unfortunately, and despite my best efforts, some years into my legal career, she'd managed to lock onto me for a couple of her cases. And I was now in the unfortunate position of working with a woman that I knew prided herself on making each new male associate cry. Literally.

To put it mildly, even on her good days Jacqueline had an explosive personality. And there could be no denying that she took particular joy in making the younger male attorneys uncomfortable enough to shed tears.

One afternoon, she buzzed my office extension. "Hey, can you bring me the Johnson file? The client is in my office. I need it right now."

Click. The line went dead.

Welp, this was par for the course now that I was assigned to her cases. The woman seemed to lack any understanding of social niceties, and that's a generous description: I was pretty certain she'd never uttered the words "please" or "thank you" to an underling.

Grabbing the Johnson file, I hopped out of my chair and jogged the short distance down the hall. Then, knocking on Jacqueline's closed door with my knuckles, I proceeded to push the door handle open with my other hand.

This "knock-and-open" system was the policy at our firm: we'd literally been told so during orientation. No one ever knocked and then waited for a partner to say "Come in." Time was money – and thus our firm culture was to knock and immediately enter.

Accordingly, after my warning knock, I pressed the door open, and stuck out my other hand with the Johnson file in it.

Jacqueline swiveled from her view of the ocean, as one of her perfectly manicured nails scraped against her all-glass, oversized desk. And then she proceeded to open her perfectly-lipsticked mouth – and begin a veritable tirade.

"How DARE you??! I'm in an important meeting – GET OUT!!!"

My jaw dropped so far I'm pretty sure it hit the floor. I looked from her face – now twisted with rage and anger – over to our client's face, who for his part, was wearing a flabbergasted expression that mirrored my own.

"Uh, sorry!" I mumbled as I beat the hastiest retreat of my life. I stepped back into the hall, feeling myself blush from my chest to my hairline, wondering what I'd done wrong.

Hadn't Jacqueline called me only moments before and demanded that I bring her the Johnson file, asap? I replayed the last few minutes, concerned that perhaps I was having a psychotic break.

Just then, Jacqui's timid secretary spoke up from the other side of the hallway. "She can be so rude! I know she called you and asked you to bring the file over – right after she rang me and I'd told her I didn't have the file."

I could feel my body swivel toward the very kind voice of the overworked secretary. Chatting with her briefly, I thanked her for validating my sense of reality.

But I remained upset all day long. And I was still simmering later that night, when I left the firm to have dinner with some women I'd met in a martial arts class, all of whom were a decade or two older than me, and had become *de facto* mentors. One of them, after being apprised of my hiccup with the female partner, uttered something I'd never before considered.

"You know, Leigh. This female partner – she sounds kind of crazy. And no doubt, she treated you badly." Her warm words moved into my jarred universe like balm for my soul. I was continuing to bathe in the buttery sympathy, until her next sentence brought me up short.

"That said, we teach people how to treat us. And you've fallen down on the job."

I stopped the fork that was *en route* to my mouth, carrying a piece of moist salmon. "I'm sorry, wait – what was that you said?" I inquired.

I'd heard my friend. But I had not entirely absorbed what I sensed was a super-important point, albeit a point my psyche was actively resisting taking in … given that it meant I was not entirely blameless in the scenario.

"I said," she repeated slowly, as if talking to a preschooler, "we teach other people how to treat us. And we're women and yeah, there's discrimination in the real world, but realistically speaking – courtesy of Title IX and various other advances in the law – in school, we're not really discriminated against much. At least not noticeably anymore in the bigger cities. Not most days."

I nodded in agreement: I'd always felt like I'd gotten a fair shake in classrooms and on campuses. And, to the extent I didn't, it certainly had not been due to any gender-based discrimination.

My friend continued.

"Teachers generally treat you well. Or at least not horribly. But then you get out in the real world, where you have a job. And bosses. And co-workers. And these characters will take advantage of you. They will seek to make their lives cushy at your expense. And, as women, we tend to say 'yes' all the time. And we fail to say 'no' often enough."

I nodded again, recognizing myself in that statement. I briefly thumbed through the last few years in my mind's eye, and honestly could not recall a time where I had ever said "no" to anyone – or to any project – at my law firm.

My mentor continued: "It's like you have a little patch of grass in front of your house in suburban America. And your little patch of grass is all nice and green, and mowed and well-taken care of. And in school – even in grad school – people are just polite, and they will walk around your lawn, and not traipse over it."

My friend stopped to take a tiny bite of her salad, and then started talking again as she munched. "But then? You hit the real world. And girl? You gotta realize people are just gonna drive their darn cars straight over your pretty little patch of grass – 'specially if you let them."

She paused again to shove more croutons into her mouth. Chewing quickly, she swallowed, and resumed her tutorial.

"I mean, they will drive a mack truck over your yard. They will do freaking doughnuts in your yard – with race cars if you let them! Until they kill your pretty little lawn. YOU are the lawn, in this example, by the way."

I nodded mutely. My friend took a minute to set down her fork before continuing.

"Ain't nobody gonna put a fence up but you. To protect YOU. 'They' aren't going to do it, because it's not in 'their' best interests. 'Their' interests extend about as far as getting YOU to do as much of THEIR work as you're willing to do – so that 'they' can get home to their families, and make more money for doing less work. And your parents aren't here to erect boundaries for you nowadays. Even if they would do that, it'd just be weird."

She had a point. And I slowly nodded again as she returned to the attack that was for my own betterment.

"You gotta learn to put up your own darned fences, m'dear – they're called boundaries, by the way. If you want to survive. In life. In your job. When you're dating. You might not like this advice, but it's true. And you're the only one who will and who can do this for yourself. And the sooner you learn this lesson? The easier your life will be."

My mentor quietly took a sip of her water. Somehow, she'd managed to finish eating, while I'd been so transfixed I hadn't taken a single bite during her earth-shatteringly profound monologue. I looked at the other two female friends at my table. They were all nodding in agreement.

Later that night, I replayed her comments in my mind. I was in charge of protecting me. No one was going to do this *but* me. And if I wanted to have anything left of me – after my life at this law firm – then I needed to start erecting some boundaries. I mulled this over. Perhaps I could start with some picket fences. Although I was at a law firm, so maybe I should just unfurl a roll of concertina wire for good measure.

I did not go back to the law firm the next morning, as somehow, I'd been impaneled on a jury in Compton, California. While I'd just moved to Orange County, the brilliant admin folks in charge of the criminal justice system had apparently used my former address in Los Angeles County to pull me into a jury pool at the Compton courthouse, of all places.

Even more shocking than being called into Compton for jury duty was the fact that – quite inconceivably – I had then ended up impaneled on an actual jury, because neither the prosecutor nor the defense attorney had exercised their challenges to strike a practicing attorney from their trial. The case wasn't exactly cutting edge: it involved a couple of young guys, who had walked into a burger joint in Compton, and demanded money after pulling sawed-off shotguns out of their pants. Interesting, but not groundbreaking.

So the morning, after dinner with my mentor, I drove all the way to Compton to see what it was like to sit in the jury box, instead of stand in front of it where I normally held court as an attorney. Then, after putting in a full day of listening to witnesses who'd seen the robbery occur, I drove back to my Newport Beach law firm.

With the words of my mentors still ringing in my ears – and the rude and completely unwarranted dress-down by my female partner from the day prior still circling my thoughts – I hit the ladies' room on the fifth floor of our building. I was planning to change from my casual "jury duty" clothes into a business suit, and then go into Jacqueline's office to erect my very first "fence."

As bad luck would have it, when I came out of the handicapped stall where I'd been changing into my power suit for my upcoming confrontation, I walked straight into Jacqueline.

"Oh!" we both exclaimed simultaneously.

Jacqui narrowed her brown eyes suspiciously while eyeballing my transformation.

"Aren't you on jury duty this week?" she asked. "And did you just change into a business suit at 5 p.m.?" she asked. She pointedly looked at her watch, and then back to me, confusion written all over her face.

"Uh, yes," I replied. "You're correct, I am on jury duty. And I did just get here. And change clothes."

Silence hung in the air, and I clarified: "I have an important meeting."

Jacqueline shrugged her shoulders, her curiosity apparently satisfied. "Okay."

She grabbed some paper towels to dry off her hands, and left. Abruptly, as always.

I finished my wardrobe change, freshened my lipstick, took one last look in the mirror, and walked back to my office. Throwing open the door, I dropped my casual clothes into my guest chair, and proceeded to carry on down the hallway toward Jacqueline's office.

I knocked, and – this time – waited to be acknowledged.

"Come in!" she piped out curtly, clearly frustrated that she'd had to voice the command to enter. The woman was nothing if not a walking contradiction.

I entered, and remained standing a few feet from her. I'd studied Sociology and Psychology in college, and knew a bit about body language and authority: I wasn't about to give up the "power position" by taking one of her guest chairs (which were intentionally geared to put the guest at a lower height than her "boss chair").

Standing awkwardly in the middle of her office, I took a deep breath, and launched into the monologue I'd been perseverating on since the night before, when my chat with friends had confirmed that this partner was a bit special. I gamely started to speak the words of the little spiel I'd rehearsed:

"Jacqui," I began, my voice shaking a bit, "I know that you have a tried and true pattern of exploding and yelling at people when you're stressed. Which you've probably had since you were a child. And I'm not naïve enough to think that I'm going to get you to change that pattern after decades."

I stopped briefly to swallow my spit, trying not to not pass out or otherwise let her interrupt me. Before picking back up – darn, was my voice *still* shaking? I took another deep breath and continued.

"But what you did – and what you said to me yesterday in front of our client – was completely unacceptable. You rang me, ordered me to bring you the Johnson file asap, and then when I did, you screamed at me for doing exactly as you'd asked. I cannot see through solid oak doors – nor into the confines of your rapidly-changing convoluted mind – but I can tell you this much: You and this law firm are NOT the only game in town. And the very next time you ever yell at me for doing what you asked?? Will be the last time. I don't care if you make the male junior lawyers cry every day and twice on Sunday – I know you keep tabs on just how many of them you can reduce to tears. You can yell at them – or your secretary – all you want: it's not my job to fix your relationships with them. But you will not ever address me that way again. So I suggest the next time you feel the pressure building, that you pause. Take a moment. And then? If you still feel that you must go off on someone, pick someone else."

Jacqueline, for her part, had rocked backward in her ergonomic desk chair. Her hand remained on her clear glass desk that never had anything on it. Her mouth was now hanging partly open – much as mine had been the day prior – and her eyes were as wide as I'd ever seen them.

She didn't say a thing.

For my part, I had never expected to get this far through my monologue without getting fired, screamed at, or both. It suddenly occurred to me that this was uncharted territory in my fearful and fearsome imaginings of how this little meeting might go. I decided the prudent course was to retreat ... before my continued presence spurred Jacqueline to terminate me (assuming she'd not already made up her mind to do so).

I quickly turned, and walked out of her office.

I made it to the hallway, thank God, before I noticed my knees were starting to buckle. I had hoped to make it back to the ladies' room, but that was a really long way away ... given how badly my knees were shaking. I changed course on the fly, deciding to attempt to make it back to my office, which was only a few doors down from Jacqueline's.

Hitting my chair, I exhaled a long and raggedy breath, unsure of when I'd last actually exchanged oxygen and CO2. It then occurred to me that Jacqui was quite the huntress: she would probably follow me.

Given that I wasn't prepared for such an eventuality, nor was I yet in a stable position where I believed I could competently continue an interaction, I dove for the black handle of my desk phone. Putting it to my ear, I figured I would pretend to be having an important conversation ... in the likely event that she darkened my door.

My instincts were spot-on. No sooner than my hand brought the receiver to my ear, Jacqui knocked and entered. "Oh, uh sorry – didn't know you were on the phone." She looked at me uncertainly, her hand still on my door handle.

I did my best to fake looking busy – wondering all the while if she could hear the loud dial tone in my ear that would make obvious my lie. "Yeah, sorry" I mouthed at her. "I had to take this call – should be off shortly."

She nodded, and withdrew, after which I gulped a few deep breaths. Should I call my mother before I got fired from a prestigious law firm? What were the accepted societal norms on such matters? I realized my mother would probably question me endlessly, and freak out a bit. Maybe a lot. Perhaps it was not the best plan to call mom: I was already doing a fine job of freaking out without extra help.

Plus, I wasn't fired – yet. No need to borrow trouble by putting the cart before the proverbial horse.

Mustering up the last shred of my courage, I rang Jacqueline's extension to let her know that I could now see her. And I wisely stayed in my office – making her come to me. Whatever the next few minutes might bring, they would definitely involve some power re-adjustments. I stayed on my turf. Plus – who was I kidding? – my knees were still shaking pretty hard, making standing inadvisable.

Jacqueline showed back up in my doorway virtually instantaneously, and proceeded to lean against the back edge of the guest chair. "So, I don't really know what to say," she began, "but first, I want to apologize."

I looked at her closely, not sure I'd heard her correctly. Could she be joking? I eyeballed her suspiciously, waiting.

She continued: "Perhaps I should explain. Not by way of justifying my actions or anything, but just to provide context. Maybe you already know, but I went to Harvard Law. And I came up through the law firms in an era where there were no women at all. I mean, we had Sandra Day O'Connor at the US Supreme Court, thank God. But, coming out of law school, I'd just assumed there would be more ... women. In the law firms. And in the courts. But there weren't. Instead, what I found was a 'pink collar' world."

I listened and nodded – knowing she was referencing the fact that even once women broke into traditionally male-dominated fields, they often tended to self-select to sub-specialties that made use of their typically better relationship skills. Jaqui continued her explanation.

"In law, what this meant is that women would disproportionately gravitate into family law, or estates and trust work. Things that involved families, and little to no confrontation. Females, by and large, did not head off to litigate in the largest law firms, the ones that represented Fortune 100 companies. Where the CEOs and executive teams of our clients were – once again – all male."

She stopped for a second. Unsure what to do, I elected to quietly nod in an attempt to get her to continue.

"So I'm not *that* woman. I didn't go to Harvard Law to handle divorces. I *like* confrontation."

Yep. She wasn't lying, I thought, as I raised my eyebrows.

"And I wanted to handle the big cases. The risky cases. The hi-tech cases, with the cutting edge legal theories, and interesting fact patterns. The high stakes litigation, with bet-the-farm type presentations."

She took a pause, slowing her roll a bit. "So, I went to work at a large law firm. But I was surrounded by men."

Jacqueline stopped again, looking over to the side wall of my office where my diploma hung, before continuing. "I felt like if I was going to make it, in a man's world, that I needed to learn how to be one of the boys. And I determined that if I were to succeed, it was because I was going to have the biggest balls of them all. And so I became even more of a 'bull in the china shop' tough-guy than I was already hard-wired to be."

She stopped again, cracking a slight smile. I realized I'd been holding my breath, and made a conscious effort to just breathe.

"But it's a new day, Leigh. And you were 100% right: I was a real witch to you. For no reason. And it *was* unacceptable. And it's time I adopt some new ways of relating, because women are finally coming into these hallways in greater numbers. Which is good! And I clearly need to change my M.O. So … thank you. I'll do better."

And with that final promise, she turned and was gone.

I stared at the door closing quietly after her, noticing how the air felt lighter, and – indeed – how I felt lighter in my body. Of course, that might have been a direct result of the fact that I'd sweat through my clothes and had been hyperventilating during the last half-hour (thank goodness I'd chosen the dark blue suit). I looked at the clock, and – for the first time in months – I decided to leave my firm at a normal hour.

When I arrived the next day, nothing could have prepared me for what was in store. Entering our firm's kitchenette, I was hit with a few "knowing nods," and various attorneys literally patting me on the shoulder, saying: "Attagirl!"

It was like a Twilight Zone. I was non-plussed.

It turned out that – while I'd been hard at work listening to evidence in the robbery trial of the burger joint in Compton that morning – Jacqueline had come into the firm, and made a point of telling each one of her male partners about how I had "balls of steel" and how I had "dressed her down" but that she "deserved it and was appreciative of it." And that it was time for her to "change her ways."

I went back to my office, thinking I should call my mentor and update her on the fact that I'd done as she suggested. But then I paused, reflecting on the fact that the lesson my mentor had shared with me was not all that different from a lesson I'd learned, earlier, in my Political Science class… with a professor who had dared to wander into the realm of Psychology when teaching about the Holocaust.

To stand up.

Such a little thing. Such a simple thing.

And yet? Such a hard and life-changing thing. If everyone had just stood up to Hitler, the Holocaust would never have happened. But instead, Milgram's work evinced that it was probable that two out of three Germans had just goose-stepped along to Hitler's bad ideas – even if they didn't actually agree with him. No doubt many people had disagreed with Hitler's notions. But so many, regardless of their theoretical disagreement, had been obedient and apathetic.

And the critical action – so infrequently taken – but which, if done, could have changed the course of history? It was the action of standing up to an injustice.

I felt the "a-ha" moment wash over me: standing up is not a theory. It's an action. A verb. You cannot think about standing up, or know that you should stand up, or believe that – if put to the test in the Holocaust or a Stanley Milgram experiment – you would have stood up. No. What is essential? Is THAT you actually stand up, and resist the bad thing.

And wasn't that essentially the same lesson that my mentor had served up over my salmon dinner? That you must stand up, for yourself, and right the wrongs, lest people just continue to take advantage.

I'd thought, coming out of college, that I'd never forget the lesson I learned after studying Milgram. But, as I reflected a good decade later from the ocean-view office of my law firm, there is a big difference between "not forgetting" a lesson, and actually applying it.

While it's important to *not* be obedient to bad ideas and bad leaders, and while it's important to *want* to stand up regardless of one's fear, unless one actually *does* the action – in real life – the lesson may as well have been lost.

And on the heels of that realization, I further understood: if everyone were to just adopt the practice of standing up to injustices – both those directed at them personally as well as those aimed at their children, spouses, friends and family – then this planet would be a much better place.

Chapter 12

It was early March 2013, and my family was arriving to live temporarily in a suburb of Sydney, Australia. We had sold my husband's business some months before. Typically, we were blessed with either time, or some disposable money. It was rare to have both simultaneously. But the sale of my husband's practice had put us in a unique position where we did indeed have a little of both, and we'd decided to un-enroll my eight-year-old daughter from third grade in Orange County, pick up stakes, and head to down to "Oz" (as my friends habitually referred to the first syllable of their Australian homeland).

Exiting the cab to walk down the driveway of our new temporary digs, a wall of humidity hit me. And just like that, I was transported back to my first session in the land Down Under.

My first time visiting Australia had been in 1994, just after I took the California State Bar Exam, a grueling three-day test. Even for someone who likes taking tests and tends to do quite well on them, the Bar Exam had been a nightmare involving three straight months of studying twelve to eighteen hours a day with no days off. I had no idea if I had passed – but at least I'd not left the testing room to repeatedly vomit from nerves, like some of my classmates.

With the test completed at the end of July, and given that I was not due to begin working for my law firm until mid-October, I found myself with a few months to unwind from the craziness that led up to the Bar Exam. A lot of my friends had encouraged me to visit

Europe. But – in a nod to my lone wolf ways – I'd chosen to ignore that advice, and instead hoof my way over to Australia and New Zealand, solo.

I had assumed that my future legal career might well lead to representation of international clients with offices in Europe, and thus a reason to visit that continent. It was far less likely, to my mind, that my work would ever cause me to visit the South Pacific. My supposition turned out to be only partly correct: my firm did have cases and clients with European contacts. But I always drew the proverbial short straw, never being assigned to cases necessitating EU travel. Which is why, at the ripe of old age of fifty, I've still never visited Europe.

But the erroneous assumption above was how I came to arrive in Sydney in the autumn of 1994, where I promptly fell in love with the country. It was enchanting. The Opera House. The Sydney Zoo. And my later travels to the Gold Coast, where I viewed the Technicolor underwater world of the Great Barrier Reef for the first time.

The northern coast of Australia was also where I'd decided to rent a little villa. The villa itself was situated on a beautiful jungle property outside the tropical town of Cairns.

The complex of which my villa was a part offered a number of different excursions, including a late-night jungle hike. Posters advertising the jungle hike had been beckoning to me for days, and throwing caution to the wind, I'd finally joined a few other guests in signing up for the excursion. Which is how we all came to find ourselves, after a very heavy dinner and drinks one evening, setting off with some "pocket torches" that illuminated a tiny semi-circle as we picked our way through the lush green jungle.

And I don't know if it was the time of year or just bad luck, but two hours into the "exciting Australian wildlife night hike" our little group had seen absolutely zero animals and insects. Bored off my arse, I thus became super excited when a really pretty, multi-colored toad leaped into my circle of light.

He cut a dapper look, glistening in all of his rainbow splendor, as he sat comfortably peering up at us with shiny little black eyes, while uttering the cutest little "Ribbit, RIBBBBIITTT" sounds. He seemed unafraid, friendly even.

A few of us bent down to stroke his little froggy head.

It was around that time that the guide up in the front of our group turned around, realizing that we at the end of the line had stopped. Sauntering back toward us, the guide mentioned that he wasn't sure what exact type of frog "the little fella was," but that "it might be poisonous."

His pronouncement caused the few of us who had pet the frog to begin frantically rubbing our hands on our pants. At which point, the guide clarified, "Well, I think it's just the frog's spit that is poisonous…."

Eww. How charming, and unhelpful. Us frog-petters looked at each other, shrugging our shoulders and vainly trying to discern how we could figure out if we had contacted the frog's invisible spit … after the fact.

A few hours later, we were tucked safely back in our villas for the evening, where I fell into a deep and dreamless sleep. And upon awakening, I did not give the whole frog affair anymore thought.

Until a couple of days later … when I realized I'd been vomiting for eight hours without cease.

Assuming I had a case of food poisoning, I debated calling my mother at home in Los Angeles. A notorious worry-wart, calling her was a last resort. But it had been a full evening of hugging the toilet bowl with no reprieve, and I now felt and looked like death warmed over. Observing my pale and sunken-eyed face in the villa's mirror, I could not honestly say I had rounded the corner and was headed for better days. In fact, judging by my appearance, it looked like I might be headed toward purgatory.

I finally broke down, placing a call to the States.

"Mom?" I inquired.

"Oh, hi honey! How IS Australia – are you having fun yet?!!" My mother's cheerful voice positively exploded into my ear.

I was pretty sure, with her being fifteen hours ahead, that it was after nine p.m. in California, while it was only daybreak in Cairns. "Well, mom, Australia is fine, thanks for asking. It's been really great, and I've seen some really cool things. But I… umm, well, I think I might have food poisoning … or … something. 'Cuz I was vomiting all night last night. And I still am this morning…." I trailed off.

"Oh dear!" her voice trilled in my ear, "well, have you taken your vitamins?"

I indicated in the affirmative, and endured the requisite sixty seconds of cross-examination that always followed this inquiry, which questions included how many vitamins, what types of vitamins, and exactly how many milligrams of each. Along with a short list of other Grand Inquisition-type questions. My head beginning to pound from the relentless inquiry, I rolled my eyes at the ceiling. Perhaps I should not have called after all, I thought.

Finally, my mother drew to a close. "Well, I'm sure it's probably just a quick flu. Or, maybe you ate something bad. Regardless, I'm sure you'll be feeling better soon!" she cheerfully chirped.

"Well, that's just it, mom. I'm feeling no better, maybe worse, and I dunno what to do...."

She immediately took up the cause for a second time. "Well, honey, I don't know. I mean this is kind of why I urged you to travel somewhere closer to home. I mean, you're like 10,000 miles away from me or something – right??? Is it 5,000 miles, or 10,000? I forget...."

"MOM! Focus, please! I really feel like I'm dying here."

"Well, honey, I ***told you*** to not go so far away! I mean I think you're literally 10,000 miles from where I am – and it's night time here – so what, pray tell, do you want me to do? From here???"

I leaned back on the pillow in my little room, sighing loudly. She had a point: what exactly was I expecting her to do, from half a world away?

Into the silence, my mother suddenly piped up: "Did you do anything different??"

And suddenly, just like that, I remembered the hike two evenings earlier. "Oh, well, your question reminded me of something. Actually, I did do something unusual...Maybe. I mean, I guess?? We all went on an evening walk through the jungle to look at interesting animals, but there weren't any. So we ended up petting a frog. And then the guide told us the little guy might be poisonous – "

"OHMIGAWWDDDD – YOU PET A POISONOUS FROG? REALLY, LEIGH? HAVE YOU NO SENSE? AND YOU'RE IN AUSTRALIA?!! HOW POISONOUS WAS IT? LIKE DEATHLY POISONOUS?"

"Mom, I don't know— "

"WELL, JESUS UP IN HEAVEN, LEIGH – AND YOU'D BEST PRAY TO HIM RIGHT NOW – 'CUZ SWEETHEART: WHAT THE HECK AM I SUPPOSED TO DO FROM CALIFORNIA? DID THE FROG HAVE A NAME... I MEAN, MAYBE I CAN LOOK IT UP, OR—"

"Mom – MOM – can you puh-leeze take a chill pill? I don't know if the frog had a name. I didn't exactly cross-examine the tour guide after he mentioned the frog's spit might be poisonous and –"

"WHY NOT? DIDN'T THEY TEACH YOU HOW TO DO THAT IN LAW SCHOOL??!" she picked up the tirade in full voice.

"AND WHAT DO YOU MEAN 'HIS SPIT' WAS POISONOUS??! IS THE FROG POISONOUS, LIKE HIS SKIN – OR IS IT JUST HIS SPIT??!"

She paused for a quick second to take a breath. Whereupon I made a valiant effort to grab control of the conversation, which was not quite successful.

"AND WHAT KIND OF FROGS DO THEY HAVE IN THIS CRAZY PLACE ANYWAY??! I TOLD YOU TO STAY CLOSER TO HOME AND NOT GO HALFWAY AROUND THE PLANET – TO A CONTINENT THAT HAS MORE DEADLY ANIMALS THAN ALL THE OTHERS COMBINED! BUT DID YOU LISTEN??? NO – NO YOU DID NOT. AND NOW YOU

ACTUALLY MEAN TO TELL ME THAT ***YOU LET A POISONOUS FROG SPIT ON YOU???!!!"***

It was amazing how crystal clear the phone connection was: I literally felt like I was standing in her kitchen in California as a kindergartener being reprimanded for some foolishness. Then again, she had a point: One should not go petting pretty frogs in the dark of night in foreign countries.

"Mom, hullo? Can we focus for a second? I just need to stop throwing up. It's probably food poisoning and –"

She interrupted me again, and said in a somewhat calmer voice:

"Honey, you should call down to the front desk of the hotel – and have them get you a doctor."

I sighed resignedly. "Uh, well, about that, mom. They don't really have a front desk."

Back to full throttle, she spouted: "WHAT ON GOD'S GREEN EARTH DO YOU MEAN 'THEY DON'T HAVE A FRONT DESK'??!! ALL HOTELS HAVE FRONT DESKS! YOU'RE NOT IN SOMALIA AFTER ALL. YOU'RE IN AUSTRALIA! OR – OR **WAIT A MINUTE**: DID YOU LIE TO ME – AND YOU'RE REALLY IN SOME THIRD-WORLD COUNTRY??!! OH DEAR LORD – TELL ME YOU'RE NOT IN AFRICA OR SOMALIA?!!!"

"Mom! MOM! I love you, but really, come on! NO – I am NOT in Africa! Like I told you, I'm on the Gold Coast of Australia, up by a town called Cairns. But it's some new resort, and they have little villa-type huts, out in the middle of the jungle. So it's not, like, all one building or a normal hotel … where I can just go downstairs to the front desk."

"Well, does this place have a MAIN Quonset hut, or villa – or whatever – that you can call? Because, Leigh, really honey," she was in full cry again, "there's just not much I can do from California ... **IF YOU WERE DUMB ENOUGH TO PET A POISONOUS FROG!!"**

Fair points, all. I had been foolish, and maybe – just maybe – my resort had a main front desk somewhere.

"Ok, yeah, I think they might have a main desk area, now that you mention it. Let me check. I'll call you back, mom."

With my head still ringing from the well-deserved mama-smackdown I'd received – but which smackdown had resulted in some good advice that I'd somehow not managed to previously arrive at in my weakened and slightly delirious state – I found the correct phone number and contacted the "main" Quonset hut. They promised to send a physician.

Changing into my last clean pair of PJs, I laid back down on the bed, waiting for the doctor to arrive. I was still vomiting at fifteen minute intervals, though there was nothing left in my poor little system and hadn't been for some time. By the point at which the doctor arrived a couple of hours later, I'd already prayed to the porcelain god another eight times.

And boy, did I look the part: hair disheveled, jammies wrinkled and slightly sweaty, face more pale even than usual, with some new and charming purplish rings under my eyes. Hearing footsteps coming up my little pathway through the open window, I dragged myself – in all my stunning glory – out of my bed, and proceeded to shuffle toward the front door of my little villa.

Looking out the screened window, I caught my first glimpse of this traveling doctor which the front desk had managed to round up for me. And then I promptly jumped back behind my wood door before he saw me.

It *couldn't* be.

I leaned my face out again, so that just my right eye was in front of the window, and took my second gander at the physician headed my way. And glory-be! The doctor walking up the path appeared to be a dead-ringer for Mel Gibson.

I gazed down at my charming outfit again, taking in the sweaty jammies with cute little bunnies on them. Lovely, just lovely: I was about to meet possibly the hottest man in Cairns … looking like an over-sized preschooler, and likely smelling like one, too.

With nothing else for it, I opened the door. And if anything, the apparition before me had somehow morphed into an even more perfect facsimile of the Hollywood superstar. For his part, the good doctor stood awkwardly on my doorstep, holding a little black bag in his left hand. (Who knew that traveling doctors in the 1990's still carried little black bags – perhaps this was an Australia thing? Or a rainforest doctor thing?)

With the sun behind his head, nicely accenting his brown hair with a slightly golden glow that stood out against the tropical and verdant jungle that was about 180 different colors of emerald green, Mr. Mel-Gibson-Doctor-Man looked so good that I nearly forgot why I'd asked him to come.

A lone tropical bird warbled out a melodic little tune as I continued to just stand in the threshold, mutely staring at the drop dead gorgeous doctor, who seemed to have walked straight out of a GQ magazine and onto the patio of my little quonset hut.

Awkwardly breaking the silence, he asked, "Are you Leigh?"

Startled out of my reverie by the fact that this living-Ken-Doll actually spoke, I stammered out a semi-cogent response.

"Yes! Umm, err, I mean, yes!"

Wow. The still-coherent half of my brain reflected on the fact that I sounded probably as unintelligent as I no doubt looked. I gave it another valiant effort.

"Umm, yes, I'm Leigh. Thank you for coming out. Please do come in – come in," I muttered, opening the door more fully to usher Mr. Gorgeous into my hot mess of a villa.

I sat down on the bed timidly.

"So what seems to be the issue?" the doctor kindly inquired.

Dang. He was so hot it was nearly impossible to think straight. Notwithstanding the distraction that he posed, I did my level-best to fill him in on my embarrassing past few hours: the inability to keep any food or water down. The fact I was vomiting about once every fifteen minutes. And finally, with some measure of embarrassment, how I hoped it was food poisoning … but was also concerned it might have something to do with the frog I'd ignorantly decided to pet on my "late night walkabout."

The doctor listened patiently, and then chuckled softly. "Well, I doubt it's the frog. Particularly since none of the other tourists have been so sick they've had to call me. It's probably just a touch of the flu or food poisoning."

I was hanging on his every word, my mind starting to gather wool and take little flights of fancy to ponder such things as whether he was married. And if not, what it would be like if I were to become married to a real-life rainforest-jungle doctor that looked like he'd just stepped off a movie set.

I couldn't help myself – I simply had to know if he was related to the Gibson family. "Has anyone ever told you that you look a fair bit like Mel Gibson?"

He laughed gently a second time. "Yeah. I actually get that a lot – pretty much every day. I don't think I'm related – but who knows? Maybe he's a second cousin twice removed or something!"

And laughing gently for a third time, he opened his little black bag. Fishing around briefly, his hand came back up with a syringe and needle as he continued:

"I think what I'll do today is just give you a little injection of an anti-vomiting medicine. I'm guessing it will do the trick."

I nodded in agreement. "Ok, great. Do you need my arm, or ...." I trailed off.

He looked at me, again with a slightly confused expression on his face. Probably wondering if air-headed blonds from California understood that the most common injection site was the bum.

For my part, I understood exactly where most injections went ... but I was not about to drop trou for a hot young doctor who looked like a moviestar. Not when I'd spent the last day vomiting, nope.

We stared at each other awkwardly for a moment. He finally opined, "Well, the arm's probably not the best location. Really a large muscle group would be best…."

Perfect – I had my out.

"Great!" I replied immediately. "Here's my thigh!" And, bending over, I rolled up my pant leg to well above my knee.

But he didn't move. I looked up to see him knitting his brows together. Then, with a shrug of resignation, Mr. Incredibly-Good-Looking finally bent forward and put the injection into my right thigh.

I unrolled my pant leg back down to cover the Band-Aid, and attempted to wrap up the visit. The doctor had now been in my villa for awhile. And I was on a strict every 15 minute "bow-to-the-porcelain-god" schedule. Looking at the clock on the wall as I felt another wave of nausea pass over me, I realized with a start that I was fast approaching the end of my fifteen minute interval.

Surely, it was bad enough that this poor gent had to see me all smelly and disheveled and in my last pair of pajamas – I was simply not about to throw up in front of a guy that looked like a movie star. Not if I could avoid it.

The hunky physician looked at me again, and told me that the fee for his visit would be added to my hotel bill. I nodded eagerly, hoping he would take a clue and start to leave.

But, rather incredulously, instead of preparing to leave, he just proceeded to sit and stare at me.

What the heck? Didn't he understand he needed to go? I didn't want to be rude, but I was already starting to do that breathing-funny thing to calm the waves of nausea in an attempt to stave off the inevitable.

Realizing that I was going to need to grab the bull by the horns in order to get him out of my villa, I smiled wanly, and said, "Thank you so much for coming out. Here, let me just walk you to the door!" It was kind of an awkward conclusion to our little visit, given that my villa was the size of a tiny postage stamp – even a raving idiot wouldn't need any help finding their way back out.

"Oh," he smiled again.

Darn, he had dimples too! And a nice tan – why, oh why did God send me a Mel Gibson look-alike during my worst hour? It just wasn't fair.

Making no move to stand up, my hunky physician then elaborated: "Maybe they don't do it this way in America, but I'm just going to wait here for another 15 minutes or so. To make sure you don't have an allergic reaction to the medicine I just gave you."

Fifteen more minutes??? Jumpin' Jehoshaphat! That just could not be! There was simply no way I could gut out another fifteen minutes without tossing my cookies again. It was inevitable – Mel Gibson's twin was going to hear me vomit. Could my embarrassment be any greater?

Deciding to give it one more college try, I mustered up a pained smile. "Okay, yeah, I guess in the U.S. they really don't care as much about patients," I intoned. "But I really think I'm fine now!" I lied brightly, in the hopes he still might leave.

He smiled, but didn't move an inch. Seeing him continuing to emulate a statue, I then gamely offered, "Or … I guess… well, I guess we could just wait…."

With an inane little smile plastered on my face – that I was pretty sure looked more like a grimace – I fought down another wave of nausea. Seemingly unconcerned with my mighty internal struggle, my kind and very patient physician just continued to sit next to me. For fifteen long, excruciating minutes.

Chatting pleasantly about the Great Barrier Reef, about his love of scuba, and about his various other hobbies. The logical part of my brain briefly catalogued that not only was he a hot dude, he had a penchant for cool activities that I also liked to partake in and discuss. But on this day, it was all I could do to not groan aloud and knead my stomach.

Finally, after what seemed like a dog's age later, the gorgeous physician finally took his leave. And I don't guess the nice fellow was more than a few feet down my garden path before I heaved my guts out one final time in my itty-bitty lavatory … hoping against hope that the good doctor had been rendered spontaneously deaf.

But the medicine he injected must have been truly wonderful stuff indeed – for that marked the very last time I vomited in Australia. Although, stepping out of bed the next day, I realized I had a little souvenir from the whole affair. Because every time I went to take a step, my right quadriceps muscle would perform this little quivery jump, which in turn would darn near buckle my entire leg and cause me to fall over.

"Ah well," I thought to myself, "no doubt they don't teach quadriceps injections in Australian medical schools…." And truth be told, some temporary instability in my right quad had been a pretty modest price to pay for managing to avoid having Mr. Mel Gibson-Lookalike-Doctor see my hiney.

Bringing myself back to 2013 and the cabbie that had just taken our luggage out of his vehicle, I smiled again at the memory of my twenty year old travel antics, and the handsome doctor I'd imagined marrying but never did. I turned to look at my daughter, who was now struggling valiantly with her little pink-wheeled suitcase on the incline of the driveway leading up to our temporary new home in Australia.

"Mama, why are you smiling??"

My daughter didn't miss a trick – she was very good at catching people's body language and facial expressions.

"Well, sweetie, as you know, this isn't my first time in Australia. And the weather right now reminded me of a funny little episode from my first visit here, more than two decades ago. It involved a pretty-colored frog, and I promise I'll tell you the whole saga, once we get up these steps. But the short version is that when we are in this country, the things that are most colorful and look like they are begging to be touched? Yeah, those things are often dangerous – and indeed, can be poisonous – so no touching weird or pretty things. Not until you're sure it's safe."

Helping her to lift her suitcase up the stairs, I added another post-script:

"And one more rule for life, based on the little story I'm about to tell you: It's fine to go exploring – but always keep your mama on speed dial. And always pack an extra pair of PJs!"

Chapter 13

The next day, my husband and I walked my child to the private school at which we'd enrolled her. Letting go of my hand, she stopped to point at the funny uniforms that the Aussies wore to school.

"Why do we have to wear a skirt when there are mosquitoes? Did men make these rules?? Because all the boys get to wear pants – and my legs are already getting bitten…." She leaned down to slap at a pesky mosquito that did, indeed, appear to be busy attacking her leg, before continuing with her observations.

"And what's with this funny little hat, with these weird flaps hanging down the back of my neck? They are SOOO annoying!"

She had a fair point: the hats were pretty funny-looking, and her legs were already getting welts from the bug bites. Nonetheless, we hustled her into her new school and prayed she'd adjust.

The hand-off went smoothly once we were on campus, and my husband and I were now back at our flat eating breakfast. He stood up from his chair.

"Well, I have that meeting – so I'll head out for a bit. See you around lunch time," he said, as he kissed my forehead.

"Okay, babe, see you later," I replied.

I watched the door close after him, glancing around the tiny living room, which was smaller than any living room I'd ever seen. Already bored, I got up and meandered into the equally pint-sized bedroom. I had already put away the clothing from our suitcases. Opening up my laptop out of habit, I stared at the blank screen.

And for the very first time in my life, I realized I had nothing pressing to do.

It was such a strange feeling. Always before, when I'd been practicing at law firms, or in more recent years when I'd helped my husband with his business, I'd been tethered to work. Even when my husband and I were on vacation, we never felt like we were truly "off the clock." There were always clients or patients to check on, phone calls to the secretaries, and endless voicemails regarding urgent matters.

The work never just stopped because we were out of town. In fact, like some prescient beast, our work seemed to know exactly when we were trying to take time off, and would invariably explode in a way that ruined a morning of the vacation here, or an evening of our plans there.

Staring at my blinking cursor, I realized this moment was absolutely unprecedented: I had no one that needed something from me. I had no calls to return. We had sold the business, and with that sale, there were finally no more tasks that needed doing. Knowing I should feel relieved, I realized I instead felt quite the opposite. For a dyed-in-the-wool Type A personality, the feeling of having no work to do was turning out to be quite unsettling.

As I began to literally twitch with the mounting anxiety of having nothing with which to occupy my time, I thought back to my last days in California, before we'd boarded the Virgin Air flight to

Sydney. Cleaning out my husband's office in preparation for transferring the reins to the new owners, I had stumbled across a women's magazine. As I'd picked it up to toss it – figuring the new owners would want to put their own preferred magazines in the lobby for patients to read – the magazine flipped open to an article about three sex-trafficking survivors. I'd stopped my cleaning streak to briefly peruse it.

The article turned out to be riveting. I ended up pulling out my desk chair, plunking down, and starting to actually read – not just skim – the article. Multiple women had been interviewed. But it was the interview of Carissa Phelps that had captivated me.

A young woman about my own age, Carissa had been raised in Coalinga, California. After Carissa's mother divorced and remarried, the blended family included eleven children, and Carissa would often leave home to avoid the chaos. During one of her times away from home, a pimp named Icey had captured Carissa, convincing her that he should be allowed to sell Carissa to help make them money – since Icey's girlfriend was pregnant and could not work.

Carissa was twelve years old.

For ten days, Icey sold Carissa on the streets, until the car in which they were riding was pulled over. The cops arrested not just the pimp, but also Carissa.

I stopped and dabbed my eyes, looking up at the ceiling tiles in my husband's office in a futile attempt to keep the tears from spilling down my cheeks. Realizing I had a few more minutes until our office's first patient was set to arrive, I picked up the article to read further.

It turned out that, after the arrest, Carissa had ended up in juvie, where she'd been enrolled in a novel program that had resulted in her receiving counseling, and meeting a mentor who would change her life. This counselor had seen something in Carissa – a combination of intelligence and determination – and encouraged Carissa to go back to school, and eventually enroll in community college and then UCLA, where Carissa earned both her JD and MBA.

The jarring ring of the telephone interrupted my reading. I set down the magazine to attend to the caller. Phone call done, I once more picked up where I'd left off.

Apparently, while in college, a fellow student in the film school had approached Carissa about making a documentary about child prostitution. And thus the documentary "Runaway Girl" featuring Carissa had been born, along with a companion book and a non-profit. And now, this amazing survivor was training law enforcement agencies and officers on how to not arrest the victims of sex trafficking – but instead get them services and help – while also training cops how to effectively tackle the problem of the pimps and the pedophiles who buy and sell victims for sex.

I set down the magazine, dabbing again at my eyes with the Starbucks napkin on my desk. I thought back to my years in college, and how I'd fallen in love with the Sociology and Psychology classes I had taken, ultimately changing my major from Music to Sociology.

I thought back, as well, to my six months at the Los Angeles District Attorney's Office during the Spring of 1994, when I'd gotten to prosecute felons in jury trials. The guy in charge of the DA's office in Whittier, a tall male Assistant District Attorney with graying hair, was an unfailingly kind gentleman. He took a minute, on my last day at the office, to lean back against his credenza, and engage me as he folded his arms across his chest.

"You sure you want to go off and work at a big law firm?" he inquired solicitously. I nodded in response to his prodding. I was sure I was going to do that, but I was less than certain that I should be doing that. And this man knew. There was so much that was being left unsaid in the conversation.

"Well," he continued, "there's no doubt that big old firm will pay well. In fact, there's no better money to be had, anywhere. So you'll definitely make good money. And you'll be able to pay off those six figure law school loans you have pretty quick." He stopped to briefly lay his hand down on a case file that was sitting on his desk, knitting his eyebrows together thoughtfully.

"But you are really talented, Leigh. Especially on your feet. And in front of the judges and juries. It's rare we get folks through this office who are as quick on their feet, or as passionate. I mean most folks who gravitate to this job, they've got some skills in those regards, because let's face it, the DA's office is all oration. We're in court, all day, every day. It's fast-paced. There's rarely briefing or written projects. It's mostly speaking and arguing in front of judge and juries. No doubt, we're perpetually overworked and under-funded. But at the end of the day? We put bad guys behind bars. That's what we do. And in so doing, we make the world a safer place."

He paused again, before ramping up toward what I could tell would be his conclusion: "And there's a unique feeling that comes from knowing, as you lay your head on your pillow each night, that you were a part of making this planet a better place. I know you aren't married and don't have kids – yet – but one day you probably will. And what I'm saying now will make even more sense then."

He looked at my entreatingly, his eyes gently and unflinchingly fixed on mine. "You'd make a darned good assistant DA, Leigh. And a truly great sex crimes prosecutor one day, after you paid your dues on some smaller cases."

I mulled over his statements, and my response. I was struggling. Particularly because, in my heart of hearts, we both knew he was right.

"I know, Rod, and thank you for your kind praise. It's not that I haven't enjoyed my time here. And you're correct: it's a good fit for my personality."

I stopped to marshal my thoughts as my mind flitted to my $106,000 of law school loan debt, and my own chaotic upbringing. And the fact that, as a first year law student, I'd chosen to start paying out of pocket for weekly therapy sessions – because I didn't want to become an adult who was as disturbed as some of the members of my own family.

I thought as well of my childhood, the raised voices that permeated every second of the day when both parents were in my house. Of being told by some in my circle that I was never "good enough," and that "no matter how much schoolin' or book-learnin' I got," I would "never be good enough." I remembered years that felt like centuries, my eyes glued to the little skeleton key slots in the old-fashioned doors in my house that acted as *de facto* peep holes into the adjacent rooms. Of the many nights I'd spent glued to those key holes, trying to see the source of the raised voices to ensure things didn't get too out of hand. Of the many minutes of my youth that I had spent wondering how much, and how badly, things might escalate that night. I re-lived the feeling of never being able to relax – of always being on high alert.

Then, my mind pulled away from my own childhood to recall the jury trial I'd watched the female Assistant D.A. in our office bring, the month prior, on behalf of a 12-year-old rape victim. She was a Junior High School girl who'd been sexually abused by the guy in charge of the Homeless Shelter at which her family was temporarily staying. I thought back to the female prosecuting attorney who worked for the nice man standing in front of me – how she'd thrown everything she had at the case in an attempt to get the pedophile convicted.

I remembered as well the surprising eloquence of the seventh-grade child who was not born here but in another country, and whose parents had sought help at the shelter – only to find their daughter victimized by the very person who had promised to help them.

My mind's eye re-visited with excruciating clarity the mental picture I'd captured of this 12-year-old as she took the stand to testify against her abuser – the memory felt as if it was seared into my soul. And I could see as well, through a cloud of rage, the clown – a literal clown (that was what he did for a living) – who'd been appointed to be the foreman of that jury. I began to sweat, recalling how this awful foreman had read a verdict which had let the defendant off the hook on all charges … despite the wealth of evidence indicating he was a pedophile who should have been sent to jail for years for molesting this twelve-year-old child.

Dragging my eyes up off the floor, I reluctantly sought out the kind face of my boss. "Rod, thanks again, but I don't think I could do a job that asked so much of me each day. And when we don't get the win, like Sally with that 12-year-old last month? Well, those losses seem pretty hard to bear. You are right – I do want a husband. And children too, one day. And it's because I want a family that I think it would be a mistake to run my tank dry, emotionally-speaking, at work each day … and then have nothing left to give to my future family when I finally got home at night."

Rod nodded once, in defeat, as I continued.

"In addition, and as you mentioned, I do have six digits of loans to pay off, and the State of California is barely paying prosecutors more than poverty wages. I'll be making three times at the law firm what I would make here." Feeling suddenly guilty, like I had something to apologize for, I added: "Plus, the big firm will be really good experience for me. I can always go there for a few years, and then come back here."

Rod extended his hand warmly and smiled, acknowledging my decision. It was a sad and knowing smile, born of years of listening to bright attorneys head off to the golden handcuffs of large law firms. A smile that almost hid the palpable sadness woven into the fact that rarely, if ever, would these young attorneys return to his office where – year after year – he slaved away, attempting to get justice for victims.

For my part, giving him one last hug, I spared telling him the real reason for my refusal to entertain his offer: the fact that I could not confront working in an environment with victims whose lives were so similarly chaotic to the childhood I'd just left behind.

Pulling myself out of my reverie that had me revisiting old memories, I focused again on the woman's magazine sitting in front of me featuring Carissa Phelps and the other sex-trafficked women. I wanted to help. I'd wanted to help since the day I'd changed my major in college from Music to Sociology. I'd wanted to help since the fateful day I'd turned down the job at the LA District Attorney's Office. Truth be told, I'd wanted to help for a very long time, and it was clear the world was not exactly becoming a better place while I dithered and procrastinated.

I also suddenly realized that while the statements I'd told my boss at the DA's office had been correct – as I truly believed at the time that I did not have enough gas in my "emotional tank" to do the work without it sinking me – a couple of decades had now passed. And I'd done a lot of work on myself in the intervening years. Sitting in the office my hubby and I were about to sell, I abruptly realized that the reasons we give ourselves to *not* do things sometimes expire, without us even realizing it.

Jiggling my mouse to wake up my computer, I brought up Google on my browser, and typed in the words "Carissa Phelps' phone number." Not expecting to find anything of value, I was shocked when my query returned what appeared to be a legitimate phone number. Doubting it would actually lead to her, but with nothing to lose, I picked up the phone and dialed the area code and seven digits.

Carissa answered on the second ring.

I explained that I was an attorney in southern California who had seen the article, and wanted to help. To my great surprise, Carissa replied she had a flight into LAX that night, and would be at a local hotel the next morning. We agreed to meet for breakfast.

Over coffee the next morning, Carissa told me more of her story, and much more about the work she was doing to educate law enforcement agencies on how to process and help victims instead of arrest them. As well, she spoke of her work to encourage law enforcement to arrest the actual criminals in the sex trafficking equation: the "johns" who – for centuries – had skated off into the night with typically no more than a slap on the proverbial hand ... so they could continue their pattern of victimizing young girls.

My meeting with Carissa was mind blowing. I had no idea that human trafficking was a $150 billion a year industry, and that 40 million people were estimated to be enslaved world-wide. Carissa's statements about the number of victims left me reeling. We concluded our breakfast by agreeing to reconvene six months later, after my travels.

And now, one week after I'd met Carissa for coffee in southern California – and then transferred the keys to my husband's office to the new owners – I'd landed in Sydney, Australia. And was currently sitting like a darned potted plant in an empty apartment the size of a coat closet, with absolutely nothing to do. But into the silence of that void, it suddenly dawned on me with stunning clarity.

What I most wanted to do? Was to help fight human slavery.

In fact, I realized that was what I had always wanted to do – but that I was now in a place where I could do so without jeopardizing my own mental health, and where – over the last couple decades – I just might have acquired some usable skills to bring to the fight.

Decision made, I turned on the internet, and looked up anti-sex-trafficking non-profits and non-governmental organizations – commonly referred to by the short form "NGO" – that were doing work in Australia and Asia.

Picking up the phone, I started to dial.

Chapter 14

"Oh – hello there. My name is Leigh Dundas. You don't know me, but I'm an attorney from California, and I was wondering if you could tell me about the work your organization performs….?"

Sometimes, I would get all the way through my introductory question before they hung up. And if I were really lucky, I could sometimes get the NGO to actually answer my question before they offed me straight off the phone. But invariably, once I got to the part about who I was – a soccer-mom attorney from Orange County, California, who'd never before lived or worked in the Australasia region – but who nonetheless wanted to help their non-profit fight the child-brothel problem … yeah. That was where the phone line would either go dead, or there'd be a guffaw of disbelief, followed by a loud click.

I couldn't really blame the Human Trafficking non-profits in Australia that I was calling. After all, I pretty much had no actual experience fighting human slavery. And while my family was on an extended visit in the region, I also could not honestly state I would be living in the area for a prolonged period of time. No doubt, the folks who picked up the phone thought I was some bored mommy from the States, looking to entertain herself for a bit, with all the staying power of a Fourth of July sparkler.

And heck, wasn't it the truth? I mean, yes, I could read, and write, and speak, and get good results for clients in court. And I was also a pretty fine salesman, I'd discovered. But were any of these talents useful in the fight to save children in brothels? Probably not.

Leaning back in my chair in my tiny Sydney apartment and looking at my watch, I realized it was almost time to go retrieve my daughter from her new school. And no wonder the folks who picked up my phone calls at these non-profits were laughing at me. It was laughable: I was really just a mom, who truly had no experience and no skills in the arena, save a burning desire to help.

Pulling out of my self-pity slide, I perked up. Darn it – I didn't care if I was inexperienced – someone must need my help! I got the name and address of the next outfit on my list, realized it was within walking distance of my apartment, and vowed to head out in person the next day. Maybe showing up in person at their office would work better than phoning these places.

And so I did: I literally pounded the pavement, in addition to doing more phone calls. For three long weeks. I called. And I knocked. To no avail. No NGOs seemed even remotely interested in my non-existent skills, no matter how passionate I was about volunteering.

It was only after my family had picked up stakes, left Australia, and was traveling along a rural highway on the southern island of New Zealand – weeks after I'd made my outbound calls – that my cell phone finally rang. Which was odd. My husband and I had relinquished our American phone numbers and cell phones when we left the U.S. and had gotten new phones once we landed. Accordingly, our numbers never rang – because no one besides our mothers had our new cell numbers.

And now, my hubby, daughter and I were all wedged tightly into our little rental car with all of our luggage – having just left a dirt biking tour through the muddy paths and overcast skies of the island that was known by the Natives as the "Land of the Long White Cloud" – and the tinkling sound of my cell phone was now echoing through the car. With a puzzled look at my husband, I shrugged my shoulders, and picked up the phone.

It was a 714 area code – the preface for Orange County numbers. That was even more weird – someone whose number I didn't recognize, but who was from our same county in California? I pushed the button on the cell phone to retrieve the call.

"Hello?"

A woman's voice came back over the line. "Oh hello, um, you don't know me. My name is Heather. And you left a voicemail on our answering machine some weeks ago now. I apologize for getting back to you so late – we were traveling and only now got your message. My husband is actually still deep sea fishing, or he would've called you … But, anyway, he and I run a couple of orphanages in Vietnam and he's going to be in Da Nang on the 23rd of this month – and we were wondering if you'd like to meet up with him while he's there?"

My eyes opened as wide as saucers. Before I could formulate an answer, the nice woman continued.

"My husband will be accompanied by the executive crew of a non-profit that fights sex trafficking – we're all friends because we go to the same church in Orange County – and they're all going to be meeting with Vietnamese government officials to discuss what can be done to address the sex trafficking issues we're seeing in the kids that are routed through our orphanages. I don't know what your schedule is like – but we'd be happy to have your assistance at the meeting."

My eyes had now grown to the size of silver dollars, and I realized I'd been holding my breath. "Wow, that's amazing! And thanks so much for calling me back. I'm very interested. Would you mind holding the line for a quick sec?"

When she agreed, I turned to my husband.

"Well?" he said, "Who is it?"

I covered the phone with my hand, as the cheap cell phones we'd bought once we landed overseas didn't seem to have a mute button.

"Um, it's the wife of some guy who runs orphanages in Vietnam, and get this! They got my message – remember when I was leaving a gajillion messages at all those NGO's? Anyway, he's Deep Sea Fishing in Baja right now – can you believe it – like, what are the odds they'd be from Orange County and fishing in Mexico right now??? Anyway, he and his friends from church are gonna be in Da Nang Vietnam on May 23rd – and they're inviting me to this meeting ... and well, I think I've just got to go!!"

I was rambling at high speed, and I'm sure doing a very poor job of relaying the facts. And it wasn't like I was ever in the business of begging my husband for things I wanted to do. But it was going to be a huge diversion of our family trip.

My husband grinned. "Yeah, I mean, I'm kinda burned out on seeing little white fluffy butts on green hills – there's only so many sheep one can look at during one's lifetime. And you've helped with my projects for so many years, it's your turn. Let's do it! But just one question: What's in Da Nang?"

I thought about his question, along with the fact that I didn't really have an answer. I was briefly reminded of how orderly my professional life had always been. How I'd always done what was expected, even when it wasn't what my heart desired. How somehow I'd always figured out how to prioritize other people's projects and desires over my own, as so many women and particularly mothers do.

I reflected as well on the strange feeling mushrooming inside my chest that was urging me, for once, to take the uncertain, unplanned, illogical, spontaneous path. And to fly to a foreign country with my spouse and eight-year-old daughter in tow.

I looked at my husband. "I don't know, babe. But I'm having a Kevin Costner kinda moment."

My hubby raised an eyebrow, the non-spoken question hanging in the air.

I continued. "Like in that movie… where Kevin Costner said, 'If I build it, they will come?' I don't know what's in Vietnam, but it's like I'm being called there, or told to go, or something like that. And I know that once I go, I'll know why I went. And that then … and maybe only then … will it all make sense."

My hubby nodded once in quiet agreement. Then my daughter yelled from the backseat, "Yeah mom, let's do it!"

I removed my hand from my cell phone where I'd been desperately trying to do a "manual mute" to prevent the sweet woman on the other end from hearing my rather ridiculous conversation.

Moving the cell phone back to my left ear, I proceeded to tell the nice lady from Orange County that I would meet her husband two weeks later, in Da Nang, Vietnam.

Chapter 15

My family looked out the window as the flight landed in Da Nang, and then stood anxiously in the aisle waiting to retrieve our carry-on bags. Exiting into the hubbub of the Vietnamese airport, we looked around. My daughter piped up, her voice sounding unique amongst the throng of people speaking Vietnamese and other languages.

"Mama, I need to go to the bathroom."

I looked around and spotted what appeared to be the universal signs for restrooms over near one end of the building. "Okay honey, let's head in that direction." Leaving my husband to retrieve our larger pieces of luggage, I escorted my daughter to the bathroom. We entered two stalls adjacent to each other. I was halfway through my business when I heard her little voice pipe up again from the other side of the flimsy partition separating our stalls.

"Mama, can you pass me some toilet paper? I think they're out."

"Sure thing, sweetie" I replied, "just give me a quick sec."

I looked to my left. And then to my right. There was no toilet paper in my stall. In point of fact, there was no mechanism anywhere in the stall, at all, from which to even suspend items like toilet paper. Interesting.

"Well, sweetheart, looks like I'm out too… in fact I think they may not carry toilet paper in Vietnamese restrooms. If they don't do it at the

International Airport, it's probably the custom throughout the country. So I'll grab some Kleenex or TP from the hotel, but in the meantime, you're going to have to rely on camping skills."

She giggled. While we'd never before traveled to non-first world countries, we'd luckily done a fair bit of camping in our lives.

"Okey dokey, Mom!" my child gamely replied.

And, not for the first time, I thanked God that I had gotten an even-tempered, go-with-the-flow kind of kid. She was not a dramatic one, taking much more after my husband than me. In fact, most of the time, she was quite easy-going.

So long as I didn't try to teach her anything directly. I had made the mistake, when she was about two years old and learning to swim, of gently suggesting she could cup her hands together so that the water didn't flow through her little fingers. I had no earthly idea that this would usher in a toddler-tantrum the likes of which I'd never before witnessed, where she insisted "I KNOW WHAT I'M DOING – STOP TELLING ME HOW TO DO IT!" (And mind you, it wasn't like I'd given her the suggestion in a tone of voice borrowed from the Marquis de Sade or Mommy Dearest – it was truly just an impromptu, kind and gentle suggestion in my usual sweet-mom voice). Similarly, my daughter had seen fit to have a nuclear meltdown the one time I suggested a refinement to her rendition of Chopsticks on the piano.

Conferring with my husband after these two moments of unhinged exorcist-like fury, I informed him that we were not going to be homeschooling like we'd harbored sweet visions of doing while pregnant. Because – while my child was a veritable angel when the piano teacher or swimming coach gave her pointers – she would uniformly dissolve into a screaming she-devil whenever we attempted to guide her learning.

After some trial-and-error, and our little discovery that she remained a calm and lovely child – so long as we left the teaching to third parties – we reviewed how lucky we'd gotten with our first child. And decided to not tempt fate by reproducing a second time … lest we get a child with my personality.

Once again – and this time, from a Vietnamese restroom – I said a quick "thank you" to God for my sweet-tempered child. Grabbing my daughter's hand, we exited the restroom, found my hubby, and then hailed a cab to the Grand Mercure Hotel in Da Nang.

After a good night's sleep, the next morning I exited the elevator into the hotel lobby to meet four gentlemen. The owner of the Vietnamese orphanages, Todd, was an American. He and his wife – whom I'd spoken to on the phone from New Zealand – owned restaurants in Orange County that were literally walking distance from the practice my husband and I had just sold.

It turned out that, some years earlier, Todd and his wife had adopted two children from Vietnam. Feeling bad that they could not adopt more of the children they'd met – who were so obviously in need – they had chosen to open a series of orphanages to provide help for vulnerable kids in Da Nang.

The second gentleman was named Ned, and though he and his wife originally hailed from Australia, they had immigrated to Newport Beach and were now running a non-profit to help sex-trafficked youth in Europe. Ned had brought two other members of their team with him to Vietnam to scope out the severity of the trafficking problem amongst the orphanages, and meet with the government officials.

After shaking hands all around, Ned and I laughed at the irony that a bunch of folks who lived and worked in Orange County, California, just happened to be meeting up in Da Nang.

"Seems more like we should be having this meeting over a backyard Barb-y on the beach in OC, eh mates?" Ned quipped.

I laughed out loud, enjoying the Australian accents and witty vernacular of his group.

Ned pointed at the doors. "Well, mates, we'd best be off if we don't want to be tardy to our meetings, eh?" And thus, our little group walked out of the hotel doors and into the hired car that would take us to our day of meetings.

We spent the rest of the afternoon touring orphanages, and meeting with government officials. I watched young boys and girls playing in dirt yards, barefoot and in shorts and t-shirts, smiling widely as they kicked a dirty soccer ball around. We went into some orphanages, and sat on beds that were wood.

"Bit hard, eh?" one of the men in our group named Connor noted, in his formal-sounding accent that made obvious the fact that – unlike the rest – he originally hailed from London.

"That's the custom in these countries," came the simple reply from Todd. "The kids are not used to mattresses like we are."

Much later in the afternoon, we found ourselves sitting in large, ornate, wood-carved furniture with red-tufted velvet seats, while Vietnamese government officials in their olive green starched uniforms greeted us stiffly. With some reticence, the officials admitted that they knew they had a trafficking problem in their country, and that they also knew it was hitting orphans and other vulnerable youth particularly hard. I remained quiet and observant throughout the day, often fighting back tears. Words were bandied about that I was not familiar with – UNODC, TIP Report – and I nodded while making mental notes to myself to clear up all these terms with which I was unfamiliar as soon as I got back to an internet connection.

(The "TIP Report," it turned out, was the Trafficking-in-Persons Report that was produced once a year by the US State Department, while "UNODC" referred to the United Nations Office on Drugs and Crime. I did further research from my laptop later that night, checking out the horrendous studies that showed that 79% of the trafficking worldwide involved sexual exploitation of some sort, and that a vast majority of the victims, not surprisingly, are female. My internet sleuthing further turned up the fact that worldwide, 30% of the victims are children, but that – in certain areas like the Mekong Region of Asia and parts of Africa – virtually 100% of the victims were under the age of 18).[64]

Throughout the long day, I listened to my new friends, as they videotaped some of the visits we made. As they spoke to the officials, to each other, and to the cameras about the breadth and depth of the modern-day slave trade.

By day's end, my heart was in pieces, but my mind was made up. I wanted to help, and I was going to find a way to do so.

When the meetings with the Vietnamese officials concluded, our little group adjourned to dinner. "Well," said Ned, leaning back in his

---

[64] United Nations, Office on Drugs and Crime. *UNODC Report on Human Trafficking Exposes Modern Form of Slavery* (stating that "in some parts of Africa and the Mekong region, children are the majority (up to 100% in parts of West Africa)…." https://www.unodc.org/unodc/en/human-trafficking/global-report-on-trafficking-in-persons.html

chair and pushing his empty plate forward a bit, "I s'pose we ought write a letter to the officials today, thanking them for their time, and posing some thoughts on a path by which we could work together to help things in their country."

Seeing my opportunity, I jumped in. "Do you have someone who does those types of things for your organization? If not – and seeing as how I was here and had a flavor for the meetings that occurred – I'd be happy to give it a whirl."

The men looked at each other, and then they looked back at me. "Do you like to write?" one of the men asked, as they waited for my answer.

I laughed softly. "I'm a lawyer, gentlemen. That's like asking a fish if he likes to swim. It's all we do – write. Well, write, and speak persuasively. I'd be happy to volunteer my time to do the letter. Truly – it would be an honor."

The group of men looked at each other again grinning, and I knew that I had them. While I'd not worked in the trafficking world, some thing were universal: fifty-year-old men did not like to write letters, from laptops, in foreign countries, in the midst of non-stop traveling. And whatever female employees their charity may have employed, those women were back in the offices in the United States and had not been in the meetings, and thus would have a difficult time writing a decent follow-up letter.

It had taken me nearly two months of cold calls, and research and outreach and rejections, but finally my persistence was paying off. When they nodded their assent, I realized I had just found my opening into this world of folks who fight human slavery.

Heading back to my hotel room, I placed a call to my former secretary to get the name of the translation service in the San Gabriel Valley that we had used on some cases in the 1990's – and which service I suspected would have translators who were fluent in written Vietnamese. The next morning, I sent the translator the follow-up letter I'd drafted in English.

One day later, he responded with the Vietnamese version.

It looked so official, and so... foreign. Ah well, I thought, as I hit the "send" button on my email: if sending the draft letter in English *and Vietnamese* did not impress my new colleagues, nothing would.

Luckily, my writing skills held up: a few hours later, I received a phone call from Connor, the Londoner in the anti-trafficking NGO, who told me my letter was a hit – particularly since their company did not have to worry about getting it translated, since I'd already thought to do so. He further informed me that they would be sending it out forthwith. I did my best to suppress a squeal of delight, which was not in keeping with the professionalism I wished to display.

"So Leigh," he then inquired, in his very proper British accent, "what are your plans from here on out? I mean, obviously, you are traveling, and you have your lovely child and husband with you. And it was amazing meeting them, by the way – do tell them 'Hello' for me. But where are you heading next, if I may ask?"

Truth be told, we had no concrete plans. My husband and I had been planning on traveling until at least July, and it was still only May. I could sense the possibilities though. Improvising on the fly, I told Connor, "Well, I believe we will be staying on in Vietnam for a few more days, and then continuing to travel through other countries in this region, probably Cambodia and Thailand. Why do you ask?"

"Ah, well, that just might be rather perfect," Connor replied. "We don't want to insert a wrinkle into your plans or anything. But there are some other folks we were hoping to connect with while we were here. But, as luck would have it, our timeline has become quite compressed. So – if it wouldn't be too much trouble – would you mind if I connected you to some folks in Phnom Penh and Bangkok, and maybe a few other places? And then, if you and your family end up in these locales – well, would you mind reaching out on behalf of our organization?"

It was all I could do to not literally jump up and down. I silently thanked God for His wisdom – and the fact that I'd listened to His voice and my gut instincts.

"Yes, I'd be happy to reach out to contacts on behalf of your entity when we are in those cities," I heard myself reply.

And smiling ear to ear, I realized I'd done it. After weeks of calling and walking all over Sydney and getting absolutely nowhere, I'd finally been confirmed in my belief that persistence pays off.

It had been a struggle – even for a stubborn Taurus and hard-headed only child. My best friend from university – the young Asian girl who'd given the opening speech on orientation night and who later became my college "ride or die" – once said of me, years after we'd graduated: "Leigh, I really do believe if someone handed you a shovel and told you to move a mountain, that you would do it. Minimally, you'd die trying."

When I'd thanked her, she informed me that it was not necessarily a compliment.☺

But she'd definitely been onto something. I'd always known I had quite a masochistic streak when it came to persisting on my chosen path, but this was why I did it – because it paid off.

Turning to my husband, who was reading in our hotel room, I informed him we would be going to Cambodia and then Thailand over the coming months, assuming he was amenable.

"If you build it, they will come," he said, winking at me as he parroted back my ludicrous quoting of Kevin Costner's movie line from earlier that month.

"That's right!" I chirped back.

I now knew why I'd flown my family to Da Nang – because I was going to have a new career in human trafficking. And even though I couldn't quite see the details of whatever the heck this new venture was, this much I knew.

It would be good. And worthwhile. And soul-satisfying.

Chapter 16

"Mama, what's child sex trafficking?" my daughter inquired, in a clear, soprano voice that rang out through the airplane. It was some weeks later, and we were traveling on a small regional Asian airline between Cambodia and Thailand. I'd been meeting with various groups on behalf of the NGO, in between sight-seeing visits, and my family had now boarded this tiny plane to our next destination.

We were the only Caucasians on the airplane: everyone around us had been busily speaking in their native tongues. That is, up until my daughter's query rang out. Funny how, when a child chooses to pose a difficult question to a parent in a crowded public venue, it seems that the background noise will often disappear… just in time for the child's awkward question to reverberate loudly through now-silent air.

Or maybe that's just my fate. But be that as it may, there was no doubt that my daughter's question had been heard by many. Quite a few folks, it would seem. All of whom had downed tools and silverware, paused their own conversations and were now looking inquisitively at the Americans squashed into too-tiny airplane seats (seats that had clearly been designed for people of much smaller stature).

I ducked further down in my cramped seat in a futile quest to become invisible, pondering how on earth to handle my eight-year-old's question. But it wasn't just my eight-year-old looking up at me, patiently waiting for an answer. Furtively swiveling my head toward the rear of the airplane, I noted with some alarm that pretty much all the passengers on this regional Asian airliner wanted to see the American lady's definition of "child sex trafficking – spun for eight-year-old audiences."

Great, just great. Did they all really understand English – how could that be? Weren't we riding on Air Laos? I hazarded another quick glance between the seat cushions. It seemed unfathomable that everyone on the plane had actually both heard and understood my child's question, but based on their inquisitive and patient gazes – and overwhelming silence – it would seem that not only had they heard my child, but that they were waiting with bated breath for my answer.

My brain struggled for an age-appropriate response as I took a gander over my daughter's head at my husband. Perched in the aisle seat, doubled well more than halfway over, my hubs was grimacing oddly … in what I began to recognize as a valiant effort to not openly guffaw. Catching my gaze, he raised an eyebrow in my direction and flipped his hands up, in a kind of "this is all you, babe!" gesture. I sighed resignedly. Clearly, my chosen mate was going to be of zero help.

Leaning back down toward my daughter, and dusting off my "uber-quiet-mommy-whisper" voice – the one which as an extrovert I rarely used – I began my *sotto voce* explanation into my curious child's ear. "Well, honey, trafficking refers to human slavery. And I know you've learned a little bit about slavery already in school, right?"

She nodded, piping up with some clarification. "Yeah, like during the Civil War, and Abe Lincoln and stuff?"

I nodded back in agreement. "Exactly, babe. Well, not all slavery was abolished, it turns out. So there's still slavery in modern times, and we refer to it as human trafficking."

At this point, I paused. I'd bought myself some time to try and decide how best to describe sex trafficking to a child so young that the "birds and bees" conversation had barely been covered.

Perseverating momentarily on how to describe the "sex" part of the human trafficking equation – in a way that would not cost my daughter decades of therapy later in her life – I decided the wise move at this juncture was to just punt.

"Well, honey, a lot of the clothes we buy, and shoes, and other items, those things are made in foreign countries. By people, including little kids, who are forced to make the products. And the workers are never paid. They are modern-day slaves, making our T-shirts, or mining for metals that go into the making of our cell phones or cars. And that happens here in Asia, and in Africa. And I'm going to try and help fix that problem, and that's why you've heard me mention the term 'trafficking.'"

Sitting up straighter, I allowed myself to briefly exhale. A tiny smile played over my lips: I felt pretty darned satisfied that I'd managed to give an answer to her question that was thorough, and yet sidestepped the sex issue. My husband gave me the double-nod from above her little ponytail, obviously complimenting my quick thinking.

My happy reprieve lasted all of about 10 seconds.

She piped up again – loudly, of course: "So, how does the 'sex' part factor in?"

While the reader may not believe her phraseology, I kid you not, that is exactly what she said. At the ripe old age of … eight.

The Cambodians and Laotians on the plane – who had just begun to chat quietly amongst themselves after seeing the excitement of the Caucasian family die down – were once more brought to a soul-deafening silence. And, almost as if on cue, the plane was rendered – for the second time in as many minutes – quiet as church.

Obviously, everyone wanted to hear mommy's answer to the second installment of this little conversation. Lovely, just lovely.

My mind flipped around anxiously, like a fish out of water.

"Darn – why did I have to give birth to such a curious child??!!" my internal voice added to my mental confusion. I shot another glance over the top of my daughter's hairline toward my spouse.

Once again, my man was struggling to stay upright in his chair, while choking back semi-audible chortles. He mouthed quietly: "IT'S ALL YOU BABE – YOU GOT THIS!" And then gave me a quick "thumbs up" sign.

Clearly, he was enjoying watching me struggle as much as the rest of the airplane was. While I've zero doubt that being married to a litigator who likes to cross-examine people for pleasure was no walk in the park for my man, he nevertheless seemed to be deriving an unholy amount of joy from watching my daughter turn the tables on me with her new-found adult-level inquisitiveness and vocabulary.

To be fair, both my hubby and I had done our part to create this little person, always priding ourselves on never "talking down" to our daughter or using "baby talk." In fact, when she was first learning to toddle, she would sometimes grab for a TV tray that we often had up in the living room. And in response, we would also grab on to the tray – and intentionally and gently jiggle it underneath her hands – to illustrate the concept of "not stable" as we said those words aloud. (I should add, lest some reader decide to report me – some eighteen years late to some agency – that this was never done cruelly: it's not like we yanked the TV tray out from under her or anything. We just made it unstable enough to make the point). As parents who believed in "show don't tell," we'd always thought nothing of such episodes: we had just been speaking to her and teaching her as we would any person of any age.

And we knew she understood the various lessons. But just how clearly she understood was made very evident during an outing one day with other parents.

My daughter was probably about eighteen months old, and we'd decided to join some other mommies and toddlers at a local Burger King. Our family doesn't eat fast food, but the local moms had decided to gather at the Burger King because it had a great play structure. Desperately seeking stimulation for both myself and my daughter, I'd decided to join the group.

And the fast food play structure did not disappoint: it was a truly glorious creation. Massive and plastic, with endless brightly-colored tubes through which the kids could crawl, that stretched from one primary elevated platform to yet other ancillary platforms. There was also a variation that included a mesh blue-colored fabric, instead of a hard plastic tube. I remembered standing underneath it and looking above my head as my daughter – on all fours, on the raised platform – extended her hand forward and brought it down gently on the blue mesh netting that bridged the two platforms.

Noticing immediately that the blue mesh net was not nearly as resilient as the hard plastic tubes through which she'd previously been crawling, my daughter at once retracted her little pudgy hand, looked down through the mesh holes at me with her eyes nearly bugging out, and yelled – "Mama, NOT STABLE!!" – as her little hand pointed at the bouncy mesh fabric.

I was so surprised by her comment – she was not yet even two years old at the time – that I literally laughed out loud, nodding my head in agreement. When I pulled my gaze back down from her perch over my head, I looked into the faces of a bunch of other mothers who were blinking in amazement.

One mom tentatively inquired, "Um, did she just use the word 'stable' … in a sentence?"

Another mother responded on my behalf, "Well, that's Leigh's kid, and Leigh's a wordy lawyer, looks like that apple didn't fall far from the verbosity tree!" We all had a good laugh, while I briefly glowed with pride at my daughter's vocabulary and insight.

But now, a few years later – and sitting wedged onto an Air Laos plane that was full of people looking on eagerly while my eight-year-old grilled me on the meaning of "child sex slavery" – I was no longer awash in pride at my daughter's intelligence and verbal talents. Rather, I was struggling mightily – as a veteran litigator, no less – to hold my own … and get out of the conversation in a way that would not leave my daughter with nightmares. Or have the other passengers laughing me off the plane.

And of course, my husband was still enjoying the show dearly. I hazarded another look in his direction. He was now laughing so hard that tears were starting to run down his cheeks. Grand, just grand, I thought, as I turned my attention back to the problem at hand. My discomfort grew by the second, as I struggled to find a way to describe a "rape for profit" industry to a child that likely didn't yet understand the concept of intercourse.

My daughter was only in third grade, after all. And while we'd covered menstruation and ovaries, and basic boy/girl anatomy, it wasn't as if she'd hit high school yet – where I knew biology teachers were unfurling condoms onto bananas and diving into all the glorious details of reproduction.

"Well…." I stammered, still stunned at how quickly and effectively my eight-year-old could reduce a person who made a living as a speaker to a verbal-crutching, hot mess of a Toastmaster embarrassment.

My daughter – quite frustrated by this unusually-delayed response from her lawyer mom – began to pipe up in her endearing voice once again.

"Oh dear me!" – my brain silently shrieked as I saw her little mouth beginning to form a word. Heaven only knew what might exit her lips next.

Resisting the urge to cower further into my seat as the rational part of my brain tried to figure out how many "inquiring Cambodian and Laotian minds" were still tuned in to our endlessly entertaining dialogue, I waited on tenterhooks for whatever gem might next fall out of her mouth.

"Is it –" she paused, and then started again, "is it like a forced date?"

My head snapped down to see my child's large green eyes gazing up at me from her seat. Wow, it would seem she had answered her own question. And with just enough data to lead to an understanding that sex slavery was definitely on the "bad" side of the equation – but not so much data that she'd need ten years of therapy.

More relieved than I could ever recall being, I nodded gently.

"Yes, honey. That's exactly what it is." And I leaned back in my seat, once again awash with the glow of having a bright child, whose mind in this instance had ultimately answered her own question correctly.

It was right around the time of the inglorious Laotian Air plane ride that Connor – the Londoner who worked with the non-profit that I'd met up with in Da Nang – suggested I contact his friend George.

An American residing in Phnom Penh, George worked with a non-profit called Love 146. I still remember our conversation over lunch one afternoon while my family waited for me back in the Cambodian hotel.

I'd asked George how the group had come by its rather unusual name of "Love 146." Setting down his bottled water, George looked into my eyes and began to speak.

"Love 146 was founded by a young gentleman named Rob Morris. It was 2002, and he was traveling in Cambodia. One night, he saw some men selling children for sex, in a brothel. Stunned that this crime could be happening so blatantly, he was moved to reach out to groups that were doing work in Cambodia to fight the child brothel industry."

I nodded, mentally taking note of the fact that I was not the only adult who, in mid-life, had been overcome with a desire to fight child sex slavery. I leaned forward to pick up my water glass, briefly nodding my head in encouragement.

"So Rob ended up getting in touch with one of the anti-trafficking groups working in Cambodia, and they were going to go out undercover that night. And they took Rob along. In retrospect, Rob learned that was probably not the best thing to do – it could have been dangerous for all involved."

George paused again in his story. I sensed a slight shift in the air, and things seemed suddenly heavier. I wondered what George was going to say next.

"When Rob got to the brothel with this other outfit, there were girls in a 'fishbowl.' That's what we call a room where there's a glass panel separating the buyers from the young girls. And these kids, they were all elementary-school age. And all the little girls were wearing red dresses." He paused in his retelling of the story, and then looked up, directly into my eyes, before he resumed.

"And pinned to each girl's dress was a number."

I blinked hard, trying to imagine a room full of girls my daughter's age, being held behind a wall of glass, so that grown men could order them by number, for all manner of perversions. My mind struggled mightily in trying to process this data – and further, in trying to reconcile that there were 40 million people enslaved in similar conditions around the planet.

George picked up the story, after a long exhale. "So all the girls were pretty numb, and not making eye contact. Which is fairly common, as you might imagine. All but Number 146. That girl – Number 146 – well she was not watching the cartoons on the TV in the corner of the room. Nor staring at her feet or at the wall. She was staring through the pane of glass – directly into Rob's eyes."

I couldn't imagine. Finding myself slightly uncomfortable, I shifted my position in my chair as George continued.

"Rob didn't know if she was scared, or in some sort of fight-flight-or-freeze mode, or if her look was simply one of defiance. He hoped it was the latter."

He stopped briefly again, taking a sip of his drink. For my part, I too hoped the girl's look was one of defiance.

"The rest of the night was spent gathering Intel, and a few days later, the other NGO raided the brothel along with local law enforcement. But most of the girls were gone." I held my breath, hoping against hope that he would not speak the words which he then proceeded to utter.

"And they never found Girl 146."

I swallowed, convulsively and repeatedly. Trying to not openly cry in front of this kind man I'd just met.

George picked up his recounting, his voice barely louder than the hum of the coffee shop. "So Rob eventually founded his own non-profit, and we remember that girl and her life, daily. Hourly. It's our name. It's our Mission: Love 146."

Rendered at once sad and mute, I sat quietly in the heavy vacuum that had descended after George stopped speaking. And in that silence, I was reminded of the words of William Wilberforce, the renowned British politician who lived from 1798 to 1859, and led England in its fight to abolish the slave trade of that era.

Wilberforce stated: **"You may choose to look the other way, but you can never say again that you did not know."**

As yet, I could not decipher exactly how my journey into this world of slavery would go. But I did know one thing, with certainty: I would do this work, no matter how hard or gut-wrenching it might be.

For I could never look away. Not now that I knew.

Chapter 17

The air was muggy and the midday sun near blinding. We were traveling by tuk-tuk to the largest body of freshwater in Cambodia, known as Ton Le Sap Lake. Our guide, Sok, was taking us to visit the orphanages located there. To my surprise, we'd been able to pay Sok in US dollars. And he was quite fluent in English.

Noting our surprise at his fluency, he put us out of our curious misery:

"My country, we had a communist takeover in about 1975, when my parents were small. The Khmer Rouge – Khmer Rouge just means the radical communist movement – they pushed the revolution, which was led by Pol Pot, who answered to the Chinese Communist Party and Chairman Mao. Pol Pot … he ended up executing about one-quarter of the people here. Almost 2 million people. My people."

My eight-year-old daughter's eyes sought mine, wide open in horror, as Sok continued.

"They targeted the smart people, the rich people. The doctors. Lawyers. Accountants. Teachers. Government workers. The CCP and Khmer Rouge and Pol Pot – they wanted to get rid of smart and rich people. Because they knew these powerful people posed a threat to the takeover – that these people might have better ability to fight back. So Pol Pot, he executed them first. It was very violent. In some places, almost no one survived. One prison – named Security Prison Twenty-One? About 20,000 people passed through there, but only seven adults survived. Most were taken from these prisons to the Killing Fields to be executed – have you visited there yet?"

We shook our heads in unison from side to side. We had not been there.

Sok picked up the thread again. "Well, those fields are just outside Phnom Penh. You should go. While you are in our country. It is where the prisoners were taken to be executed, but because the Communists were so poor, they didn't like to use bullets – because bullets were expensive. Instead, my people were killed through blows to the back of the head, with things like axes or tools. Until the people died where they were, and were shoved face-first into shallow graves."

Sok brought his history lesson back around to the point that had inspired it: "So we take dollar now, and we speak English. Because since the Communist takeover, our country's educated people were dead. So we've struggled to rebuild. We rely on tourist; we take American dollar."

My daughter and husband's eyes were like saucers, possibly even more surprised than even I had been by Sok's pronouncements, as the others in my family were completely unfamiliar with Cambodian history. But not I – for I had indulged my penchant for reading by buying every book on the Cambodian genocide I'd encountered when we first landed in southeast Asia (including the gripping autobiography by Pin Yathay entitled, "Stay Alive, My Son," where the author tells the true story of his family's evacuation from the City of Phnom Penh with the lie that it would only be "for three days" – and the subsequent genocide and starvation of all seventeen members of his family – followed by his harrowing escape from the Khmer Rouge communist work-camps).

And Sok spoke truth: Cambodians took our US dollars without need of us ever exchanging it into the local currency, and when it came to the spoken word, English was the hands-down common denominator. We would frequently encounter groups of German or Italian tourists speaking heavily-accented English to Cambodian tour guides, who would answer back, also in heavily-accented English. Neither speaking the other's language fluently, but everyone speaking just enough English to get by.

Sok pointed to the edge of the lake at which we'd arrived. "That is Ton Le Sap. It is the largest freshwater lake in southeast Asia. The Mekong River feeds the Ton Le Sap River, which comes into this lake. In our dry season, it's only about one meter deep, or 3 feet for you Americans." Sok chuckled benignly.

"The people who live near here are originally from Vietnam. And they like to fish. But because they are very traditional Buddhist, which is against killing, they will only catch what they can eat, and wait for the fish to die – they do not kill with their hands."

"Here," Sok pointed at a tiny little canoe, "your daughter, she get in here, and sit there." Sok pointed to some horizontal slats that were obviously the little boat's *de facto* seats. "And you, here. And your husband, he sit there." Once more, Sok pointed, and then agilely leaped in and took up an oar. "Now, we go. And visit orphanage," Sok announced, some excitement in his voice as he dipped the oar into the water of Ton Le Sap.

I looked across this very shallow, greenish-tan, mud-colored lake. Sok had said this was freshwater, but it did not seem so fresh. It looked just about like liquid … mud, if my eyes were not deceiving me. Lifting my gaze from the murky water, I started scanning the landscape. To my surprise, I saw what seemed to be a bunch of houseboats on the horizon. I squinted, and analyzed my internal voice's decision to characterize the apparitions I was seeing atop the lake as "houseboats."

Such would be an overly ambitious phrase: what I was seeing were more like "floating tepees" or "floating shacks." Tiny, ramshackle wooden huts that had been attached to the top of horizontal pieces of lumber which had been lashed together to float on the lake. The structures were definitely more "Huck Finn" than "Lake Powell houseboat."

Sok saw my narrowed gaze, and elucidated.

"Ton Le Sap is home to the poor. Poorest of poor. They cannot afford land taxes, so they live on water. Floating. And the orphanage we are going to visit is the same: it floats on water. And the kids are all orphans whose parents died. And one teacher, he lives there, floating, all the time, with the kids."

I'm sure my face registered my shock at what I was seeing. Whole villages appeared to live atop this muddy lake, on floating pieces of wood banded together. We approached one of the larger platforms some minutes later, and alighted from the canoe.

Walking inside, we were surrounded by young Cambodian children my daughter's age. Instant new friends, it seemed. And despite my daughter speaking exactly zero Cambodian words, and the orphans speaking zero English, all the kids bounded off together down the edge of the platform. It was a relief to see that, despite the hardships, children everywhere were… children.

Sok proceeded to give us a tour. We went classroom to classroom in the floating orphanage. Given the language barrier, I understood little of what I saw written on the chalk boards. But I did understand the math, once we got to the math classroom. And I understood as well that the children in this literal backwater, a generation or two after a genocide had ravaged their country, were learning math that was far in advance of what my daughter and her friends in America were learning in their private schools. Interesting, indeed.

From the classrooms, we went to the living quarters, and then the kitchen. There were large blue plastic barrels standing upright near a propane stove. I inquired about them.

Sok pointed, and replied, "That is their drinking water."

"But where does it come from?" my husband asked.

"The lake," Sok answered. "The orphans live on the lake. The lake is their drinking water. It's also where they go to the bathroom. It's where they wash their dishes. This same water provides everything, including the fish that they eat. They live here, all day, every day."

I gazed downward, viewing anew the tan and muddy water that was clearly visible as it lapped languidly between holes in the wooden planks under my feet.

"And what do they eat, besides fish?" I asked.

"Mainly rice," said Sok. "And the fish. Meat is really rare. You can buy a bag of rice for $30 US and it will feed them for a month."

My husband, clearly as moved by the orphans' plight as I was, eagerly worked out the transaction. He was wrapping up when my daughter bounded back into our midst with her new friend in tow – a little Cambodian girl with long black hair and one pink strand.

"Mama, can we have your phone? I think a tourist gave her temporary hair dye, but they don't have a mirror, so she's never seen what the dye looks like in her hair …" my daughter rattled off, rapid-fire.

I stared at my child, in utter amazement that the two girls had been able to communicate all this with simple gestures, and who knows, maybe some telepathy or mind-reading skills.

"Sure!" I replied, digging my cell phone out of the pocket of my shorts.

My daughter grabbed it eagerly, reversed the camera, and snapped a photo. Turning to her new friend, she showed her what the pink strand of hair looked like, while the other girl squealed in amazement, preening.

I laughed again, fascinated at how similar some things were the world over, despite other obvious differences.

"Here, let me take your photo, gals," I said. They posed, arms around each other.

I showed my daughter's friend the shot. She was clearly entranced.

I turned back to Sok. "I can send this to them, so she can have a copy," I offered.

He smiled, "There's no way to get it to them. They don't have any phones."

"Not any – not even the teacher?" I queried.

"No," he said simply.

Undeterred, I replied, "Well, I could print out a copy and maybe mail it – to you, or to them?"

"We have no mail service," Sok noted, smiling sadly, "it's very different from America."

I nodded in acknowledgement, my mind still struggling with the fact that there was literally no way to even get a paper copy of the girls' photo to them.

"Almost time to go," said Sok, as my daughter and her new friend hugged each other hard.

We turned to walk across the platform to get back into our tiny canoe for the trip to shore. My husband reached the canoe first, and took a big step off our platform and into the canoe, causing it to tip precariously. I followed, and was standing partially in the canoe, one leg in the tiny vessel, and one leg still on the orphanage platform, so that I could help my daughter step into the moving canoe without falling.

As I was standing there none too solidly, my husband pulled at my sleeve. More than a tad frazzled that he was trying to catch my attention while I was trying to get my daughter safely on board the canoe with no missteps, I ignored him.

He plucked again at my elbow, saying quietly but urgently: "Leigh. Listen."

I turned toward him, still exasperated at his interruption. But my quick retort died on my lips, as I pivoted my body further in his direction and looked at the scene to which he was pointing.

Our canoe had docked parallel to the floating orphanage, and on the far side of our little canoe, an even tinier canoe had drawn up alongside my husband. In it was a woman who was emaciated, and wearing a threadbare T-shirt so thin you could see her skin beneath it, along with equally threadbare pants.

Before her, in the front of the canoe, stood a tiny toddler.

Half-naked and unbothered, the little girl stood sucking on a bottle full of dirty lake water.

My husband reiterated, "Listen. I think she's about to repeat what she just said."

Time stood still. To my right was my daughter, dressed head-to-toe in her favorite colors of pink and white. My daughter's hair was pulled back in a neat ponytail, secured with a matching pink and white hair-band. The other woman continued to sit, rocking gently in her dilapidated canoe as she stared pointedly at my child. She then turned her head slowly back to her daughter, before she swung her gaze around to once more settle on mine.

"Thousand dollar, you take?" the woman said, extending a bony leathered hand toward her offspring.

My heart ripped in two. I heard my daughter's rapid intake of oxygen, followed by her quiet voice whispering into my ear.

"Mama, did she just offer to sell her daughter to you?"

I nodded mutely, beckoning my child to step fully into our canoe as I extended my right arm to catch her lest she fall. At the same time, I looked back at the older woman. Upon further inspection, she was probably my age or younger, but looked twice as old, having spent a lifetime clearly undernourished and outdoors, in the ruthless baking sun of Cambodia.

I choked back tears, mouthing more than enunciating the words to the woman in the canoe: "I'm sorry" – I said, as I shook my head sadly from side to side and repeated once more: "I'm sorry, I – I can't."

The woman blinked at me, and then began to paddle slowly away as my family watched, becoming tinier on the horizon. Where was she headed, and what would she do? And what, pray tell, would become of her little girl?

The questions raged on relentlessly in my heart and soul during the boat ride back. And throughout the afternoon and evening, all three of us – my husband, daughter and I – took turns crying.

We knew, intellectually, that the answer to the problem was not for us to purchase a child. And we knew, as well, that the poverty we had seen was a poverty unlike that which pervades America. There were no shelters near Ton Le Sap Lake, no food stamps, no charities, no churches.

There was simply a poverty so severe that if you did not sell your child, she might well die. We were shaken, to our core. It was a lesson that never left us, even now – ten years hence.

And some months later, when we returned as a family of three to our house in the States, we walked in the door expecting to feel like we were "home" – only to realize we now felt like were in a foreign land. We'd been gone for the better part of a half year, and we'd been living amongst people who lived very differently than Americans.

I like to think I keep a fairly tidy house, with very few chotchkes, lots of empty surfaces and no real clutter. It's definitely not a hoarder's house, nor is it chock full of stuff.

But my husband and I both took one look around the living room upon our return from Asia, and said almost in unison, "Time for a Goodwill run."

Having spent nearly a half-year living out of two suitcases, and seeing communities like that on Ton Le Sap Lake, all three of us suddenly understood that truly everything we owned was a luxury. The only things one actually needs in order to survive on this planet are clean water and some occasional food (and much less food than we, as Americans, typically consume). Clothing and shelter? Those items are only really necessary if one is living in a cold climate – otherwise, even the latter items are unnecessary.

Having had the good fortune of this experience when my daughter was eight, I am convinced now that many of the problems I see in today's younger generation stem from a failing of American teachers to actually show the ugly upshot of political systems like communism, and a failing of us as parents to do the same. Put simply, most Americans have spent one too many summer vacations going to the Grand Canyon and Disneyworld with their children.

This is categorically not how the rest of the world lives, and our children have a biased perspective – which is not their fault – for it's all that most of us have ever shown them. But it's a very narrow viewpoint, and a particularly dangerous one in today's world.

Currently, 51% of surveyed youth have a positive view of socialism and believe our economy should be "mostly socialist."[65] As someone

---

[65] Glaeser, Edward L. How to Talk to Millenials about Capitalism, The Social Order (Spring 2019), https://www.city-journal.org/millennials-embrace-socialism.

who has now lived and worked in many communist or formerly communist countries, I can attest that the fact that half our American youth are so deluded is one heck of a problem.

But not my child. We came home from Cambodia with lessons instilled in all of us that no amount of reading or watching documentaries could impart.

Lessons that, indeed, have never left us. I remember going shopping for "back to school" items the autumn after our travels.

We were in South Coast Plaza when my daughter pointed at a Hello Kitty Backpack, and said, "Oh mom, I need a new backpack."

I looked down, smiling, and inquired: "Do you need it?"

She paused for a second, and then looked up, matching my smile. "No, it's just a want, not a need."

Lest the reader think I did this all the time, I did not. And it wasn't like my husband and I never bought our daughter another new backpack. But after our travels in southeast Asia, my child understood intrinsically the difference between a "want" and an actual "need" – and also realized that 99% of the items that we Americans think we "need" are actually simply "wants."

Never was that fact more on display than the Thanksgiving holiday of the year we came back from Asia. My daughter's fourth grade teacher had asked the kids – without the parents' knowledge – to make a list of the "fifteen things" for which the children were most thankful as the holiday approached. Then, the teacher had sent the list home with the kids the Wednesday afternoon before the long weekend.

Unpacking my daughter's backpack that night, I discovered the gift from the teacher. I opened up the colored construction paper creation – with the little handmade paper turkey on top – and began reading the lined paper glued to the middle, which was the list of fifteen things for which my daughter was grateful.

High on the list was "clean drinking water." Because, as my daughter had astutely noted in her scrawled handwriting, so many people in the world "lack access to clean water." "Schooling" was also very high on the list – because "so many kids" do not have access to education – "particularly girls" my daughter had noted. "Food" was also on the list. Toward the very bottom I saw "parents" and "grandparents" featured – apparently we were also items for which my daughter was grateful.

I smiled, reflecting back on the fact that I had often wondered if "seeing too much hardship" at age eight in Asia was going to leave my daughter needing decades of therapy. So far, it looked like it had occasioned the exact opposite: a child who "got it" – and understood that the fruits of American materialism did not even come close to making the cut on a list of items for which we should be grateful. Using a magnet to tack my daughter's creation to the front of my black refrigerator door, I chuckled aloud at the notion that my child appeared to understand Maslow's Hierarchy of Needs in a way that few college students did.[66]

The truth of the matter is that we *can* change the world in which we live. And the corollary to that statement is that one of the best and

---

[66] Abraham Maslow was an American psychologist best known for his theory of the Hierarchy of Needs, which posited that humans are motivated to fulfill their needs in a hierarchical order. This order begins with the most basic needs before moving on to more advanced needs. From the bottom of the hierarchy upwards, the needs are: physiological (food and clothing), safety (job security), love and belonging needs (friendship), esteem, and self-actualization. Maslow believed that needs higher up could not be satisfied until the lower ones – like food and clothing – were met. Mcleod, S. (Mar 21, 2023), *Maslow's Hierarchy of Needs.* Simply Psychology. https://www.simplypsychology.org/maslow.html

easiest ways to do so is by educating our children with truth. And we do that best by showing them, not telling them.

I thus encourage the reader to take your children – and yourselves – on the roads less traveled. And further, to "travel" the roads that led directly to the mistakes in our planet's history. To witness with one's own eyes the historical evolutions and atrocities that we, as an evolved species, have no business ever repeating.

Yes, my friends: take your family, and especially your little ones, *there.*

To *those* places.

For it is then – and perhaps only then – that our children will truly understand the mistakes of our ancestors, and hopefully, grow up to be good stewards of this planet. Stewards who understand that our only actual job is to navigate ceaselessly toward justice.

Toward freedom.

The e-mail which follows I authored on February 20, 2018, when I crawled back into bed at 4 a.m., after visiting the brothels in the Red Light Jihadi District along the Thai-Malay Border, and found myself unable to sleep. Initially, I planned to just send the e-mail to my husband and a few friends, to update them on my status.

But then I ended up cc'ing half my Rolodex – Christians, Jews, Mormons, atheists, judges, lawyers, journalists, pastors, soccer moms, dads, doctors, accountants, Americans, Europeans, Australians, Asians. Upon awakening the next morning, I was astounded to find fifty-eight replies, every single one a permutation of the following:

"You brought tears to my eyes – how can I help?"

Proving to me once again that regardless of race, religion, or walk of life, the good people of this planet are united by minimally these two things: (1) our capacity to recognize evil, and (2) our desire to help rescue those victimized by it.

And on the darkest of nights – like when six months to the day after I wrote this email I received word that the lady trapped in slavery – who I speak of in the following email, and who had just committed her life to Christ – was then "disappeared" … well, it is then that the above truths give me hope that the good people of this planet will yet persevere … to find a new and peaceful dawn.

Email to My Friends – February 20, 2018:

Hey all,

I know some of you have been wondering what I've been up to since my departure awhile back. I've now made it (safely) to what is Ground Zero of the SE Asia Red Light Jihadi district, where radicalized Muslim bombers seek to liberate a separate Islamic state via a religious war with a history dating back as far as the Gaza Strip upheavals (1940's)… and with a death rate just as high: more than 6,000 dead in the last few years alone. Since my last trip to this town of 140 child brothels, the two "hotels" (brothels) that I stayed at last time have been bombed, and the situation has deteriorated further.

Tonight, we were able to go out into the community. For those interested in what this region looks like (warning, somewhat disturbing content follows), I've attached a few pics below.

The first photo captured my partners and me doing outreach to the girls of the town – a street with nothing but brothels lining it – as the young girls got dressed up to go to work.

After the sun went down, we traveled to a veritable no-man's-land: a dirt alley so dark, abandoned, and filthy that one walks away questioning whether hell is truly reserved for those who've passed.

At the far end of this blackened alley hides a brothel that is nearly unfindable. In this literal hole in the wall, barricaded behind steel gates, works a woman from a land far away. This is not unusual: the vast majority of the girls trafficked into this area hail from Laos (or similar areas). And when these child sex slaves do not die of disease or murder and instead reach adulthood… they end up in places like these.

She is my age, almost exactly.

But she has lived a life that is beyond incomprehensible: her husband owned a breaking house (which is exactly what its name implies)... she is a domestic violence survivor... and she's been working in this town for decades. In the second photo, you see her next to me and two young ladies from our outreach program, on the brothel floor, as she gets made up to greet an arriving customer.

And the last photo? Well, it's something you're not likely to see again.

It is the back room of a child brothel... capturing in garish colors and unflinching light the juxtaposition that keeps me coming back to this work.

These children are being raped for profit, multiple times a night, by men five to ten times their age ... in what is unequivocally the fastest growing criminal economy on this planet. Their only witnesses?

The teddy bears lining every corner of their rooms.

Yes, slavery exists in first world countries. Yes, American teens deserve rescue as much as anyone else. But the reality is that the girls – nay, the children – living in these rooms you see, lying side by side on mats on the floor, hugging their well-worn stuffed animals to their chests like life preservers...well, these children cannot and do not self-rescue.

That's the unvarnished truth, my friends.

Unlike the slavery situations in Eastern Europe, these little girls are never going to sweet-talk a customer out of his phone to place a call for help. Because the customers who come for them are not drunk frat boys led astray on a backpacking trip through Amsterdam. No: these girl's customers are hardened pedophiles. And the sad truth is that unlike some American trafficking victims, these girls are never going to run away... because where would they run? They were not kidnapped nor baited and switched into brothel work – they were quite simply sold into these child brothels by the very people who were supposed to protect them: their parents.

And so while every single one of the 40+ million people on this planet trapped in human slavery undeniably deserves rescue, I choose to spend my time on this most vulnerable population. These girls, in these towns, sold into the hands of pedophiles...who stand no chance of escape absent a miracle, outside intervention, or both. And the efforts are working:

Tonight, one of the controllers of the brothels tentatively agreed to allow our nurses in to check on the health of the girls. This is unprecedented (and much needed). The woman in the second photo has now agreed to come to Sunday services, and is making plans on how to escape this town which is truly a hell on earth. And in recent weeks, one of the madams here just closed up shop, stating – after decades in the business – that it "just felt wrong to continue."

So that's what's up on the dark side of the moon, 10,000 miles from home.

For those inclined to pray, the girls of this town certainly need it. And for the rest? Well, warm and fuzzy happy thoughts are surely appreciated too. Until we meet again (or I find another rare pocket of cell/data service)....

Leigh

BEER

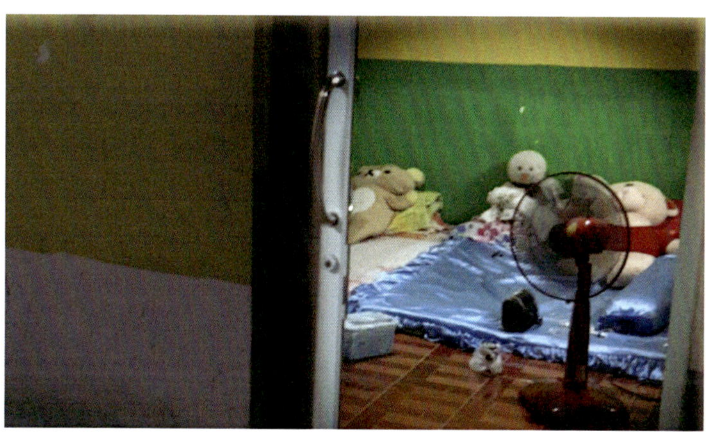

Ton Le Sap means "Great Lake." The lake's river basin is home to 3 million people. Many live in land dwellings like those in first two photos below. We were told by our Guide that "tin roofed" dwellings house "rich people" – usually because they've sold a child into slavery. Poorer locals live on floating dwellings, like the one on which my daughter is walking (bottom pic).

Children living on the floating orphanages of Ton Le Sap; my daughter and I visiting the orphanage (bottom photo).

As seen in the first image, the water of Ton Le Sap Lake ranges from 30 feet deep ... to only 3 feet deep in the dry season. The lake provides the orphans with fish, drinking water, and serves as a *de facto* restroom & clothes washer.

My daughter, below, with a Cambodian girl she befriended while at the Ton Le Sap Floating Orphanage/School.

A 3-year old boy with his pet python asked my daughter to hold his snake, but she replied: "No, thank you – I don't want a living necklace – I'll let mama try it out."

Killing Fields Memorial outside Phnom Penh, Cambodia

During the rainy seasons, bones of those executed by Pol Pot & the Communist Khmer Rouge Regime still rise to the surface of shallow graves where they were executed. The remains are collected by locals and placed into this multi-story, glass case.

I did not know – when we began the tour with my then eight-year old daughter in tow – that it would conclude at this memorial. As a compromise, we'd allowed her to listen to the self-guided audio cassette – and we'd <u>only</u> allowed her to listen to the tracks that my husband and I had vetted as being okay for her age.

But when we came upon the structure at the end of the tour, my daughter took off running up the stairs to see the memorial. When I caught up, I found her eyeball to eye socket of a skull.

She turned her face to mine, asking quite hauntingly:

"Mama, how did this happen?"

I replied that it was a result of those in power abusing the trust of the citizens – and the people not realizing this "until it was too late." In the picture below, if you look closely, you will see my daughter – standing nose to the glass – with me off to the left.

My husband and I worried for many years about this trip – and whether it had scarred my daughter, or was going to crop up years later as an incident that would necessitate therapy. But my daughter is now eighteen, in college and successfully adulting. And in hindsight, I've come to believe that we in the West tend to over-shelter our children.

My daughter understands poverty. She understands that the majority of this planet does not live in the comparative luxury that surrounds even the poorest of those in America.

More importantly, after the fateful visit to the Killing Fields and seeing similar conditions in a variety of countries, my daughter understands communism and dictatorships. And – despite being at a liberal university – I am proud to state that she is NOT one of the 51% of our youth who think (upon being surveyed) that "it would be cool to live in a socialist or communist country."

Because at age eight? She came face-to-face with the results of communism.

In Bangkok, with the Royal Thai Police & colleagues from my NGO, who were signing a First-of-Kind Memorandum of Understanding which I had authored that allowed our NGO to do groundbreaking anti-trafficking work in southeast Asia.

Below are exterior shots of some of the buildings and brothels in the Red Light Jihadi District located in the Deep South of Thailand. Nearly all buildings in certain towns – from stores to banks – have been converted into *de facto* brothels, many with bars or cages covering their windows. There were 140 child brothels in this town when I started working here in 2013.

The Red Light Jihadi District on the Thai-Malay Border is a region fraught with religious tension. There are radicalized Jihadi Terror Training Camps in the area, similar to those in the Mid-East which are depicted in blockbuster movies. In south Asia, the radical Jihadi camps keep their skills sharp by bombing the brothels in nearby towns. The pictures you see below are the result of such bombings which occur almost daily: 330 bombs went off in this town the first year I began working there.

The below pictures are from Thailand's *coup d'etat* in Spring of 2014 (its twelfth since 1932). Tensions became high during early February of 2014, when I was on the ground working with the Thai Government.

A general election had been scheduled for that February which could not be completed due to protests, and a few weeks later, military martial law was declared.

The picture below is of me in a brothel in the Red Light Jihadi District. The young girl to the right of me in the photo had just been forced to have a nose job, as the sex buyers in the region prefer a certain type of nose (which certain ethnicities do not possess). Accordingly, the brothels force the girls to undergo nose and breast surgeries.

The pastor with whom I work in this region – seeing that the young girl had only recently had nose surgery – proceeded to work out an agreement with the mamasan that allowed the girl to <u>not</u> work the floor that evening while her nose was still fully packed with gauze, so long as the pastor and I kept buying drinks every hour (and as a result, the girl insisted on a photo, which we do not normally do).

Tampa Re-Awaken – June 2021
10,000 in Audience

Post Falls, Idaho Re-Awaken – Sept. 2022

Defeat the Mandates Rally – March 2022
25,000 People in front of LA County Hall

Dundas Keynoting with General Flynn in 2021 Supporting Pastor Jackson Lahmeyer's U.S. Senate Race

General Flynn – 3-Star General, Former 25th US National Security Advisor, Intelligence Director for Joint Special Operations Command, and Defense Intelligence Agency Lead – Calls Leigh Back On-Stage at the San Diego Re-Awaken Event, Stating:

> **"I mean – this is a WARRIOR.**
>
> **She is a JOAN OF ARC.**
>
> **She is a CHAMPION for this country.**
>
> **I mean she is UNBELIEVABLE. God has given us her – to be able to fight for you – and to be able to fight for this country.**
>
> **So thank you – very much – for all that you've been doing!"**

With Robert F. Kennedy Jr. at State Capitol (2019), protesting SB 276 which gutted medical exemptions for most vaccine-injured children in California.

Keynoting at Re-Awaken Event with Eric Trump (2022)

Dundas Organizes 4-Day Nationwide Walkout from November 8-11, 2021 – To Oppose the Biden Administration's Unconstitutional Vaccine Mandate That Was Being Forced on American Workers.

East Coast Protests in Support of Nationwide Walkout

Below, Dundas Announces to Multiple Standing Ovations that – at the end of the one-week Nationwide Walkout – the US received its first win on the subject when the 5th Circuit Federal Appeals Court ruled Biden's mandate was flatly unconstitutional.

When I asked Holocaust Survivor Vera Sharav what she thought about Orange County CA & New York in tandem resurrecting "passport systems," she said:

"Oh – that is a NAZI plan. That is how Hitler started hunting MY PEOPLE."

I responded by asking if she'd be willing to allow us to make a TV commercial with her, and she agreed.

After raising almost $250K for the ad-buy, below is what aired hourly in our county on CNN, MSNBC & Fox, during prime-time, for one week:

> **"I'm a child survivor of the Holocaust.**
>
> **One of the discriminatory actions against Jews was special 'passports' to identify, discriminate and persecute us.**
>
> **It makes me shudder to think that places like Orange County, California, are considering digital vaccine passports. If enacted, these passports will create a two-tiered society and deny citizens equal access.**
>
> **Those who disregard history's lesson are doomed to repeat it."**

Screen Shots from the Holocaust Survivor TV Ad

Vera 30 second spot vers3 oven at end.mp4
ARBEITSLAGER
0:02 / 0:30

Our Holocaust Survivor TV Ad caused 2,000+ people to arrive at the next County Board Meeting, after which the Board abandoned the digital vaccine passport plan.

Leigh Taylor Dundas, Esq.

From 2020 through 2023, Leigh undertook a Freedom Tour, during which she gave more than 200 speeches. In summer of 2021, she circled the United States twice, giving a unique speech for each day of summer.

She has also been a keynote speaker at all of Clay Clark's Re-Awaken America Tours and the Defeat the Mandate (LA) Tour, speaking to between 3,000 and 25,000 people at a time.

Cumulatively over the past 38 months, she has spoken in 100 big cities and small towns, in more than 25 states, changing the lives of over 100,000 people who attended her speeches in person – while reaching another estimated 20 million people through broadcasts via live-stream, internet, and podcast platforms.

To learn more about her work or support it, go to: **FreedomFighterNation.org**

Chapter 18

When my daughter was two years old, and sleeping in the back of the truck on our way home from a boating trip to Lake Mead, I'd had an idea for a screenplay centered around a sex-trafficking plot. I had never written a screenplay, but I was entranced with my idea. And as the notion would not leave me alone, I'd finally relented and put pen to paper. But life with a two-year-old and a professional career was busy, and I'd never had the chance to finish it. Every time I went to do so, life intervened.

And I do mean *intervened.* The last time I'd decided to have "uninterrupted writing time" and finally finish my screenplay was a year or two after I'd first started writing. My daughter was at grandma's house for the evening, my husband was out with his mother, and I was home alone for once.

Mentally overjoyed at having found five or six hours in a row to just write, I turned off my cell phone, and plunked down on the couch with my laptop, only to hear our house phone ring.

I debated answering it. But after reminding myself that this was "Non-Negotiable Writing Time," I decided to let it go. Thirty seconds later, it was still shrilly singing across my living room. I was cursing my decision when the answering machine finally picked up. After the torture of listening to my own voice on the outgoing message "We're not home – leave a message!" I promptly heard the voice of one of my best friends from childhood.

"Leigh, it's Shari. Call me. Paul died."

All my friends, including me, were within a few years of the magic age of 40. And we all had young children at home – in fact, my friend Shari's daughter was still a baby.

Throwing my laptop off of me, I practically dove over my kitchen counter in an attempt to grab the handset before the call ended. Just missing her call and with a beeping dial tone in my ear, I quietly cursed the delay as I punched into my phone the ten digits to Shari's cell phone number.

My brain staunchly refused to believe that her husband had died – how was that even possible?

Shari answered immediately, providing terse details.

Apparently, her husband had made dinner for her and the baby, and then he'd gone into their bedroom to unpack his suitcase from his recent business trip. While in the bedroom, he'd suffered a fatal heart attack, which Shari had discovered some time later when she wandered into their bedroom.

My mouth was hanging open as I listened to the facts Shari recounted. Promising to go straight to her condo, I abandoned my screenplay for another day.

Her husband's death was quite the shock for our tight-knit circle of childhood friends: we'd all ended up stopping our activities that month to band together and assist my girlfriend in preparing for the funeral, picking out a casket, and otherwise dealing with the unexpected and incredibly challenging turn of events. Some years later, Shari and her daughter are now thriving… but such were the types of barriers that I would invariably encounter whenever I tried to finish my screenplay about sex-trafficking.

But it was now 2013. And my family was in Cambodia, and I'd discovered a fabulous little café run by an NGO that employed teenage survivors of sex trafficking who were learning new vocations while they healed and got counseling. The café was full of chill music and quiet corners, with big plush pillows and window seats into which tired tourists could burrow to escape the hubbub of Phnom Penh's incessant street noise. It was truly an oasis – Starbucks could've taken a lesson from this little café – and I'd found myself spending the better part of a week in this coffee shop frequented by ambitious young expats working for Cambodian NGOs. It was here that I hunkered down for the first time in years, able to gratefully disappear into my writing and finish the screenplay.[67]

But on this hot afternoon, I was ready for a change of scenery after being indoors all week staring at my laptop. And our guide Sok's statement about visiting the Killing Fields had been weighing on my heart.

So, after some discussion on my phone with my husband, who was back in the hotel room, we decided to make the half-hour trip to the Killing Fields. This, despite the fact that we had no babysitter – and thus my eight-year old would also have to come along for the ride.

That said, I'd done some research online, and discovered that it was basically a self-guided tour through some grass fields, with an audio-cassette tape and ear phones. So with that in mind, my hubby and I reconciled taking our daughter to the Killing Fields with the knowledge that she could just do the walking part of the tour, sans audio-information.

---

[67] While I wrote the screenplay because the idea for the script would not leave me be, I must confess I've no idea what to do with it now. With that said, I believe the world could stand to learn more about human trafficking, and I would love to see the script turned into a movie one day. If readers have thoughts in this regard, feel free to contact my agent at Robert@BigIdeaSpeakers.com.☺

No sooner had we alighted from the Tuk Tuk did the plan fall apart. "But I want to hear the tapes too!" my daughter lobbied.

"Honey, this is some very heavy stuff they're talking about, and it's not really age-appropriate –"

"But it's not fair for you guys to get to hear it and for me not to hear it – how am I supposed to know what's going on if I can't hear??!!" my daughter replied, quite emphatically and persuasively.

My husband and I looked at each other, while my daughter swiveled her head from my countenance to his. After more discussion where we attempted to explain to her that we would recap the salient points, followed by a fair bit of decent lawyering from our third-grader in response to our entreaties (which my husband never failed to rejoice in by ad-libbing with little gems delivered *sotto voce* like – "Now you know what it's like to be married to you!" followed by a throaty chuckle), we'd finally managed to reach a compromise where we – the parents – would listen to an audio-track to preview it. Then, if it wasn't too graphic, we would permit her to also listen.

With the agreement thus hammered out, and my daughter now content, I turned back toward the fields, eyeballing them anew. They looked innocent enough. In fact, they looked just like the flat fields of grass that one would see back home in Southern California.

Except for the little sign next to us with the years of the genocide posted on it – 1975 to 1979. Staring at the sign, I reflected on the fact that I had actually been alive at the time of the genocide. A mere toddler when the Communist Takeover of Cambodia had begun, sheer luck had planted me on the opposite side of the planet, in nearly identical fields that – instead of being the site of much bloodshed – had been the site of my favorite memories. I sighed, feeling my mind skip back down the decades in search of the comfort of happier places....

"Leigh, I'm bored with swimming – we've done every trick we know how to do off the diving board!" cried my friend Cynthia. Cindy lived up the hill from me. Her house was about a 15 minute walk by rural road – or a full 40 minute trek across the open fields (if one wanted to avoid the road that teenagers would oft-use as their own private race track).

Today, Cindy had walked over to my house to play, and we'd spent the better part of the afternoon swimming. But she was right – we'd exhausted our supply of fun things to do in the pool.

"Wanna make some mud?" I inquired. While swimming was fun, digging in the dirt and making mud was always a fan favorite.

"Yeah, let's do it," Cindy replied, starting off down my driveway toward the south end of the property in search of "The Hole" that my friend Kevin and I often played in. Sometimes – as today when Kevin was busy elsewhere – my girlfriends and I would take over digging in "The Hole."

"You get the big bucket, and – hey – does that faucet still work?" Cindy said, pointing at a rusty pipe sticking out of the ground that had a metallic circular knob attached.

"Pretty sure it does," I replied.

She wandered over to give it a yank. "Yep – it works!" she responded after twisting it.

We pushed a series of large buckets toward the faucet that was now spluttering high pressure rusty water out its side, proceeding to add the liquid to the dark brownish-black soil that was plentiful in the deep shade found underneath my parents' canopy of century-old avocado trees.

"Hey – now that we've got so much of this – why don't we become mud monsters?" Cindy offered.

I stood up from where I'd been mixing water into dirt to ensure the perfect thickness of mud, while occasionally picking out the odd piece of root that was detracting from the mud's consistency. I was still in my wet bikini bathing suit – Cindy and I had not changed after exiting the pool – and I mulled over my friend's idea. I'd done a lot of things with mud, but never had I slathered it over my body before. But what the heck, it sounded like fun.

"Okay," I replied, "why don't I paint you with the mud first, and then you do me?"

Cindy nodded eagerly, and threw her arms straight out from her sides. She looked a bit like one of the criminals waiting for a pat down that I watched on the police show CHIPS each night. Staring at her briefly, I proceeded to bend over and dip my hands into the gloppy mud in the bucket, and then rub my muddy hand over her very white skin. Calves, thighs, arms, chest – everything exposed was plied with the thick black mud.

"Okay," I noted, "it's probably time to do your armpits and your face, if you want to be fully covered. And maybe your hair. Those are the only parts of you that are still white or blond, and not yet muddy…." I trailed off.

"Yeah, let's do our WHOLE BODIES!" Cindy practically screamed in agreement. "And then we'll look like AWESOME SWAMP-THINGS!!!"

I figured she was referencing some horror movie she had seen that I was not allowed to watch.

"Sounds good!" I yelled back, matching her enthusiasm, as I proceeded to cover the rest of her body. Two minutes later, I took a step back to eyeball the transformation.

It was pretty impressive.

Cindy, like me, was not just Caucasian, but nearly albino. Melanin was an item I was pretty sure our bodies had never known, even in summer time. But the rich loamy earth had turned into a nice black paste, and now Cindy looked like one of the aboriginal tribesman that I'd recently seen on a documentary. The only thing which still remained white on her body were her eyeballs. And her teeth... which became visible whenever she opened her mouth to speak. It was cool. And kind of terrifying, all at once.

"Okay, my turn to do you!" Cindy replied.

"Okay," I responded, a little less enthusiastically. I preferred touching to being touched, especially with slimy mud, but I couldn't very well ask her to not return the favor. To her credit, her enthusiasm made the process pretty quick and painless. I was covered in mud in no time flat.

Transformation complete, we elected to run over to the glass front door of my house, to see if we could see our reflections. Lo and behold, we could, in fact, see ourselves in the mirror-like door.

And I'm not gonna lie, we were a pretty frightening sight: two albino girls turned black-as-night with mud. Including our blond manes, which were now wet but also caked with drying blobs of muddy goop that had clumped up and stuck to strands of our hair. Swamp-things, indeed.

"This is SOOOOO cool!" Cindy exclaimed in delight. "We should go to the top of your driveway right now, just like this. And jump around and scare the cars that come around the corner!!!"

I mulled over her suggestion. It had been a decent amount of work, this body-painting with mud, and the end result was pretty spectacular. It would be somewhat sad, indeed, for us to just rinse it all off. Quite a waste, actually.

Yep, scaring innocent passersby sounded like a much better use of our time, which stretched out endlessly in front of us on this hot and languid summer afternoon.

"Okay, let's go!" I concurred.

Racing down the flat part of my driveway past the house, we then began to ascend the asphalt driveway – making our way up toward the road. It was a steep grade of a driveway, that ended at a much higher elevation, in the middle of an almost U-turn in the main rural artery that snaked through our hills. When my family first moved into the house, we'd come home from running an errand one day to hear our neighbor tell us about a car that had taken one of the curves too fast, flown off the road, dropped down about 100 feet, and luckily managed to land "right side up" in the flat part of our driveway that bordered my parent's bedroom.

Apparently, the flying car had just missed crashing into the side of our English Tudor roofline.

My parents – duly shaken by my neighbor's colorful re-telling of the whole affair – wasted no time in finding a solution to such craziness.

The next day, the whole family piled into our car and went down to Sackett & Peters, which was our local hardware store. There, my parents shelled out a decent bit of cash for a bunch of Italian Cypress trees, which they then immediately planted alongside the length of the road that bordered our property. This immediately created a *de facto* living fence to forestall any future such incidents.

Now, a full decade later, our Cypress trees had grown considerably. In fact, they were about two stories tall, and a fairly effective blockade – courtesy of my parents planting them only six inches apart. And the trees had not just grown upward over the years, but also outward and into their neighbors, intertwining to create a solid green line that stretched hundreds of feet along the road, effectively protecting our property from any other crazy drivers that might inadvertently try to leave the tarmac and catapult toward our roof.

Which was great. Except for the fact that it made our driveway hard to see into and out of – given that the mouth of our driveway opened up in the middle of a hairpin turn ... the approach to which was now completely obliterated by the solid tree line.

But the trees and area behind the trees also made the ideal hiding place for me and Cindy, and we wasted no time tucking ourselves in behind the green line. We waited breathlessly for the sound of an approaching car.

"I think I hear one coming – get ready!" Cindy whispered conspiratorially.

"Okay," I responded.

Then, when the sound of the engine was almost upon us, and it seemed the car was about to come around the bend and into view as it crossed the top of our driveway, Cindy and I leaped from our hiding spots, timing it just right as the car sprang into view after clearing the Cypress tree line.

Jumping up and down wildly, we screamed "Ugga Bugga Ugga Bugga!" and all manner of other inanities.

We were immediately and intensely rewarded for our efforts by the car swerving, with the driver looking backward over his shoulder at us in frank horror.

Success. We high-fived each other, and went back to our hiding spot, eager to try it out on the next unsuspecting passerby.

Minutes elapsed – ours was not a well traveled road – and then suddenly we heard the sound of another car approaching. It sounded like the windows were down, because we could also hear muffled children's voices. And the car was going slowly.

Cindy eyed me, one eyebrow cocked in anticipation. I could read her mind. "This," she was thinking, "is gonna be epic."

I lifted an eyebrow of my own, and nodded in agreement.

The car rounded the hairpin turn, revealing itself as it lumbered past the Cypress trees. We jumped out. And as I did, I noticed it was a very slow-moving, olive green 1970's station wagon. Full of kids.

Perfect – Cindy and I would have an audience of our peers.

We began thumping our chests with ever more fervor, as kids are wont to do when faced with a good audience. And we leapt even higher into the air than the first time, all the while vocalizing like the tribal warriors we imagined ourselves to be.

I don't think the mother who was driving the station wagon heard us. At least, not initially. But, boy oh boy, her kids sure heard us.

And saw us.

"Ohmigawwwddd – mommy, MOMMY, what IS THAT??!!" screamed the little boy, pointing his index finger out the open window, the whites of his eyes now evident. "Ahhh, ohmigosh, they're MONSTERS – MOM, THERE ARE MONSTERS – MOM THEY ARE RIGHT OVER THERE!!" screamed his sister.

In retrospect, the car must have been moving at the speed of a three-toed sloth, because we were able to hear every word that each of the kids said, and it was taking an incredible amount of time for the car to lumber past us.

The mother turned her blond head toward the back of the car. No doubt, in order to reassure her children – who were sprawled amongst the endless backseats of the 1970's station wagon – that monsters were only imaginary.

At which point, swiveling her head over her shoulder, her gaze must have fallen upon us. In all of our black-mud, gloppy-haired, native-on-a-war-path, screaming-like-a-banshee selves.

We were Swamp-Things, on Steroids. And this? Was our best audience yet.

We whooped it up even louder, beginning to chase after the car. The mother's face – before setting eyes on us – had initially carried quite a placid and almost serene look. No doubt, the very same look she used to reassure her passel of children each night that monsters could not possibly be residing in their closets.

But on this fine summer's day, upon alighting on the horrific vision of Swamp Things chasing after her station wagon, her serene expression had crumbled. Arched eyebrows rose ever higher on her pretty face, eventually plastering themselves against her hairline, while the whites of her eyes grew to enormous proportions, as she too began screaming.

"OH MY, OH NOOO!! OH – DEAR ME? WHAT ***ARE*** THOSE ***THINGS???!!!!*** her voice cried out, a fair amount of hysteria woven into her words.

Ohhh, this was rich. Just too good. Better than we had ever hoped possible, when we'd first hatched the notion of jumping out at passing vehicles. Cindy and I trailed off to the side of the driveway, clutching our sides and doubled over in laughter, which caused some of the caked-on mud to flake to the ground.

"That was SOOO GOOD!" yelled Cindy. "We scared them something CRAZYYY!!!"

I just nodded while trying to catch my breath – I was still laughing too hard to even reply. We stood there, giggling and replaying the fruits of our labors, until we heard another sound in the distance.

"Listen, I think it's another car!" said Cindy.

We got quiet. It was, indeed, another car. Awesome. We retired to our hiding spot behind the row of trees, and waited. As the car decelerated for the corner, we prepared once again to jump out from behind the tree line. At the last second, though, I hesitated. I'd noticed that this car's engine had slowed down. A LOT.

Though still a child, I was very practiced at listening to cars coming around our corner. After all, I spent about four hours each day, running my Big Wheel to the top of my driveway with my best buddy Kevin. And I'd been doing that for years on end. My ears were now fairly experienced at noticing differences between cars and trucks, at recognizing differing speeds, and at recognizing the shifting of gears or engine braking.

"Oh well," I thought, "maybe it's just another cautious driver going really slowly."

Brushing all hesitation aside, Cindy and I flew out of the trees like deranged Peter Pans on cocaine. Thumping onto the asphalt driveway, we started jumping up and down and screaming... only to observe that the car was a most familiar color and model. And – horror of horrors – it was not continuing to pass across the top of my driveway. Rather, it had been slowing down because it was about to turn *into* the driveway.

Behind the wheel, my mother's face registered shock – but not nearly as much shock as my elderly grandparents, who she'd apparently thought to kindly bring back to our house with her this glorious and fine day.

For their part, the grandparrents were firmly ensconced in the backseat, while their faces were leaning toward the center of the vehicle to get an unimpeded view of the Swamp Things. From the expressions on their collectively-horrified faces, Grandma and Grandpa looked about ready to sustain a heart attack, or stroke. Or both.

"Aiii-yahh-ah-ah-ah-oh-OHH-NOOOOOO!!!"

Our merry tribal yells devolved into fear, underscored by the certain knowledge that we were soon going to be in a lot of trouble. Cindy and I promptly turned tail and bolted down the asphalt driveway, our little bare feet slapping hard. Hitting the bottom of the drive, where the grade lessened and the pavement became flatter, we could have continued in a straight line, past the house and back to the faucet where we'd started the whole charade. But we knew the faucet didn't have a hose attached, so it would be hard to get ourselves clean. Thus, like birds of a feather, we telegraphically and in unison made a left turn and diverted into the backyard ... where the shining clear blue water of the swimming pool beckoned to us.

With a final horrified glance over our shoulders, and still in our swimsuits – and also still pretty darned muddy ... despite a fairish amount of clumps having flaked off our bodies during our mad dash down the driveway – we jumped into my mother's gleaming swimming pool.

Later that afternoon and evening, there were some not-so-pleasant conversations with my parents, who explained how clumps of mud – once liberated from children's bodies in massive amounts – apparently do bad things to pool filters.

Smiling at the memory, I brought my mind back from its reminiscing to the present moment, gazing at the grassy fields of Phnom Penh which – instead of housing children playing harmlessly like I had growing up – were the site of mass graves into which the Communists had executed the Cambodian people.

Clearly, the children born in 1972 in Phnom Penh had experienced a vastly different upbringing from mine ... and I was torn between wanting to understand it, and simultaneously wanting to flee from it.

Chapter 19

I leaned down toward my daughter, who was gesturing at her little cassette player – asking if my husband and I had finished the first segment, and whether it was okay for her to listen to it. The first audio-track had been pretty historical, with few if any graphic details. While I couldn't imagine that it would hold her attention at age eight, neither was I concerned that it would leave her with nightmares. My husband and I nodded in response to her question, watching as her little hands adjusted the headset over her ears, and seeing her beam out a smile of satisfaction as she found the button with the green triangle on it to start her audio-track. She nodded up at me as it began to play, and we proceeded to walk through the Fields.

Some hours later, and near the end of the tour, we were surprised to notice that we'd been able to let my daughter listen to all but one or two of the tracks. Just as my husband and I began to quietly congratulate ourselves on successfully navigating the trip to the Killing Fields with a young child in tow, we spied an imposing structure.

And of course, my daughter made a beeline for it.

The Killing Fields Memorial is seventeen stories tall, and stands over 200 feet, or 62 meters. It is made of glass. In my memory, when I think back on it even today, what I see in my mind's eye is a giant clear Rubik's Cube, towering well above the tiny human visitors to the area.

Within the tall glass structure are shelves, placed about every foot or so. The shelves hold the bones of those who were executed decades ago into the shallow graves. And each year, when the torrential rains come, the flood waters wash away some of the topsoil, allowing more bones of the dead to float to the surface. For their part, the Cambodians collect the skeletal remains of their ancestors from the fields, along with various bits of tools and clothing, and then they place the bones gently inside the towering Memorial.

There are 17 levels inside the imposing structure. And on the shelves which are eye level to visitors sit 9,000 skulls. Only skulls. Arranged by gender and age – many infants and children as well as adults were killed in the Fields. The skulls are also arranged by how they were murdered, i.e., a hole in the skull made from the fatal blow of a machete, versus a hammer or a bullet.

The Memorial at the site bears words that roughly translate into the following:

"Never will we forget the crimes committed during the Democratic Kampuchea Regime."

Nor should we forget: the communist Khmer Rouge debacle was a horrifying example of the atrocities that far leftist states create. Pol Pot's radical vision – like many leaders of socialist and communist countries – was to implement a classless society via agricultural reform in order to turn Cambodia into a self-sufficient rice production machine. In his quest to accomplish his goals, Pol Pot and his communist colleagues recruited illiterate young peasants to do their bidding, deluding these young men into thinking they were fighting for a just cause – a perverted Robinhood variation of the "poor against the corrupt rich."

Under Pol Pot's direction, the young male Khmer Rouge communists of 1970's Cambodia, clad in black pajama-style pants, quickly morphed into the murderous arm of a genocidal state which sought to erase all city people. Or any others who might pose a threat to the communist takeover – like professionals and intellectuals, such as doctors, lawyers, and teachers. All were exterminated promptly, as were artists and followers of religion. Anyone with lighter skin, or smooth hands, or who could speak a foreign language, or who wore spectacles – as those were indications of a "higher" class – all such people posed a threat to Pol Pot's ability to take over the country. And thus, during the violent Communist takeover, these professionals were the ones the Communists sought to exterminate first. Those that were not immediately executed were driven out of the city into the countryside to work on communal farms, while the uneducated peasant farmers were put in charge of management.

Not surprisingly, the communist experiment failed spectacularly. But not before it managed to kill one-quarter of the Cambodian population in the 1970's.

While my husband and I had managed to hide the worst of these details from my daughter by advancing past certain tracks on the audiotape, there was no avoiding this Memorial structure.

As my daughter approached the structure, I ran to join her. Standing next to the Memorial, we were both now eye-to-eye with the skulls of children who were likely my daughter's age at the times of their deaths.

After many moments spent looking at the skulls of these children, cut down in cold blood by communists, my daughter tore her gaze from the horrifying glass shelves in the case, and looked up at my face.

"Mama?" she inquired softly, "how did this happen?"

I knelt down next to her. "Honey, this happened because those in power lied to the people. And by the time the people figured it out, it was too late."

I took a breath, and plunged onward. What was the saying about being "in for a penny, in for a pound?" Looking at her, I continued.

"You need to be very careful who you listen to, in this lifetime, sweetheart – and what they tell you."

She nodded, her eyes on mine.

"Just because someone is in a position of power over you does not make them right, nor does it mean that what they tell you is truthful. As this shows us." I pointed to the structure, and then the fields beyond.

My daughter's eyes followed my gestures, and then came to rest again on mine.

"The communists got the city folks to leave their homes by telling them it was 'only temporary' and 'just for a couple weeks.' But it was a lie, though the people didn't know it yet. And so they allowed themselves to be led from their homes in the city, and out into work camps. Where those in power… did – did … this."

I took another breath – trying and failing to control my emotions.

"The communists starved them. And executed them."

I stopped, noticing that my daughter had still not moved a muscle, before I pointed to the Memorial one last time.

"Just because someone in power tells you to do something doesn't mean you should. You have your own moral code. And it's up to you – not the people outside of you who tell you things – it's up to you to make sure you live justly, and ensure that injustices are not happening to you and others. Even small injustices. Because if you don't stand up to them when they first start to occur, then it can lead to things like this."

She nodded solemnly, quietly.

I sighed, and began to stand up, feeling older than my years. My husband's eyes met mine – and we inclined our heads at the same time – arriving telepathically at the same conclusion: Either we were going to be footing the bill for a lot of therapy in our daughter's later years ... or she was going to assimilate these lessons in a way that could never be un-learned.

My bet – and hope – was on the latter.

As parents, we learned much that day. Indeed, we learned much from that whole trip. It's a far different cry to be standing in the Killing Fields talking about the hazards of e.g., "wrongly trusting those in power," or "going along with the crowds" – or being "wrongly obedient to bad orders" – than it is to be having that conversation in the back of the car on the way home from school in Orange County, California. "Showing," as my favorite professors used to say, "is so much more powerful than telling."

And while I was not sure, back in 2013, that the path I chose to take with my daughter was the correct one? With the benefit of hindsight, I now doubt myself less.

I've learned that children are able to track with concepts and responsibilities much greater than that which we – as parents in cushy, western societies – tend to understand. Don't get me wrong – I'm all for preserving the magic of childhood (my daughter, now a freshman in college, has never actually watched a horror movie).

But by the same token, and perhaps somewhat incongruously, I believe that by NOT showing our children how the majority of the real world lives – including our historical societal mistakes – we are depriving our children of the very understanding they will need in order to better the condition of this planet.

And with that being said, I now encourage everyone I meet to show your kids more. And then take their newfound understanding and compassion – and desire to assist – and mold it into helpful actions: Beach clean-ups. Elephant rescues. Care packages for domestic violence survivors or vulnerable youth. Building homes for the poor.

Because in the final analysis? We cannot shield our children from everything for eighteen solid years… and then wonder why, as adults, they lack the understanding and tools to help. It's a gradient, no doubt.

But if you're going to err? I humbly submit that it's better to err on the side of showing them all the various facets of the world – the beautiful and the sad.

And then?

LET. THEM. HELP.

Chapter 20

It was now later in 2013. We were home from our travels in Asia, and the non-profit I'd been privileged to cross paths with in Da Nang, Vietnam, had allowed me to continue to do volunteer work for them as my family traveled through Cambodia and Thailand. Upon my return to Orange County some months later, the entity had then offered me a job as their General Counsel.

While I was, technically speaking, stateside again, I had also been tasked with helping our NGO open its newest office – in Bangkok. Thus, I was now splitting my time between our entity's headquarters in Newport Beach, where I did normal desk-jockey legal work, and southeast Asia, where I would perform slightly more unusual tasks, like hiring a crew of former law enforcement officers to gather Intel on the towns with the worst child-brothel problems.

Our eyes were firmly set on a tiny town in the south of Thailand, pitched along a river that divided Thailand from Malaysia.

While overseas, I'd met a pastor named Lars who did some work in this town. Lars was a man of great faith. Originally of Finnish descent, he now resided with his wife near Chiang Mai, a town in the north of Thailand.

Years earlier, Lars had moved to southeast Asia after having lived in Australia where he'd worked as a general contractor – before hearing God's call to help the people of Thailand. I still remembered our first conversation in a Starbucks in Bangkok the month prior.

"So, how'd you come to be working against the brothel trade in Thailand?" I inquired curiously. "There are so many Christian ministries like yours in the country, but from my research, very few are doing any work to help the girls who are enslaved…."

Lars grinned and leaned back in his chair. A tall thin man, with pale freckled skin, twinkling blue eyes and a ready smile – and a still-detectable Finnish accent – he set his coffee cup down.

"Oooohhhh, well," he spun out the first vowels with a very long "o" sound, so characteristic of those from the Nordic countries. "Now, that's a story. A story you'll likely find interesting."

I settled into my chair, waiting expectantly.

"You see, I was a contractor in Australia. That's where my wife and I lived, and we were raising our kids. But I'd heard the call, God's call mind you, to come here. To do work in Thailand." He chuckled again.

"But it took some convincing for my wife Marjatta to agree. She'd been born here, in Thailand, to missionary parents, before moving to Australia once she became an adult. And Marjatta felt like she had, how do you say? Well, she felt like she'd 'paid her dues' doing time in second- and third-world countries."

He uncrossed his legs, laughing again. "But I said to God, 'God, I heard your call, but I don't really want to live *without* the love of my life – so please make sure that she hears the call, too!'"

He laughed uproariously again, and then took a sip of coffee. "And, wouldn't you know, God is so, soo gooood!" Again, the long "o" came from his mouth, followed by another impish grin. "And so Marjatta heard God's call … and here we are!"

I laughed along with him. Lars' humor was incredibly infectious.

"But I still haven't answered your question, eh?" he intoned, a more serious note creeping into his voice. "So one afternoon, when I was flying back to Bangkok from Australia where I'd been visiting relatives, well I fell asleep on the plane. And I had a dream."

He leaned forward, pushing his coffee toward the center of the little table. "And in this dream, there was a big map open on the table, a table kind of like this," he said, pointing to the iron and wood table underneath our drinks. "And I saw what appeared to be a fiery finger of God, reaching down, and pointing with great passion at a spot on the map. This spot on the map, it appeared to be a small town, eh? And then, I awoke from the nap." He raised his eyebrows briefly, taking another swig from his cup.

I leaned forward to interrupt him as the teenage students to our left grabbed their backpacks and departed their table. "You're telling me that your work against the brothel trade is the result of a dream from God?" I asked, incredulous.

Eyes a-twinkle, Lars replied. "Oh yes. You must understand that I had never had a dream like that. But it was so real. It was literally like God was telling me to go to this place on the map. And so I wondered, when I awoke, if there really was such a town, in that spot on the map, with the same name that I had seen in my dream."

I was riveted – hook, line and sinker. "And – " I asked, leaning in – "was there such a town?"

"Well, Leigh, that was the question! So I got home to Marjatta, and we decided to look! And when my wife and I unfurled a map of Thailand, what did we see? Way down in the deep south of Thailand, along the border, there was a town. A town with the same name that

I had seen in the dream, if you can believe! And that is what confirmed for me that this – this?! Well, that THIS had been no ordinary dream. No! I had been called by God to go to this place. And so we did. Me and Marjatta – we went there!"

"You did?" I asked, nearly speechless at his amazing story.

"Yes, yes we did," Lars continued. "We actually drove. And looking back, it was probably silly. We were the only white people who'd ever traveled so far down south in Thailand, at least in recent history, according to what the locals told us. And what we saw when we arrived broke our hearts. As soon as we arrived in the brothel town, we saw a truckload of girls pulling into the, well uhh, the dirt alleyway, I guess you'd call it."

I inclined my head to the side, my eyes full of questions that I wasn't brave enough to ask.

Lars toyed with the handle on his coffee cup briefly, and then looked up to meet my eyes once again. "We didn't know what we were seeing, initially. But it was a group of girls, standing in the back of a pick-up truck. In their village finest. Their nicest garb. And they were unloaded, Leigh, right after this truck came to a stop. They were all young, very young. And they looked scared. And after these girls were unloaded, they were marched – more like herded, really – into a brothel right there in the alley. I'm certain that they were from Laos, Savannakhet – that's where about 90% of the girls trapped in the brothels of this town come from, I've since come to learn. Because it's so poor in Laos ... the parents in the Savannakhet province, many are so poor that that they will sell their children to the brothels for money."

My eyes blinked back tears. I found myself once again at a loss for words.

Lars' voice intruded into my silent reverie. "You should come," he said, simply, his eyes on mine.

I nearly jumped, so startled was I by the suggestion. "Me?" I replied, dumbly.

"Yes," Lars calmly reiterated, not taking his eyes off mine. "You should come."

He had said it again, simply. Hopefully.

Lars laid the flat of his palm gently on the table. "You should definitely come. And we? Well, we will do good work together down in the south – I can just feel it!" he pronounced, smiling once more.

To my surprise, I found myself agreeing without hesitation, and Lars mentioned that we would depart on our trip to the south of Thailand the following Monday. We wrapped up our meeting with no further adieu.

Later that night, I phoned my husband from my hotel room. (There's a fifteen hour time difference between Bangkok and California, so the only time to catch a loved one is late at night or in the early morning hours.) I excitedly recounted my conversation with Lars, and my decision to accompany him to the brothel town.

"Where exactly is this place?" my husband asked, a note of suspicion in his voice, as he stumbled over the foreign name.

I replied with the particulars, but I could tell it did not mean much, as my husband was not remotely familiar with the geography. His thoughts soon turned to more important matters.

"Well, honey, it sounds interesting, but is it safe?" he asked.

Typical, I thought. My man was former military and – true to form – safety concerns always topped his list. He'd been a teenaged officer in the Army – a rather rare accomplishment for someone not actively deployed in a war zone I had come to learn – and he had spent a total of ten years in the service and Reserves. While this experience had seemed uber-cool when we were dating, it was now laying like a wet blanket over my plans to travel to a brothel town.

I kept a measured tone in my voice, as I replied to his worried question. "Well babe, nowhere over here is exactly 'safe,' but this pastor goes down there a lot, and he's still standing!" I smiled and brought my voice up in pitch to lighten the mood. To no avail.

His voice came back over the wire, full of uneasiness. "I don't know honey. I'm not telling you not to go. Obviously it's up to you. But I minimally think you should do some research first."

An annoying pronouncement, but he had a point. It was bad enough I was spending half of each month 10,000 miles from home. If some research would set his mind at ease and not further upset the marital apple cart, so be it.

Deciding to get the answers to his questions hammered out asap, I walked out of my hotel room and caught the first elevator down to the Business Office. Jiggling the mouse on one of two computers in the tiny room, I typed the name of the town into Google.

Not much came up. In fact, I couldn't find anything at all about the town. Then again, Google didn't always work well in foreign countries.

A nice young man – an employee of the hotel – opened the glass door to the business office. I looked up at him, feeling like I recognized him from my earlier passes in this room where the printer had jammed on me.

"Can I help you?" he asked kindly.

"Well, I'm not sure…" I said, looking up hesitantly as I lifted my hands off the keyboard.

I continued. "The computer is working fine, but I'm thinking of traveling to a certain town – and my hubby – well, he wanted to be sure it was safe before I went visiting it. Do you think you could do a local language newspaper search, you know, in Thai? In your newspapers? To see what comes up?"

The young man nodded politely. "Sure thing, ma'am. Just write down the name of the town on this piece of paper, and I'll look it up for you."

I did as he asked, and proceeded to start checking my backlogged emails while he disappeared to hopefully find the answers to my questions.

Two minutes later, he was back by my side. Eyebrows furrowed together, he stood nervously in front of me, palpable waves of concern rolling from him. But maybe I was misreading things.

"What did 'ya find?" I asked brightly.

"Well, umm…. Permission to speak freely?" he replied.

What? Did he just ask me for permission to speak?

"Sure, yeah." I replied, struggling to keep my tone casual in the face of his obvious disquiet. "Just tell me what you found."

"Okay, well, let me start by saying I'm male. Obviously. And I'm Thai. And I'm fluent in your language, and my own. And I live here, in this country…." He trailed off.

Wondering why he was pointing out the obvious, I nodded again in the hopes of encouraging him to spit out whatever he was anxiously chewing on.

Taking a deep breath, he finally blurted out what had clearly been on his mind for the last couple minutes: "Well, I'm a big strong guy – born and raised in this country – and … well … ***you couldn't pay me to go to this region."***

He said the last part quickly, with a rush of air leaving his lungs. And then, he apparently decided to clarify his reasoning.

"It's known as the Red Light Jihadi District. Red light, becaue of the child brothels in it. And Jihadi? Because radicalized Muslim insurgent bombers from Malaysia – who are basically at war with the Buddhists in the south of our country – well the Jihadis just bomb the heck out of this region. They kind of use the brothels – and any tourists – as target practice."

He had my attention now. My complete, undivided attention.

"They bomb it A LOT. They had about 330 bombs go off this year, already," his eyes flashed, "and if I were you? I would not go."

Nodding once more, with a little half bow, he turned and took his leave.

I sat numbly in his wake, shivering a bit in the cold air-conditioning of the business office. Well, this was a facer – I'd promised the pastor I would go, while also promising my husband that I would *not* go if it the town turned out to be dangerous. I again pondered what the young man had said.

Bombs, he'd noted. Apparently, 330 bombs. No two ways about it – that was quite a large number.

It wasn't like only one bomb had gone off in the preceding months.

By his math, the region was experiencing about one bomb per day, all year long. This was definitely not what my husband would call "safe." And even I, as a clever-tongued attorney, would be hard-pressed to spin it as such. Plus, how would I ever explain it to my child if I were hurt, or worse?

Decision made, I pulled my cell phone out of my bag, and texted the pastor. Tapping out some vague excuse to the effect that "something had come up," I made my apologies and bowed out of our upcoming trip.

Two days later, I was home, safe and sound in Orange County. After a twenty-eight hour flight, I'd made it back in time to tuck my daughter into bed. And now, after a half-hour of reading her favorite stories aloud, I was laying on her pink quilt, staring at the glowing planets we'd suspended from her ceiling. She was nestled into my left armpit, breathing heavily and no doubt beginning to sink into a sweet slumber.

She'd asked me that night as I tucked her in, "Mama, why do you keep spending so much time in Thailand?"

My response had hung in my throat. I felt caught between two desires – to stay in Orange County and be a "normal mom" on the one hand – and a competing need to do something about the sex trafficking problem that was so horrific in Asia, on the other hand.

My reply to her had been lackluster, and did little to reconcile my guilt.

"Well, honey, you have a good life. In part, because you were born here. But the kids born in other places, places like the ones we've visited? As you know, many of them don't have such good lives."

She nodded, as both my mind and no doubt her mind flashed back to our visits to Ton Le Sap Lake and the Killing Fields of Cambodia.

I picked up again before I lost my will to finish. "And there are little girls who never get to live their lives, free. Like you do. Like I do. And it's a horrible thing. To never be free. To not be able to learn, or play. To not be loved … or have dreams for what you want to do when you grow up. And I—I guess I just feel the need to do something about it." I paused, trying hard not to cry as I gathered my thoughts.

"And I'm sorry, honey. Because I know when I'm over there helping those little girls, I know that also means that I'm not here. With you."

She nodded quietly, as I turned my head, swiping at my eyes before she could see the tears forming – and hoping against hope that I had not left her with the notion that she was less important to me than these other girls, because that was certainly not the case. Breathing a silent prayer to God, I hoped that the lesson she would take away is that we had a duty to help, even if it wasn't always easy.

Now, a few minutes after this difficult exchange, the little person who mattered most to me was sound asleep, still nestled warmly beside me. Why then, was I so sad? I could feel the hot tears I'd held back earlier beginning to escape the sides of my eyes and roll down my temples into my hair, as I lay on my back beside my daughter.

Why, indeed, did I feel called to do this work? None of it made much sense. I had no connection to Asia: I'm not Asian, nor are any of my family members. And unlike Lars, I was not married to someone whose parents had worked in Asia. I literally had zero connection to the region: I was the proverbial soccer mom in Southern California – the person least likely to be picked to do such work.

But then I thought back to my legal career. There were plenty of corporate litigators in America, shoveling money from one big client to another – depending on which party won the particular courtroom battle on any given day. But just how many of these talented lawyers were willing to take their skills and do something life-changing in a third-world country? None that I knew. I could enumerate literally none – out of the hundreds of lawyers I knew – who were willing to do such work.

And I thought again of my childhood. A childhood that left me knowing exactly what it was like to feel the impotent rage against someone bigger and stronger who was behaving unjustly.

Didn't I have a duty to change things, if I could? Was I perhaps put in this time and place for a reason – for work such as this?

At all earlier junctures in my life, I had always taken the safe route. And I supposed it was forgivable even now, should I elect to pull back from this work. I could easily justify bailing on a war zone with the legitimate excuse that I had a young child and family to attend to.

But was playing it safe my highest and best use?

That was the question that would not leave me, even as my eight-year-old child rested snugly against my chest.

Was one life more important than another?

I had been gifted my life in California – as well as the child sleeping beside me. But I could just as easily have been tossed down into the chaos half a world away. If I believed my child deserved freedom, wasn't it at least partly my duty to try and ensure that same existence for others who were not so fortunate?

And if not me, then exactly who would pick up the tools and go fight these evils?

Sitting safely in Orange County was no longer my highest use, nor my best use. And I knew it.

Slipping my arm out from under my daughter's angelic countenance, I tiptoed down the hall. Finding my purse, I pawed briefly through it in search of my cell phone, and then tapped out a quick email to Lars, telling him I would be back to Thailand in two weeks' time – and stating that I wanted him to take me into the Red Light Jihadi District.

Still somewhat torn, but more satisfied than I'd felt in quite awhile, I powered down my phone while pondering the new reality I'd discovered.

That perhaps I had not lived the life I'd lived only to grow up and play things safe. That perhaps there were skills that I had from years earlier – not to mention hopes that I'd harbored for decades – that I'd not yet made good on.

It was time to do so.

Chapter 21

It was the late 1980's. I was sitting in the den, in front of my Apple computer, where two large floppy disk drives the size of small shoe boxes purred next to my elbow. My English professor in college had given us a Take-Home Final, and I was staring at the blinking green cursor on the black screen, debating what topic to address next.

Noting that I was down to the final couple of hours and really needed to wrap it up, my thoughts were suddenly interrupted by a sound from outside the house. I inclined my head in the direction from which the sound was emanating. It sounded like voices. Unhappy voices.

My parents had never had a great marriage, nor even a good one. They'd both been raised by at least one parent who was physically abusive, not to mention emotionally cruel. Finding each other in the 1960's at a roller rink in southern California, they'd become a couple. And then, after a whirlwind six months, they'd headed off to the altar. Counseling to rid themselves of their personal baggage, or even coach them into better communication patterns, had apparently never entered their minds, nor was it the trend back then. Sucking it up – and repeating generational patterns – that was more the norm.

After their precipitous trip to the altar, followed by a singularly disastrous and unhappy two decades spent fighting non-stop, my mother and father had finally concluded that perhaps they were not the best mates for each other, and separated. My father had temporarily rented a motel room in the Inland Empire near his body shop, and my mother had stayed in our house. And it was around this time that she and I had gone to a family friend's birthday party, where my mom had run into an old friend of hers from high school, Don.

My mother and Don had spent their teenage years hanging out in groups, going bowling and to dances, but never becoming an official couple. Fast forward twenty years, and Don had separated from his wife on the east coast, while my mother had also just separated from my father. After reconnecting at the mutual friend's birthday party, Don and my mother had promptly decided to try out the dating status that had eluded them in their younger years.

Now, with my ear cocked intently to the side, I was surmising that my father had come to visit, only to discover Don's truck in the driveway. My internal warning system went into overdrive: I knew this was likely to end badly.

But – looking at the clock – I also knew that if I didn't continue typing my final exam, I would not meet the necessary page requirement. Which would result in an "F" grade for the English Literature class. I continued typing, or at least I tried to, as the voices outside escalated.

"Darn it, Sara, really?! I want him GONE!" my father yelled.

"Now, Caleb, calm down. Don was just visiting and having some lunch. I don't know why you're so upset. You and I agreed to separate, after all…." my mother intoned gently.

At least she was keeping her cool, I thought. I watched my black poodle, Inky, slink out of the room in an attempt to leave behind the sound of raised voices coming from outside the den wall.

"I don't freaking care – get his gosh-darned truck outta my flipping driveway!!" my father yelled, for the second time in as many minutes.

Well, shoot. This was escalating, and quickly. Then again, it always did.

"Look, why don't you leave," my mother suggested calmly, "and we'll chat about this tomorrow?"

"I'm not leaving!" came the instantaneous and rage-filled reply. "This is still MY darned house, and Don can be the one to freaking leave it – where the hell is he anyway?? I'll come drag him outta there," my father continued, in bellowing tones loud enough to be heard miles away. "I swear I'll just drag him right the heck outta there if he's not man enough to face me...."

I shoved my fingers in my ears, trying in vain to focus on my English exam. But more expletives and raised voices ensued – and then my mother's boyfriend Don came running into the den where I was typing, throwing open the coat closet door.

"It would seem that your illustrious male parent has a gun, and I'll be tarred and feathered if he has a gun and I don't," Don expounded, as he rummaged in the closet looking for a shotgun. Which he found, without much effort.

Darn, I thought, looking at Don holding the shotgun. This was definitely going downhill fast.

"Do you know where the shells are?" Don queried, looking over at me shrewdly.

I did know, but I wasn't about to say. I swiveled my head back toward the computer screen, pretending to have not heard him. To no avail.

"Nevermind, I think I found them!" Don triumphantly stuck his head out of the closet, holding some red cartridges that he started jacking into the weapon.

"Lovely, just lovely," I muttered under my breath. I wondered briefly if my English professor would understand why my exam was late, if I endeavored to explain it to her. I envisioned the conversation. Nope. It would just sound too crazy. Because it was.

My ruminations were cut short by yet more raised voices that seemed to be now coming closer to the house. I stood up, silently. And like a leopard hunting its prey, I moved toward the window. Inching the curtain back, I saw my father storming down the driveway. As Don had mentioned, he was indeed brandishing a gun in his hand. More loveliness – why, oh why did the crazy-train have to come to town when I had a final exam to complete?

Letting the curtain fall closed, I kicked off my shoes, and sprinted silently in sock-feet to the front door that my father was, without a doubt, also heading toward from his position on the outside of the abode. Slamming into the foyer like a freight train, I twisted the knob on our front door that would throw the mechanism into a locked position, while simultaneously leaning into the door with all my weight to ensure the lock moved as soundlessly as possible. And then I high-tailed it back to the other doors in the house to ensure they were all locked.

Finishing my pass through the house, I arrived back to the den, slightly out of breath and – gasping quietly, but with my mouth wide open to lessen the noise of my breathing – I began to mentally take stock of our various windows, wondering which if any had been left open.

My brain's internal calculations indicated that there might be some windows still open – maybe. But I couldn't get them closed without being obvious. And loud. Windows in houses built in 1929 – with their sills and hardware slathered with 12 coats of paint – did not shut easily or quietly, I'd learned. I just had to hope that they were already closed.

But it suddenly occurred to me that even if all of the windows were shut and all the doors were locked, they were all made of glass – so locking them was an imperfect solution at best… given that a bunch of testosterone-fueled men were running around with guns in their hands.

Taking stock of the den from the threshold of the doorway, I saw my Apple computer beckoning. As I made my way further into the room, I spied Don who had largely stayed put – in his half-in-half-out stance near the closet. I could also hear the voices of my parents, both still angry and raised, from outside the house, and cringed as I heard my father flogging the same points, ceaselessly. Persistently perseverating on perceived wrongs was my father's strong suit, I'd noticed over the years.

"Darn it, I know Don's in there – why don't ya come out and face me like a man, Don?!! And quit cavorting around with my wife. Or are you too scared???"

I looked out a different window. My father still had his weapon, and Don, for his part, was still cradling the shotgun while standing in the threshold of our den closet. At least Don didn't look inclined to go outside and trade words with a crazy man holding a gun. A small blessing for which to be grateful.

I decided to capitalize on it. "Um, sorry, Don – it sounds like my father is not particularly sane right now. Why don't you just stay where you are? I think I'm going to go check on things again."

Knowing I should probably leave the den, I noted that my parents were continuing to make their way around the outside of the house, yelling and screaming, gun and arms waving in the air – with my father still looking for an unlocked door through which to enter. Thus far, my parents had managed to not kill each other in the fifteen years I'd been alive, but I wasn't prepared to bet the farm on that continuing. Particularly since a new variable – Don – was involved.

I weighed the options, along with the fact that I still needed to finish my college English Final. I cursed my bad luck – why today of all days? I was not that far into my college career, and I was not about to let my crazy dysfunctional family dynamic derail my opportunity, or even cost me a decent grade. But the planets did not appear to be lining up in my direction. Something needed to be done, and fast.

Abruptly leaving the den, and still in my socks, I padded silently out to the kitchen phone. Picking it up, I dialed the number for a family friend whose husband was currently employed as a lineman for the phone company – but who had also worked as an L.A. County Sheriff in the decades prior. Our good friend Molly answered, and I quickly recapped the current drama.

Molly, for her part, promised to grab her spouse and immediately head over to our place. Putting the receiver down and looking at my watch, while also bending my ear to the goings-on outside, I realized that I wasn't sure that this plan was going to work quickly enough: Molly lived a good fifteen minutes away.

I stealth-walked over to where the raised voices seemed to be coming from, and could hear my male parent still at it.

"I swear to God, if you don't bring Don outside to talk to me, man-to-man," yelled my father, "I'll just go in there and drag him the heck outta there! And if you make me do that, Sara, I may as well just shoot him while I'm in there!!"

I pulled the curtain back more, trying to get a read on my mother's expressions to see if she was actually considering this rather horrid idea to put all three of them in the same space. Catching her face and body language, I could tell that she knew that having Don and my father in the same room was a bad plan. For her part, my mother appeared committed to the idea of holding her ground outside the house, while continuing to attempt to reason with my male parent.

I went back to check on Don. Still in the den. Good. Though he was looking a bit pasty and sweaty. Well, that wasn't really surprising: I was certain he wasn't used to grown adults running in circles around buildings, hunting the other adults that were inside. Though my family did not always have a good fix on reality, I certainly did – and I was aware enough to recognize that today's little contretemps diverged greatly from a "Leave It To Beaver" existence.

The voices continued to escalate outside. Now my father was rattling the doors, cussing out whoever had locked them.

"Darn it, Sara?! Did you really lock me OUTTA MY OWN DARNED HOUSE?! Am I not TRUSTWORTHY?? I'm STILL your husband – my name is still on the darned deed! That's it – I'm COMING IN!!"

Oy. I'd weighed the consequences of locking the doors against not doing so. And five minutes earlier, it had seemed like a good idea to bolt them. I still thought it was the better idea … but maybe not: it seemed to be causing quite the blood pressure increase on the part of my father. Who was now jiggling the door as if his life depended on it.

That said, the 1929 door wasn't budging. I muttered another thankful prayer for old houses with rock-solid construction and steel hardware. I figured the door would hold – so long as my father didn't decide to just put his fist through the glass, or shoot it out. Looking at the clock, I realized it had only been a couple of minutes since I'd called our family friends for help, though it seemed an eternity had passed. But I was aware of how time can do funny things during such escapades.

Hearing a new and dangerous note in their voices, I decided I didn't trust this to end well. Nor did I trust that our family friends would arrive in time from their house across town. Things were degenerating too rapidly. With no small amount of embarrassment and humiliation, I tiptoed back to the phone and, with trembling hands, dialed 9-1-1.

"9-1-1 operator, what is the nature of your emergency?"

Mortified at having to make the call, I stuttered out my very short reply: "Umm, yeah. Family dispute, weapons being brandished."

"Okay," the nice 911 operator replied, "and what's the address, honey?"

I quickly supplied our address and then set the phone down, leaving the line open, but not being willing to stay glued to it – lest I miss some environmental cue that would warn me of further escalations.

While it seemed to take forever, in reality it was probably only a matter of minutes before LA County Sheriff's units suddenly overtook our driveway. Looking out the window, I saw every inch of available space was now full of police cars, their red and blue lights still rotating. Doors to the police cars had been left standing wide-open, while burly men in Sheriff's uniforms with hands on their holsters started streaming around the exterior of the house. Don was still largely hanging out in our den closet, but making brief appearances to check on the unfolding scene outside.

I sat back down at my computer. If I picked up where I'd left off – and typed my freaking fingers to the bone – I might make the cut-off for my Final, and yet have a hope of pulling an "A" in the class. With half my mind on my Final, and the other half ruing the day I'd been born into such a dysfunctional family, I attempted to focus.

Little did I understand that at age fifteen – and forcing my fingers to fly into the 120-words-per-minute typing zone in order to try and save my English Literature grade – I was learning skills that would later prove invaluable.

In retrospect, and with the vantage point that comes from hitting the half-century mark, I can look back and understand that the many years of my childhood I spent on high alert were not a waste. Being attuned to every foot-fall, every raised voice, begat a decent skill set. I'd spent many minutes of my life parsing muffled sounds to deduce whether it was laughter or crying I was hearing through a wall or a door, deciphering whether it was a joyous guffaw… or perhaps a prelude to something violent.

I had learned to read every frown, every raised eyebrow, in every room that I ever stepped into. I'd learned to listen to both the tone and the vocal pitch, to telepathically back-fill the needed data … when the words coming through the walls were too muffled or indistinct to discern. I'd perfected the art of sleeping while listening, always keeping some part of my mind attuned to the goings-on outside my bedroom.

I knew that anger and love each left their own unique imprint on a room, even well after the time the folks attached to such emotions had vacated the space. I knew to keep my back to the wall, to listen to every word, to pretend to be involved in other tasks in order to escape being noticed. I never entered rooms without having an escape route planned, and I knew better than to ever second-guess my gut instincts.

I had spent all the formative years of my life playing chess, with people, predicting whether they might do "x" or "y" and calculating different firing solutions for each. My early years had taught me well how to deflect, how to argue, how to stand up, and how to disappear. And they taught me as well that injustice is a sin, but to fail to stand up to injustice is by far the greater sin.

Most of all, I had learned how to fight, and to win, with my mind and my mouth … because those are the only tools you have when the aggressor is three times your size. And I learned the hard way that it was equally important – when people screamed lies at you – for you to never sign off on their version of reality. And to instead always maintain your truth. Even on the nights your own voice was silenced so that it was just you … keeping your truth alive … inside the hollows of your own mind.

Yes, I had learned many lessons over the years. Not least, that in protracted battles, it is often one's integrity, persistence, and hope for a better result which will carry one to victory … if one simply refuses to give up.

Yes, little did I know at age fifteen that these skills I'd been unknowingly accumulating during my childhood would prove handy in the early years of my career, when cross-examining witnesses as an attorney. And even more handy three decades later, when I would come to confront the criminal cartels that run the brothels of southeast Asia, and also battle the pedophiles who frequent such places … and the Jihadis who bomb them.

Chapter 22

Fresh off my flight from Hong Kong, I met Lars at the Starbucks in Suvarnabhumi Airport, the major international hub in Bangkok that most tourists pass through when entering Thailand. Anxious but resolute, I stood with my hand on my carry-on bag.

Spying me from a distance, Lars called out warmly, "Ah, Leigh! You ready?"

Noting again how unfailingly hopeful and energetic Lars was, despite working in some of the most emotionally-challenging areas in the world, I matched his bright tone. "Yes!" I replied.

Truth be told, though a bit nervous, I was ready to go to the south of Thailand to see the brothel towns. Making our way through the vast airport, we cleared security and stood in line for Thai Smile, the regional carrier that would transport us and our few belongings to the Narathiwat Province located in the deep south of the country.

Having boarded the plane and taken our seats, Lars suggested a quick prayer. Given where we were heading, connecting to God – and all that was good and right – did not come amiss. I gratefully nodded my agreement, and Lars began a quick prayer. As he concluded, the flight attendant came by, handing us waters. Lars took a quick sip, before opening his little tray and spreading out some paperwork.

Leaning my head back on the seat, I decided to close my eyes for just a quick moment. I was thus surprised to wake up ninety minutes later as the plane was descending – I supposed I must have been pretty jet-lagged to have fallen asleep so readily on a midday flight. As the plane came to a halt, I noticed we were at the end of a runway. Looking out the tiny window, I saw a narrow portable staircase being moved toward my side of the plane. Clearly, this was a tiny airport; no jet bridges were in evidence. Lars and I stood, and grabbing our luggage from the overhead bins, began to file out of the plane and down the awkwardly narrow staircase.

Standing on the tarmac, Lars pointed toward the building.

"There, over there, that's where we head, inside the airport."

As we neared the doors, beads of sweat began to dot my forehead. I quickly wiped them away with the back of my hand, as Lars looked over at me.

"You okay – you want to stay here, in the South?"

I was pretty sure I did, and nodded resolutely. Lars seemed satisfied with my non-verbal answer.

"Okay, well that's good. Because see the airplane over there?"

I looked back over my shoulder at the end of the landing strip, where his finger was pointing.

"That's our plane, the one we just got off of. It's doing a U-turn now, and it's about to come back down the runway, and be wheels-up, *en route* back to Bangkok. It's the only plane that comes here from Bangkok – there's literally only one flight a day into this place. And one flight out. So your next possible flight out of here? Well, it's not until this same time – tomorrow."

I swallowed hard, hoping I did not look as rattled as I felt by the notion that I couldn't leave even if I wanted to. I was in a province where bombs went off daily. And I truly felt like I'd arrived in a foreign land. Looking around, I noted that I was surrounded, without exception, by people who were not Christian, and not Buddhist. Here in the deep south of Thailand, it was one-hundred percent Islamic territory.

I began to take note of other things as well. Like the fact that there was not a single woman outside or inside the airport who had her hair exposed. In fact, all the females I could see were wearing very traditional types of Islamic dress – niqab, hijab burka – all types of coverings were on display, hiding nearly every inch of every woman's dermis.[68]

The only thing that remained *un*covered were their eyes.

Well, and me – I was not very covered. I gazed down at my cargo shorts and T-shirt, resigning myself to the fact that I likely stood out like a sore thumb.

"We'll go now, eh? And get the rental car...." Lars suggested.

I followed along for a few feet. Abruptly deciding I should hit the ladies' room, I made a right turn. "Meet you at the rental desk," I called, peeling away to enter the bathroom.

I'd learned in Asia it was best to make use of the facilities wherever and whenever you found them. I knew we had a three-hour car ride ahead of us, and I was guessing it was through pretty rural areas. Thailand was not like Southern California, with gas stations and rest

---

[68] Niqab is a black, restrictive garment that completely covers the face of Muslim women (with the exception of the eyes). Hijab refers to head coverings worn by Muslim women, and burkas are an enveloping outer garment which fully covers the body and face.

stops peppered every few miles. Using the airport bathroom seemed to be the wise choice, all things considered.

Pushing open the scuffed and creaking door, I found myself confronted by a wall of women, who promptly began looking at my arms and legs studiously. Ducking into the nearest available stall, I withdrew into my little private realm, trying to remember if I'd brought any pants or long-sleeved clothing with me to this region. I doubted it. With dawning clarity, I suddenly realized this could become a very long trip for me, given the limitations of my wardrobe.

Exiting the stall a moment later, I walked over to the sink, and put my hands below the tap. Cranking on the metal faucet, I waited. And waited. Finally, a splutter occurred, along with a *Pffft* of air and – before I could snake my limbs back out of harm's way – a violent explosion jerked the faucet's head up and down … and then proceeded to shoot out a nasty stream of rust-colored water, directly onto my hands.

Charming.

I quickly wrenched the faucet back to the "off" position, and dragged my gaze along the wall, hoping in vain to find a paper towel dispenser. No such luck. Instead, I found the entirety of the females in the restroom now gazing sadly at my left hand … which kind of looked like I'd dipped it into French Onion Soup. They had also set to murmuring none-too-quietly – some were even pointing at me – and it wasn't difficult to read their minds. Even though all I could see were a lot of eyeballs, I was absolutely sure they were having a chuckle at my expense.

Rubbing both hands on my shorts, I left the humid bathroom in search of Lars. It was a miniscule airport, and he'd not gone far.

"Okayy!" he sang out from the rental car desk, "I've got the key, now, eh? And the car – she is just over there!"

Well, that was some good news at least. We threw our luggage in the trunk, and got into a little 4-banger Toyota-looking vehicle (although I soon came to learn that all the cars, despite looking similar to American models, had different manufacturer and model names in Asia).

It didn't take long before we'd exited the airport roundabout, and were hitting the open highway. At which point, the car began to pick up speed. A lot of speed. A whole, whole, whole lot of speed.

I tried to peek at the speedometer unobtrusively, but the driver's compartment was on the opposite side of the vehicle from what I was used to, and there was a gear shifter in the way, as well as the steering column. All of which were serving to obscure the dial of the speedometer. And the dial appeared to be in kilometers. I gave up trying to determine how fast we were traveling, but as someone who had spent a fairish amount of my youth going exceedingly fast in all manner of vehicles – boats, cars, off-road vehicles, motorcycles and quads – my intuition told me we had to be traveling in excess of 100 miles per hour. Well in excess of that speed.

Lars looked over at me indulgently. "Would you like me to explain?"

I nodded simply – I wasn't used to conservative Christian pastors around my mother's age driving their vehicles like Mario Andretti.

"Well, firstly, we are in Muslim territory. And it's not just Muslim country. That, in and of itself, is not a problem at all. It's the fact that we are entering radicalized Islamic-insurgent-bomber-training-compound-type country."

I took the last fact in. This, no doubt, was what my husband had warned of. And this is also why the young man in the hotel business office had indicated he would not personally travel to the Deep South.

"It's a lovely country, as you can see," Lars said, waving his hand at the beautiful jungle that we were whizzing past at the speed of light. "But it has been a bit ravaged by the religious tensions. In fact, right over there – you can see the remains of a Buddhist temple that they bombed."

I quickly rotated my head in the direction he was pointing, to better observe the missing roofline and partially-standing walls of the temple. "But before you're tempted to demonize anyone, around the next corner, I will show you the mosque that the Buddhists took revenge on."

The mosque was also a sorry sight, I noted, as we flew past it.

"So you see, both sides eh – the Muslims and the Buddhists – they are having a religious war down here in the Deep South. Not unlike other religious wars throughout the ages," Lars aptly noted, "with much bloodshed, and retaliation, and loss of life."

He suddenly slowed the car's pace. I didn't understand why. But as we cleared the next bend, his deceleration made sense. Because stretching out in front of us – perpendicularly across the road – were long rolls of concertina wire, about 4 feet high. And lines of tack strips, with concrete barriers placed in between them.

Our car was forced to go at a snail's pace, turning nearly at 90-degree angles, wending its way back and forth from one side of the highway to the other, in order to stay in the violently-curving narrow lane that had been demarcated with the cleverly-deployed barriers.

The whole thing was starting to look a bit like a war zone. My impression was heightened as two very tall, raised watchtowers came into view, with men standing atop them holding automatic weapons. "All Along the Watchtower" – U2's 1980's song from my favorite CD, Rattle & Hum – came unbidden into my mind, along with the opening lyric: "There must be some way outta here…."

I looked outside the car, craning my head a bit. There was no way out, I noted. Not from this zone, nor from the area as a whole. As Lars had so aptly pointed out, earlier in the day, when our plane made a U-turn and raced down the landing strip, wheels up and back to Bangkok.

Our car slowly approached the elevated wooden watchtower, as Lars rolled down his window.

His head turned briefly in my direction as the window descended, and he said quietly to me, "You stay silent, eh? I speak fluent Thai – I'll talk to them."

I nodded again. For a natural extrovert, I found myself more silent than I'd ever been in my life.

Leaving my window rolled tightly shut, I eyeballed the men in dark green military fatigues carrying automatic weapons, who were approaching our vehicle on both sides. Actually, upon closer inspection, they were not men – they appeared to be teenage boys. In uniform. With heavy-duty weapons in hand.

"Sawadee Krap!" Lars hailed them in the standard greeting of the country. The men nodded almost imperceptibly, but said nothing.

"Mai jer gaan nan leuy khrup," Lars continued pleasantly. (Which phrase I later learned meant: "I haven't see you in awhile").

One of the younger guys cracked a bit of a smile, knowing that, of course, it had not been his exact same team who had last encountered this blond and happy Finnish pastor.

Suddenly, dogs began barking, and I swung my head around searching for the source. The barking seemed to be emanating from my side of the car, and I looked out my passenger window to spy two-man teams holding leashes of loud slavering German Shepherds, who for their part, were working their way quite thoroughly over each of the wheel wells and down the length of the car.

The pastor continued to make small-talk. "Wanee rawwwnnn!" Lars laughed, drawing out the last syllable, as he pointed out the windscreen toward the cloudless blue sky.

The young guy in camo pants and jacket nodded, agreeing with Lars' assessment that it was, indeed, quite hot this afternoon.

I turned back toward my side of the car, noting in relief that the men with dog teams appeared to be done. Or maybe not – as they were now taking a large mirror on an extension pole and running it underneath the vehicle.

Lars leaned over, and whispered quietly. "Ah, what they are doing now is ruling out things that go 'Boom.'"

I opened my mouth slightly, stupefied at the notion that anyone would think *we* were the bombers. Then, moments later, the guy who had been chatting with Lars waved us through, apparently satisfied that we posed no threat.

Lars picked up the conversation as if nothing unusual had occurred. And I supposed for him, what had just occurred was not particularly out of the ordinary.

"So, there'll be a few more of those checkpoints," Lars intoned, "because that's how they try to keep the bombs to a minimum. And that reminds me: I never finished answering your question." He looked in my direction, as he once again pushed our rental vehicle toward its top speed.

Speaking louder as the RPMs climbed, Lars noted, "So there's a religious war going on between the Muslim and Buddhist factions. That's the backdrop, I suppose you could say. And then there's the training camps for the Jihadi bombers that are across the river, mainly on the Malaysia side. And they need to practice their bombing skills. So sometimes, they will all save their money, cross the River, and buy a girl that they will share for the night, in one of the child brothels of this town we're going to," Lars explained.

The clear blue sky of the day seemed at odds with the words coming out of my new friend's mouth. I continued to look quietly in his direction, waiting for the next installment in this reality about which I knew so little.

"After the men are done buying girls for the night, they will then bomb the brothels, to expiate their guilt perhaps. I suppose Sigmund Freud could have some adventures trying to understand the inhumanity down here," Lars noted as he leaned forward, scanning the road. "But other times, the bad guys will just lie in wait, off to the sides of the road, like here… or there."

Lars motioned again with his left hand through the windscreen. "And these bombers will just stay concealed … until a good-looking target car comes upon them." Lars stopped speaking.

I inclined my head toward his side of the car. "You mean, like a car full of Caucasian people?" I asked.

Yes," Lars replied matter-of-factly. "Or a car full of cops. Or military. And then? The bombers will push a button – remote detonating the bomb they placed roadside."

I contemplated what he was actually saying – the answer to my earlier question about our seemingly excessive rate of travel now becoming all too clear.

"I see. So, basically, you're just outrunning the bomber's trigger finger?" I clarified.

"Exactly," Lars said simply. "That is exactly what I'm doing. Or should I say, praying and hoping to do."

"How has that worked so far?" my voice queried, far more tremulously than intended.

"Great!" replied Lars, "I'm still here – yes??"

I guessed that I must have waited a moment too long to respond, because Lars added, "It will be fine – you'll see! Let's pray!"

And, with that, he began to pray aloud, still driving fast but with his eyes wide open, while I closed my eyes and bowed my head in prayer, listening to his heartfelt entreaty:

> "Father God, we thank you for the blessing of this day, and for the reinforcements that are arriving to help the Girls trapped in the brothels. Father, we thank you for Leigh, and her desire to learn about the plight of the girls down here, and along with her NGO, help bring the girls resources....

Lord, you know there is much darkness in this land. And we ask today for your guidance in vanquishing the evil that exists here in the Deep South of Thailand, and for your protection over the girls – and over us – as we do some work. In *Thessalonians*, we are told that you are a faithful God, and we know that to be the case, in our hearts. Dear Lord, we ask today that you continue to strengthen and protect us – as well as the people of the Deep South – from the evil one.

And for our part, Father, we will do our best to be neither afraid nor fearful as we walk into the dark places of the planet. For we know – as we are told in *Deuteronomy* – that our Lord walks with us. And that you, Father, will neither leave us nor forsake us. Father God, please be with us today … and in the coming days as we journey into this region. And be also with the young women, who know not the Freedom we do. Help them be free in their hearts, in the comfort that only You can provide, when there is no one to comfort them. Until we can hopefully help free them – in all respects. Thank you, Father God. Amen."

I lifted my head, renewed by the quiet sense of love and contentment in what we were doing. I had known many pastors, in many different cities spread across this great planet. But I realized, with a start, that I'd not known any quite like Lars.

The man was a vessel for God's love, and he lived every day to please God. He had told me, earlier in the day – when speaking of the coffee shop which his ministry had opened in the suburb of Chiang-Mai and which café employed orphans and others who had been cast from the main roads of society:

"I try not to preach – in the 'preachy' pedantic sense – when I am meeting one-on-one with folks. I try to just live my life as I think Jesus would have. And if I have to choose between lecturing about Jesus, or behaving as I believe Jesus would have, I choose the latter. I guess I just believe that people will come to know Jesus when we act as vessels of Jesus' love for others. We get further by doing good than talking about doing good, eh?"

Interrupting my quiet reverie, Lars chuckled quietly and downshifted again as we approached another watchtower. And as I braced for more dogs and young men with automatic rifles, I reflected on Lars' thriving ministry – proof that his method worked. I found myself wanting to emulate his approach, wanting to stay in Thailand permanently, wanting desperately to help … in this land that was so foreign to me.

Three hours hence, and a few more watchtowers and bomb-sniffing dog inspections later, Lars and I finally rolled into the tiny town that was our destination. I let go the breath that I hadn't realized I'd been holding, relieved to have arrived safely. My relief lasted only a moment, as I remembered that there were no hotels in this town, only brothels.

And that the "hotel-brothel" we were pulling up in front of would be my home for the next few nights.

Chapter 23

Lars and I checked into the brothel, securing two rooms on one of the higher floors in the building.

"It's got like nine levels, kind of like Dante's Circles of Hell, if you will," said Lars, as he put away his credit card. "But I've learned that the upper floors are better. The lower the floor, the worse the activities that occur. And on the bottom is a nightclub, which generates a lot of noise. So today? We go higher up. It's better that way."

I just nodded again, feeling a bit shell-shocked by all the bombed-out buildings we had passed in the car, combined with my first time setting foot in an Asian brothel. I was really going to have to find my voice – it was like the proverbial cat had stolen my tongue from the moment I'd de-planed in the Deep South. We went upstairs to the rooms to freshen up, Lars accompanying me the whole way.

Exiting the elevator and walking down the hall, I saw Thai or perhaps Malaysian men, casually standing in thresholds, naked but for the tiny towels covering their nether regions. They were chatting easily with each other, one hand often holding a cigarette, the other hand typically resting on the narrow shoulders of what appeared to be young teen girls. It was like some demented frat house scene from a movie, except for the fact that the men were three times the age of the young girls. And the young girls, for their part, looked timid, resigned, and scared.

Lars looked into my eyes, and I noted a heavy sadness that I was certain was also reflected in mine.

"We start by changing what we can," he said. "You'll be safe here because you and me ... we are too old for these men's tastes," he noted, trying to lift my spirits.

He was right: we were too old for these pedophiles. And his rule sounded like a good place to start – to "change what we can."

I pondered his rule for living, as I closed the door to my "hotel-brothel" room. I felt instantly relieved to be able to block out everything – particularly the cloying cigarette smoke, and the images of young girls standing near men old enough to be their grandfathers. Reassured by the fact that Lars' room was proximal enough that he'd be able to hear my screams should anything untoward occur in my universe, I let out another pent-up exhalation.

As I took stock of my surroundings, my feet made a beeline for the bathroom. I was overdue for a shower. And I could not wait to properly wash – my experience at the airport with the rusty tap water hitting my palms was still making me cringe.

Looking down at my hands, I figured that they probably carried a truly unquantifiable germ load by this point. Doing some quick math – I'd told Lars I'd meet him in the lobby "in a bit" – I figured that I likely had a good quarter hour in which to score a quick shower.

Pushing my head into the tub-shower-combo, I twisted the knob on the wall that I assumed would turn on the shower, noting as I did that all of the fixtures in the tub – and indeed even the toilet bowl – said "American Standard." Taking another look at the toilet, I noticed that it appeared to be identical to the ones I'd grown up with in the elementary schools of the 1970's: a black seat ring. And underneath, a white, sturdy porcelain bowl. And the classic "American Standard" logo baked onto the enamel in scripted gold cursive. I was pleasantly surprised by the brothel's bathroom hardware.

Turning back toward the tub, I eyeballed the water coming out of the shower head. It looked like clean and clear water, but after my experience earlier in the afternoon, I was wary. I leaned into the tub, taking a sniff at the spray of water. It smelled normal enough.

Decision made, I stripped down quickly, and hopped into the shower, feeling the tension leave my head and neck, and all but reveling in the opportunity to wash off – not just the germs – but the ever-present layer of sweat that permeates one's universe when trekking around tropical countries.

A few minutes later, feeling relatively happy and clean, I stuck my head out into the bathroom, looking for the towels. There were none. Just some large wash cloths.

My mind flashed back to the Thai men, standing in the hallway with their little loin cloths. No wonder the towels around their waists had looked so tiny – this place only had weird hybrid hand-towels masquerading as small bath towels! Looking warily at the pile of two glorified hand towels on the sink, I decided I did not want to use them to dry off – I frankly didn't trust that any amount of bleach or detergent had rid the towels of whatever less-than-pleasant experiences they'd been put to in their earlier life cycles in the brothel. I stood next to the toilet, a bit flummoxed at how I was going to get dry without the use of towels.

That's when I spied the toilet paper.

I rapidly bent down and yanked hard on the little square of toilet paper. The dispenser promptly started humming like the bobbin on a sewing machine and – looking at the whirl of toilet paper that had been unleashed into my universe with one single albeit quite violent jerking motion – I reflected that perhaps it wasn't really necessary to pull at the TP as if I were attempting to start a recalcitrant lawn mower engine. Because now, I'd unleashed a ghostly swirl of white squares that were busy floating about my head and torso … in a sort of Rhythmic-Gymnastic-Competition-Gone-Awry kind of way.

Putting my hands up in the air, I endeavored to catch the white squares that were now flying everywhere. It was touch and go for a few seconds, but I managed to tame the mini-hurricane of toilet paper I'd set in motion. With my right hand now swaddled in a huge wad, which looked suspiciously like an albino oven mitt, I began dabbing at my skin … in a vain attempt to "towel off" with toilet paper.

I rapidly realized that there was a reason human beings did not generally use toilet paper to dry off after showers: it was singularly unsuited to the task. Then, glancing at my cell phone and noting the time, I realized that at the rate I was going, I was likely going to be late to meet the pastor in the lobby.

Just as I was trying to figure out if I should abandon the oven-mitt-TP-plan in favor of toweling off with some of the clean clothes from my suitcase, I spied movement out of the corner of my eye.

Was that a cockroach? Glory be, it was!!

But this was no ordinary American cockroach.

No, this was an Asian roach. And there he stood, in all of his stunning buggy-ness, on the carpet outside my bathroom threshold. He appeared to be about the size of a mouse. Was it me, or did everything seem super-sized in tropical regions? And holy heck, how exactly did people deal with cockroaches that were the size of rodents?

I eyeballed him anew, as he stood there looking up at me, his enormous antennae quivering in my direction, almost like he'd never seen such an apparition before. I pondered the fact that the bug seemed almost human, and appeared to be giving me some serious side eye.

Risking a glance toward the mirror above the sink, I checked out my appearance. I was quite a sight alright: naked, still covered with large droplets of water from the quick shower, which droplets had not yet fully evaporated and were still enveloping large portions of shoulders and back – and now also bedecked with charming little white tufts of cotton stuck all over my skin. Kind of like a toilet-paper-and-lint-nightmarish apparition on steroids.

It was hard to take my eyes off my ugliness.

I continued to stare and – assessing my shocking appearance in the mirror one last time – I realized that it was no wonder I had caught the attention of a passing member of the insect population.

Cursing quietly, and grabbing the tiniest corner of the hand-towel – that had probably been all sorts of places I didn't want to even think about before it landed in my room – I flapped the towel so it would open. And then waved it in the direction of the cockroach.

No dice: Roach Boy didn't move. He just kind of sat there, bored, with a "Lady – is that all ya' got?" stare aimed in my direction.

I flapped the hand towel again. Much more violently and assertively at the Arnold-Schwarzenegger-esque bug that was still managing to give me some truly stupendous insect side-eye. Again, no dice.

But after a few moments, seemingly bored, or perhaps just inclined to take pity on the ugly idiotic foreigner – who after all had managed to use an entire roll of toilet paper to dry herself off … and who still bore unfortunate lint-ish remains of such inanity about her arms and legs and torso – the roach cast me a final look before turning and lumbering back into the crevice from which he'd materialized.

Briefly scanning the floor to ensure he wasn't recruiting any new friends to come see me in all my hideous splendor, I attempted to dust off the remaining tufts of TP that were still stuck all over my body. Then, I got quickly dressed.

Taking one more quick pass in the mirror before yanking open my door, and noticing that I was flushed and heaving like I'd run a marathon – I'd put drying off with toilet paper and having a Mexican-Stand-Off with a roach right up there with a Cross-Fit session for its cardio conditioning capacity – I silently cursed my decision to take a shower and ran for the stairs.

Lars was waiting patiently for me when I arrived in the lobby, looking like a calm, collected, sane person. The same, however, could not be said for me.

The rapid-fire shower and TP debacle – capped by the cockroach stand-off and my flat-out run down eight stories of stairs in the brothel – had left me more sweaty and disheveled than when Lars and I had first arrived.

Observing my kind pastor friend who was now looking at me a bit quizzically, I debated explaining the source of my delay. As I couldn't really figure out a genteel way to describe my adventures, I settled on mentioning only the cockroach portion of my quarter-hour rodeo.

"Oh yes, the roaches – sometimes, they are bigger than the rats!" Lars exclaimed, laughing.

I wasn't so sure it was a laughing matter. "Um, yeah," I retorted rather unintelligently. "The bug was really rather large –probably the size of a normal mouse in America," I elaborated.

"Yup, that sounds about right!" exclaimed Lars, laughing again. He was unfailingly upbeat, and could find humor in the most unlikely things and places. There was a lesson there, I was sure of it.

We exited the lobby, and began to walk the roads.

The small brothel town, as I was to learn, was comprised of endless rows of dirt alleys, populated by run down buildings. Each building had a series of roll-up metal doors – doors like those one would see on an auto body shop in East LA. Lars explained that, as dusk approached each evening, the metal doors would be pulled open to reveal little make-shift bars that served beer, local-language karaoke … and girls.

For a price.

I strolled slowly next to the pastor, my orientation continuing as the hot tropical air flowed around us, bringing with it the tinkling sounds of tiny birds. I stopped and inquired about the birds.

Lars lifted his hand to shade his eyes, squinting up into the higher regions of some of the nearby buildings. "Ah, yes. The birds. Many in town devote the upper levels of their buildings to birds. The tiny birds you hear are kept to make birds' nest soup. And the other items stored on the top floors of these buildings, behind the wrought iron bars, are the very youngest of girls. The girls who are not free to roam the bars at night, but who are nonetheless for sale … for the right price. You will see teens tonight, and even some pre-teens perhaps, in the brothels. But you won't ever see the really young ones on display. But they are here – make no mistake – under lock and key. Up in the upper floors of the buildings you see ... with the bars on the windows."

My eyes took in the dilapidated surroundings, feeling the hot and humid late afternoon air that clung to our skin and our shirts, and which brought with it a sticky, dank odor of decay and mildew. The visions of worn-down buildings were starkly juxtposed against the beautiful jungles and songs of tiny birds. I felt my mind and stomach somersaulting with the cognitive dissonance stemming from a land that was in many ways so lovely, and in other aspects, so lost that the beautiful things – tiny birds, and young girls – were kept under lock and key.

Prisoners to their own respective fates.

Chapter 24

It was a couple weeks later, and Connor, my British colleague, had landed in the brothel town with a film crew in tow. We were about to make a short documentary about the lives of the young girls caught in the slave trade. I'd spent my earlier trip with Lars figuring out which brothels and rooms we would use for filming.

Now, Connor and I were standing in a dirt alley. One of the girls from the brothels was waiting for me, and I'd promised to meet her shortly after 9 p.m. I told my colleague I would catch up with him in a bit.

"You can't go out by yourself, Leigh," said my colleague from London.

"Excuse me?" I replied, turning more fully to face Connor. "What exactly do you mean, 'I can't go back outside?'"

Connor sighed loudly as he began to explain. Apparently, his fiancée had also traveled with him on this trip – she was completing her Master's Degree and was set to study some of the dynamics that were driving the brothel industry. Unfortunately, though, she had become separated from Connor earlier that evening, getting lost in the maze of dark alleys that ran the length and breadth of the brothel town.

While Connor and his bride-to-be were luckily reunited, Connor had apparently decided to handle the earlier problem by creating a bright line rule whereby none of the female employees of our NGO were now allowed outside the hotel-brothel at night.

But I was the only female employee in Asia right now. And I was not happy with this new, out-of-the-blue line in the sand that was hampering my work. How was I supposed to get anything done? Perhaps it had eluded my colleague, but one can't really work in a brothel town only during the daylight hours – nothing happens in the daytime. All of our work was at night. How in the heck was I to get anything done, if I had to remain in my room all evening?

Aside from the logistical difficulties posed by the new rule, the perceived unfairness of it grated on me as well. I'd spent my life in large law firms, firms filled with men who could be at best paternalistic and patronizing, and some men who at worst could be harassing and discriminatory in their behavior. I'd paid my proverbial dues over many years.

And having spent two decades holding my own, I now found myself railing internally at this male savior who'd decided to come along in the middle of a foreign country, making up new rules for only the females, which made executing my job nigh on impossible. Although, I had to admit: at least the Christian men in my NGO were coming from a well-meaning place. As I looked at my new co-worker, Connor, I felt my mind drifting back to earlier days, at the US law firms, where the discrimination was equally overt, but not so well-meaning.

Chapter 25

It was the 1990's, and I was representing an out-of-state chemical company whose proprietary recipes and data had been stolen by a competitor. The other parties to the lawsuit were represented by a variety of Oregonian attorneys – three old, white, male, fuddy-duddy types in brown and black suits.

I tried not to roll my eyes as I opened the door to my firm's conference room, taking in the typical y-chromosome heavy presence. The only other woman in the conference room, besides me, was the court-reporter. She looked to be about twice my age. It was pretty standard on these environmental cases I worked – I was frequently the only female attorney in a room full of men who were double or triple my age.

And today was no exception: all three of the male attorneys looked to be older than sixty. And my witness – the person my client had offered up to be deposed by the other side's attorneys – was an 85-year-old engineer. This should be fun, I thought to myself, setting my notes on the conference table.

I sat down, and we were about to swear in my witness for his deposition, when the older fat male attorney had an epiphany.

"Gee whiz, these note pads that this high-end Newwwpooort Beach law firm has" – the attorney emphasized the vowels in the first word intentionally – "are quite nice. They've got a nice stiff cardboard backing on them, so the yellow pages don't bend at all when you're writing on your knee!"

I looked at him, stoically, while opening my laptop. This was not exactly an epiphany – I was pretty sure stiff-backed notepads could be procured from any Office Depot or Staples.

But these guys were clearly backwoods-Oregon types – maybe Oregon didn't have big box stores like ours?

Regardless, I didn't respond to his comment. I wasn't here to chat. I was here to keep my witness as silent as he could be, while still allowing him to answer any properly-framed questions.

My witness and I had met earlier in the week to prepare for his deposition. As an older male engineer, he was a 'man of few words.' From my perspective, such folks were usually a dream to defend in depos, because they didn't talk a lot – which meant that opposing counsel had to work harder to uncover data. I expected today's depo to be easy enough to defend. Leaning over, I caught my witness' eye, silently adjuring him to follow the rules I'd laid out during our earlier meeting.

Our prep session had followed my tried and true formula. I'd approached it like I always do, much as a first-grade teacher approaches her class when instructing on the basics.

"Your job is to NOT talk as much as possible. Every time you open your mouth, you give them data, and make their life easier. And that is not what you are here to do – rather, you are here to answer their questions with the minimum, correct amount of information. And moreover, to answer ONLY the question they posed," I warned, "so please, do not gratuitously give out little bits of info they never asked for."

Taking a sip of my tea, I continued my tutorial. "A depo is NOT a conversation. I repeat: Depositions are *not* conversations. As humans, all the time in casual conversation, we kind of 'read the other person's mind' if you will – and proceed to answer questions the other person has not yet formed, without making them spell it out for us. That's called being polite. And those are fine rules – for normal conversation."

I looked sharply at my engineer; he appeared to be tracking with what I was telling him. I carried on. "But those are NOT the rules when it comes to you being deposed."

"When you are being deposed, you answer *only* the question asked. The rules are: 'Yes.' 'No.' 'Green.' 'I don't know.' 'I don't remember.' And –" I held up a finger dramatically for effect, "'I need to go to the bathroom.'"

He looked at me quizzically. I began to explain.

"You don't ever respond to their question by saying, for instance, 'Well, the answer to your question is yes… but sometimes in the rain, well then, the answer would be no….' No, you don't do that. Instead, you give short, one word answers. Understood? You make the other side ask for the details in later questions – you don't volunteer details before they ask you a concrete question. So if opposing counsel asks you, 'What color was the car?' You say, 'Green.'"

I leaned forward, still looking into my engineer's eyes. "You do NOT say, 'Well, it was green, but it looked like it had a metallic clear coat, so depending on the light, I guess it could've appeared blue or turquoise….' NO. You don't say any of that – one word answers. Got it? You say, 'The color was green.' And make them ask about the exact shade."

My engineer nodded, and I continued.

"If the opposing attorney asks you, 'What size was your coffee table in 1950?' you may answer – assuming you still remember the answer accurately. But, if you do not remember, you say 'I don't remember.' That statement, deconstructed to its base, means that – at one point in time – you knew the answer, but because of the passage of time, *you no longer know the answer.*

I paused briefly and readjusted my seat.

"Now—" I tilted my head to the side, "if the opposing attorney asks you how big *my* conference table in *my* living room is, then you answer 'I don't know.' Because you've never been in my house, and would have no way of knowing. You do NOT say 'I don't remember,' – because that wording implies that at one time you knew the answer and have since forgotten it, which would be impossible ... since you've never been in my house."

I concluded my monologue: "People use these phrases 'I don't remember' and 'I don't know' imprecisely and interchangeably all the time. But you will not do that, in your upcoming deposition this week, because they actually have very different meanings, and you must remember that."

Reflecting back on my prep session, I felt like I'd been thorough, and now that we were in the deposition, my eighty-five-year-old engineer seemed to be holding up just fine.

But I could not say the same for the other attorneys. Every question they posed was objectionable, and my job – my only job – was to note the objections for the record (and instruct my witness not to answer, in severe cases).

"Objection, asked and answered," I interceded, for what felt like the umpteenth time since the depo had begun.

The fat older Oregon lawyer sighed, clearly becoming rattled and losing his train of thought. Bonus for me, I thought wryly to myself, just as the older guy burst out again, arguing against my objection. "I did not ask that question yet!"

Another point for my side: the more the attorneys talked or argued amongst themselves, the less my witness would be talking.

I responded to the other attorney's argument, simply stating, "Yes, you did already ask that question." And then, for good measure, I proceeded to quote verbatim the exact phraseology he'd employed the first time he'd asked the question, all of about a minute earlier. After which, I asked the court reporter to confirm my opinion by also reading from her transcript the exact question the fat older lawyer had already asked.

The Oregon attorney's eyes narrowed. Clearly, he didn't like me. And he didn't care for my objections.

"We don't object like that, all the darned time young lady, when we're up in federal court in Oregon – that's not how we do it," he intoned gravely, staring at me from behind his heavily-lidded eyes and bushy eyebrows. Apparently, he mistakenly thought that schooling me might get me to change course.

I remained unconcerned, and responded in a bored tone to his statement. "Well, sir, we're not in court, we're in a deposition," I said. "And the objections were warranted. You only get to ask a question once. Not multiple times … because you didn't like the answer given. And the fix, by the way, is quite simple: I suggest if you don't like me objecting to your questions, then you start phrasing your questions in ways that are not objectionable."

I raised my eyebrows. "I'll make it simple: just don't ask compound questions, or questions you already asked before. And then I won't pose those objections."

I concluded my little lesson by smiling politely at the fat older lawyer, while blinking my eyes innocently, knowing full well the combination of my smile and words would make him even more upset. Out of the corner of my eye, I saw the court reporter also smiling briefly at my rejoinder. More points in my favor – opposing counsel was starting to look like a horse's behind ... and even the other folks in the room were starting to notice.

Some time later, a break was called, and all the men including my witness went off to the little boys' room, while I hit the ladies' room. My engineer had been instructed to not even make small talk with opposing counsel while in the men's room. The ladies' room and men's room shared a tiled wall, and for my part, I kept my ears open in a vain attempt to try and figure out if I could distinguish the voices coming indistinctly through the wall. Hearing occasional muffled male voices, but nothing intelligible, I prayed my witness was keeping quiet.

Upon leaving my stall, I found the court reporter washing her hands. "I know it's probably not my place to say," she piped up, "but my-oh-my! The opposing lawyers are a back-woods group of good ol' boys – and I just love how you're keeping your cool! I've never seen someone so on-point, and incapable of being thrown off course by their intimidation – and you're so young!" She stuck her hand out, "I'm Brenda, by the way...."

I took her hand and shook it, thanking her for the compliment. It wasn't the first time I'd heard such a sentiment. I'd always had a decent poker face, and an equally decent ability to stay on course.

We returned to the conference room, where two more hours of deposition ensued. The fat older attorney continued to remain functionally incapable of asking a clean question, and so I'd been on a proverbial roll – objecting pretty much nonstop, in a dead-pan voice, which tone I had noticed had a tendency to upset him even further. And which tone I thus continued to employ. But it wasn't difficult work; I was, in fact, quite bored.

All of a sudden, into my engulfing torpor, the court reporter interjected: "Umm, hold up folks. My machine appears to have gone dead. I can't seem to transcribe anything right now."

We all looked around. This was definitely not a common occurrence. As the court reporter began to fiddle with her machine, my deponent – true to his engineering background – decided to take a look under the table to see if he could debug things. His frail old-man voice wafted up to us from his bent position peering under the table. "It looks like the electric cord to her machine fell out of the floor jack," he observed.

Beginning to scooch to the edge of his chair as if he were going to hit the floor and crawl under the enormous conference room table to fix it, I placed a hand on his shoulder. My witness was ancient, and truly a little frail fossil of a man. I wasn't about to let him crawl around under the heavy wooden table.

"Here, Fred, allow me. You're the deponent – your only job today is to answer questions. Just … just stay in your seat – I've got this."

I slid forward off the conference room chair, pulling the skirt on my business suit to just above my knees so I could bend more easily. I was now on all fours under the table, and I reached forward to grab the cord that had somehow become disengaged from the electrical outlet.

As I moved to fix the cord, the older fat attorney pulled his chair out a bit from the opposite side of the table and, dropping his gaze down toward me – with perfect timing – whispered:

"You're a real piece of work now – aren't ya' little girl? Why don't you make yourself useful while you're under there?"

Chuckling, he nodded once, and used his hand to tap his thigh near his crotch, his implication unmistakable.

Charming, just charming.

I placed the court reporter's three-pronged end of the cord into its rightful spot in the outlet, and climbed fairly quickly out from under the table and back into my chair. Whereupon I asked the court reporter if her machine was functioning again. When she indicated it was, the fat older attorney began to open his mouth – clearly under the assumption he was going to resume questioning my witness.

Before he could get a word formed, I interjected:

"Let the record reflect that opposing counsel appears to have intentionally disabled the court reporter's ability to transcribe these proceedings by using his foot to disengage the court reporter's cord, thus rendering her steno machine inoperable. During the time she was incapable of transcribing the proceedings, I crawled under the conference table to fix the problem. At which point, opposing counsel referred to me as a 'real piece of work' and further adjured me to 'make myself useful' while I was under the table, and – through hand gestures – appeared to clarify that I was to do so by 'servicing him' as he pointed at his crotch."

I watched in satisfaction as the fat older attorney's face turned eight different shades of eggplant. Apparently, he'd not thought I would have the gumption to put his sexual reference on the record. Of course, he'd once again erred.

"For my part," I carried on, without taking much of a breath, "I'm not inclined to take him up on his offer, which harassment is likely in violation of local court rules in Oregon – I know it would be in California – although I am inclined to seek sanctions at this point for his inappropriate conduct."

Silence ensued for a long moment. After which, the deposition began to go more smoothly.

The court reporter high-fived me on the way back into the bathroom at lunch. "I don't know how you work with counsel like that – he's horrible!" she remarked.

I smiled tiredly. "Oh, you have no idea – last month, my bra was hanging from the ceiling...." I retorted, while rolling my eyes and reaching for a paper towel.

The court reporter leaned toward me conspiratorially. She clearly wanted to hear the tale.

I reflected on the fact that she'd had my back all day. It was the least I could do to oblige her with the rather incredulous story.

Chapter 26

Throwing the paper towels into the metal bin affixed to the wall of the ladies' room, I took up the story that the court reporter was dying to hear.

"Well, I'd been working on the same high-tech case with the same supervising attorney here in my law firm, for a few years. We'll call the guy Rick, to protect the guilty." Brenda chuckled, as I continued. "Rick was basically my boss on these cases. And he's, like, this really mild, unassuming Christian fellow. He's got a wife, a few kids, the whole nine yards. At least, that's how I always viewed him."

I watched Brenda as she leaned back against the sink counter. As she settled in, I picked up the story.

"But then, around this time last month, I was heading down to the basement, where the gym is located in our building. It was after hours, and most of the lawyers were already gone for the day. My plan was to squeeze in a quick work-out before heading home. I always changed clothes in my office because the gym didn't really have proper locker rooms. So I put on my sports bra and spandex and T-shirt, and headed down to the basement, leaving my business suit and bra in my office, tucked into my gym bag."

She finished toweling off her hands, neither of us making a move to exit the bathroom; it seemed we'd reached a tacit understanding that we were going to stay in the cozy environs of the ladies' room until my little tale concluded.

"So, what'd Rick do?" she inquired.

"I know, I know," I laughed, "so far the facts aren't that scintillating. And frankly, at the time, I had no idea my evening was about to go to severely sideways. 'Til that point, it was just another night at the firm. That is, until I exited the elevator after my work-out, and hit the lobby. Where it was like I'd entered the Twilight Zone…."

"Oh?" Brenda asked.

"Yep. Rick was standing near the secretarial cubicle – the one that is just past the receptionist's desk in the elevator lobby. So as I leave the elevator, I run smack into Rick, who says, 'Notice anything different?'"

I smiled, thinking back in disbelief to the events that unfolded after those fateful words. "At the time I was sweaty, and hot and hungry. So I just kind of walked past Rick, shaking my head and ignoring his question. But undeterred, he pointed at the ceiling with his index finger, and said quietly, 'Leigh, why don't you look up?'"

Brenda set her purse on the counter next to the sink. Her eyebrows raised in implicit encouragement to continue.

"And so I did look up. And there, hanging from the absolutely enormous brass chandelier in the elevator lobby of our little high rise building here in Newport – right above the thick Oriental rug, and the mahogany desk of the receptionist who'd already left for the day – gently swinging in the breeze from the air-conditioning was my bra. Which Rick had scotch taped to the brass arms of the chandelier … for all to see."

"He did not!" Brenda exclaimed in disbelief, her words echoing around the tiled walls of the ladies' room.

"Oh, but he did, Brenda. He did – he'd hung my bra from the brass chandelier," I replied, remembering the absurdity of it all.

"And that wasn't all. You see, it was really quite a masterpiece. Because, from the little pink bow of my bra, right in the center, Rick had stretched a 2-inch piece of Scotch Tape vertically downward, to which he'd attached his business card."

Brenda's eyebrows raised so far up her forehead in shock they were nearly touching her hairline. "Well, I've never heard – I mean… I just, umm – wow!" she interjected.

"I know, right? I'd never seen the likes! But wait, there's more."

Brenda's eyes stayed riveted on mine as I continued.

"Believe it or not, from his business card, Rick had run another 2-inch piece of Scotch Tape downward – to which he'd attached a single dollar bill, oriented vertically."

I stopped and looked at her shocked expression. She seemed stunned.

"It was quite the creation: my bra, then below that, the business card, then below that, the dollar bill. I gotta say, the dollar bill was a nice touch – it gave the whole work of art kind of a high-end, strip-club vibe," I joked.

"What'd you do?" she asked, tossing her lipstick back into her purse, her eyes still glued to mine.

I squinted at the ceiling, trying to remember exactly what I'd said on the night in question.

"Well, I think I told Rick something along the lines of: 'Take that down, right freaking now, before some partner sees it!' Because I, for one, was not about to be caught standing on the receptionist's desk after hours – undoing his little masterpiece."

I grabbed a paper towel to dab at my lipstick before continuing. "I mean, can you imagine if one of our senior partners had decided to come back to the firm to pick up some work after dinner – only to see me standing atop the receptionist's desk, fiddling with my bra?" I said, pulling a bobby pin from my French Chignon and using it to secure a piece of hair that had gone astray.

Brenda said, "Wow, you weren't kidding – that's quite the story!"

I checked my reflection in the mirror as I continued. "Oh, the story's not over … because after he took my bra down from the chandelier, then he decided to wear it."

"He did WHAT???!!!" she shrieked.

I laughed with her, and carried on with the re-telling. "Yeah, true story. I don't know just exactly what kind of a mental breakdown Rick was having that night, all I know is that he really appeared to be in the midst of some kind of psychological decompensation moment. I mean – who does that?? He was supposed to be up for a partner vote later that week, if you can believe it!" I rolled my eyes, remembering the absolute lunacy of the night.

Brenda shook her head again, apparently speechless.

"So yeah, Rick – in his abundant wisdom that evening – decided to put my bra on over the top of his clothing. He literally put it on over the top of his white buttoned-down shirt and red tie. And then, for good measure, he pranced up and down the interior hallways for about ten minutes."

"That is simply ... unbelievable," Brenda said, finally finding her tongue.

"I know. And it gets even worse."

Brenda's eyes widened some more, no doubt wondering how much worse this tale could possibly get.

"Yup, believe it or not, while still wearing my bra on the outside of his business clothes, Rick walks up to the night secretary, who happens to be a black woman. And he asks her whether she is familiar with a word in the dictionary "reneger" – which means "one who reneges on their promises.'"

The court reporter opens her mouth, and then closes it. Apparently, I've again rendered her speechless.

Chuckling again, I carry on. "So, at this point, the night secretary – she's a pretty tough cookie from New York – she says to him, 'Rick, honey, I'm not sure that I was aware of that particular word 'reneger' – thank you for sharing that lil' tidbit with me, by the way. But this much, I DO know: Boyyyy, you about to get yo' ass fired!'"

We both laugh loudly at the choice words the New York secretary had employed in her dressing-down of Rick.

"Well, so, uh, has he been fired yet?" Brenda queried, after we'd both caught our breath, and our tittering had died out.

"Pretty much. For my part, I gave Rick the option of apologizing the next afternoon. I mean, it was pretty apparent he'd lost his darned mind for a few hours, and I figured he might've recognized that fact by the morning after. But nope. Rick told me that he 'didn't see the need to apologize' because he 'didn't think he'd done anything wrong.'"

"Wow, talk about shooting yourself in the foot, and then making it even worse!" Brenda astutely noted.

"Indeed. But word travels fast around here – especially on a story like that one – so a few hours later the partners got wind of it, and yes, Rick was then 'given the opportunity to seek employment elsewhere.' He got the old heave-ho, and now I think he's working at firm that is very, very far away."

The court reporter looked at me one last time, her hand reaching for the door as she made to exit. "Wow, that is just… I don't even know what to say. You rock. Here's my card. Don't hesitate to call me whenever you need work – I'll gladly transcribe your proceedings."

As we shook hands a final time and parted ways, I reflected that I had indeed successfully navigated the waters of a harassing workplace well enough. In fact, so well did I survive the law firm environs that – after six years of employment – my secretary Cassidy came into my office one day to offer up a backhanded compliment.

"Well, girl, you beat the odds," Cassie stated, while handing me the memo she'd edited for my client.

"What are you talking about, Cass?" I said, grabbing the document and dropping it on the corner of my desk, as I bent to retrieve my purse from my desk drawer.

"Oh, don't you know?" she bandied back.

"Nope. No idea what you're talking about," I replied, "but I'm about to be late for lunch. Although now you've piqued my curiosity, so do tell. Quickly though."

"Okay, well you know how you were 19 years old when you first got the job offer to come and work here for the summer? And then when you started full time, you were like, what, 21 or 22 years old?"

I nodded, not quite sure why she was running me through my own *curriculum vitae.*

"Well," she continued, "um, I don't really know how to politely say this to you, but no one thought you'd last. We all took bets on you."

I stopped rummaging around in my purse for my keys, and looked up at Cassidy.

"What do you mean – took bets on me? Like you were betting on a horse or something? Like you were betting against me lasting?"

She nodded. "Yep, that's about the long and short of it. Everyone placed bets on how long you'd last before leaving the firm – a week, a month, a year, maybe a few years at the outside. And the last bet just ran out."

My hands stopped moving. Rather dumbfounded, I just stared at her as she clarified.

"The longest bet was six years, and you just beat it. Because you're still here. And none of your colleagues who started with you are still here – which we didn't expect and is kinda even more impressive. The secretaries were the ones who thought you'd last the longest, but even we didn't think you'd go this long."

Well, gee whittakers – this was a facer. I'd been working my buns off, billing 2,500-3,000 hours a year, for going on six long years... amongst people who were supposed to be my colleagues ... but who also so believed I would not make the long haul that they had money riding on it.

Charming. But not altogether surprising.

I smiled. "Yeah, well, I guess they didn't know me, did they?"

"No," Cassie replied, grinning back at me. "They didn't."

I looked at my watch – I could stand to be a few minutes late to my lunch. "Did I ever tell you the story about the students, or the rats?" I asked.

"Nope – but I got time if you do!" Cass replied, plunking down in my guest chair.

Chapter 27

I picked up the story without hesitation.

"So in the 1960's, some elementary school teachers were told that certain kids in their class were smart, and that these 'smart kids' could be expected to have 'growth spurts of intellectual achievement during the year,' based on the students' results on some Harvard Test they'd taken."

Cassie looked at me closely, her attention clearly aroused as I continued.

"But actually, the test was nonexistent: the children designated as 'smart growth spurters' were chosen at random. And the question the researchers were trying to answer is whether the expectation of the teacher – patently false though it was, given that the smart kids were actually ***not*** smart but just randomly designated – would have an effect on the children so labeled. Turns out, it did."

"Really?" Cassie interjected.

"Yep," I continued. "Expectations matter. Even unspoken expectations, it turns out. And it wasn't like the teachers were going around all year saying 'Hey smart girl, let's have you answer this question,' or 'Hey dummy, this easier question over here is for you.' No, the teachers were being fair. There was no overt favoritism going on. For their part, they were being even-handed in their treatment of the 'smart kids' and the 'not-so-smart' kids."

Cassie lifted her hand from her lap, and placed it face down on my oak desk, her eyes glued to mine, while she ignored the pretty tableau of the Newport coastline visible through my window. For all the downsides of working my tail off at a law firm seven days a week, the gorgeous ocean view from my fifth-floor high rise did not count among them.

"So did the kids perform better, just 'cuz the teacher thought they were smart?" she asked.

"Indeed. They performed much, much better. The average kid in the class who had not been (falsely) labeled as smart gained only twelve overall IQ points in their first grade year. But the kids who had been deemed 'smart?'"

I smiled, and paused expectantly, "those children gained nearly thirty IQ points. ***By year's end, the kids labeled as smart ones were performing 2.5 times more intelligently on standardized tests.*** Not because they were smarter – but rather, because someone had believed that they were. Expectations matter, Cass. They always have. And they always will."[69]

"That's fascinating – how do you know all this stuff?" she asked.

"Well, I also think it's fascinating," I replied. "And after taking a college course that went over this material, I realized I was just not meant to be a piano major. And I changed majors – just so I could study all this weird stuff, full-time." I laughed. "That was before my left turn into law school. And now, about that rat study…." I trailed off, raising one eyebrow.

---

[69] Rosenthal R. (1968). *Pygmalion in the Classroom: Teacher Expectation and Pupil's Intellectual Development.* Holt, Rinehart & Winston, Inc. https://gwern.net/doc/statistics/bias/1968-rosenthal-pygmalionintheclassroom.pdf

"Yeah, do tell," Cassie replied. Shifting in her chair, she crossed her legs for what was turning into a longer conversation.

"Well, there was a researcher by the name of Curt Richter. At least, if memory serves, I think that was his name. Anyhow, he decided in the 1950s to try and figure out how long rats would swim before they gave up the ghost and drowned. So he threw some of his domesticated lab rats into vats of water, and noted that they died after . . . ." I paused for a second, looking up at my ceiling as I tried to recall the facts from years ago. "I believe they died after 15 minutes, on average. Richter wasn't all that impressed with their performances, so then he got the idea to throw some wild rats into the drink. Thinking that perhaps the aggressive wild rats would out-perform his fat and lazy lab rats."

I paused again, as our firm's mail clerk opened my door and dropped mail in my box. As the door closed behind him, I continued.

"So the researcher goes out and catches some wild rats. And proceeds to throw them into the vats of water. And – strangely – the wild rats performed even worse than the lab rats had. The wild rats actually swam for less time – and died more quickly – than Richter's domesticated rats."

Cassie looked at me quizzically.

"I know," I replied in response to her unspoken question, "it doesn't make any sense. You'd think the wild rats would do better than the coddled and fat lab rats. And it was puzzling for Curt Richter, too. But after contemplating this unexpected anomaly, he figured out that maybe – just maybe – the lab rats' better performances had to do with the factor of hope."

"Hope?" Cassie queried.

I nodded. "Hope. Richter surmised that because his lab rats got two square meals a day fed to them by their loving human caretakers, that maybe – in their little lab rat brains – they had hope. Hope that the humans who would buzz by their cages supplying food twice a day might similarly buzz by and save them from drowning. Richter's theory was that maybe it was the secret promise of hope that had caused his lab rats to swim longer than the wild rats."

My black desk phone buzzed loudly and suddenly into the quiet of my office. Cassie made a move toward my phone when it rang, saying "I'm so sorry, Leigh – I know I should be getting that…."

"No worries." I quickly lifted my right hand and pushed the button that would send the caller to voicemail, since I did not want to interrupt my chat.

Shrugging my shoulders, I carried on. "So anyway, Richter decides to test the hypothesis that his lab rats harbored some form of hope that was powering them to swim for longer spans of time than their wild counterparts. And he re-does the experiment. But this time, just before the lab rats are about to sink to the bottom of the tubs and drown, he rescues them. Towels off their little furry heads. Whispers some – I dunno exactly – but some sweet-nothings in their little rat ears, telling them what 'good rats they are' and how he 'believes in them.' In short, he reinforces the notion of a hope of rescue that he suspected the lab rats were harboring that made them swim longer."

I took a dramatic pause. "And then? After rescuing them? Richter proceeded to throw them immediately back into the drink."

Cassie tilted her head inquiringly. "He did?"

"Yep. He rescued them, and then tossed them right back in. And of course the big question," I paused again while arching an eyebrow, "is whether the lab rats were going to swim fewer minutes on the second pass. Which would've been understandable – given that the rats had basically just run the equivalent of a marathon during their first swim session. Or, alternatively, whether the rats would swim for a longer period of time, now that Richter had just reinforced the notion of hope by saving them during their first dip in the water."

"And?" questioned Cassie, leaning further forward.

"They swam longer, Cass. A lot longer. Wanna guess exactly how much longer?"

Cassie shook her head side to side. I let the tension build.

"They swam – wait for it Cass – they swam ... THREE. DAYS. LONGER."

"THREE DAYS?!!" Cassie near-shouted, disbelief etched in every fiber of her being.

"Yes, three days," I said, smiling quietly."[70]

---

[70] *The Hope Experiment.* https://www.penpenny.com/jivan-ghadage1/The-HOPErdquo-Experiment-During-a-brutal-study-at-Harvard-in-the-1950s-Dr-Curt-Richter-placed-rats-in-a-pool-of-water-to-test-how-long-they-could-tread-waterOn-average-theyd-give-up-and-sink-after-15-minutesBut-right-before-they-gave-up-due-to-exhaustion-the-researchers-would-pluck-them-out-dry-them-off-let-them-rest-for-a-few-minutes-and-put-them-back-in-for-a-second-roundIn-this-second-try-how-long-do-you-think-they-lastedRemember-they-had-just-swam-until-failure-only-a-few-short-minutes-agoHow-long-do-you-thinkAnother-15-minutes10-minutes5-minutesNo60-hoursThats-not-an-errorThats-right-60-hours-of-swimmingThe-conclusion-drawn-was-that-since-the-rats-BELIEVED-that-they-would-eventually-be-rescued-they-could-push-their-bodies-way-past-what-they-previously-thought-impossibleI-will-leave-you-with-this-thoughtIf-hope-can-cause-exhausted-rats-to-swim-for-that-long-what-could-a-belief-in-yourself-and-your-abilities-do-for-youFootnoteThe-experimenthttpci (quoting Richter, C. (1957) *On the Phenomenon of Sudden Death in Animals and Man*, *https://citeseerx.ist.psu.edu/viewdoc/download?doi=10.1.1.536.1405&rep=rep1&type=pdf*).

Cassie flopped her elbow over the arm rest as she leaned back theatrically in the chair. "That just doesn't seem possible!" she declared again.

"I know, my friend. I know. But such is the power of hope. Hope matters. Expectations matter. I think you've heard me talk in the past about my parents' marriage. Well, my father never thought much of me. I was always the 'no good, piece of scum that would never amount to anything.' According to him, I could do no right – I was just a 'pea-brained, good for nothin' idiot.' Despite my education."

"Oh, Leigh," Cassie chimed in, a sad look on her face. I shrugged off the display of sympathy with which I was so uncomfortable, and continued.

"It's all good, Cass. Because my mother? Well, she believed. In me. She believed, hard. And she loved – fiercely. Protectively. She thought I could walk on water. I couldn't – but darn if I wouldn't die trying for her. I don't think I was particularly gifted. I mean, I went to college with nine-year-old kids. You know – *actual* geniuses."

Cassie interrupted, "But, surely, your IQ! And your test scores –"

"I hear where you're going, Cass, I really do. But my point is simply this: I think it was way more nurture than nature, in my case. I don't think I was born special. But my mother believed I was, and so I became. And in a way, having two polar opposite parents was eye-opening, and soul-stretching. Because I had a choice: I could believe my father. Or…? I could believe my mother."

I shrugged my shoulders, briefly recalling the1970's of my youth, as I stared off into a corner of my office. Bringing myself back in to the present moment, I decided to wrap up the lunchtime story.

"So, in the final analysis, Cass, I chose to believe what my mother said. To believe in the good that she could see. Even when I couldn't necessarily see it myself. And then I learned at some point – whether in defiance of my father's expectations, or in honor of her expectations – I learned that it was my responsibility. To myself. To have expectations. To have … hope."

I looked at my secretary, my voice quiet now. "And I do. And so should you. ***So should we all."***

Cassie stood to take her leave, discreetly wiping a tear on the back of her right hand.

As she hit my threshold, I asked her, "By the way, can you call Joe and tell him I'm running late for lunch?"

"Sure thing! It's the least I can do – since I'm the one who made you late!" she laughed again, her left hand reaching for my door handle.

"Oh, and Cassie?"

She stopped, turning back to face me.

"Part two of that lesson is that I don't bet against myself. Ever. I *expect* that I will win – because even if the battle doesn't start in my favor? I've learned I get one heck of a lot farther by expecting that it will go in my favor. And you can feel free to tell the partners they shouldn't bet against me either."

She laughed. "Touché, my friend. Although I'm guessing the partners might've figured that one out by now…."

Chapter 28

Twenty years later, standing in the middle of a dark alley in a brothel town in the south of Thailand with my colleague Connor, I forced myself to quit remembering the battles I'd successfully navigated in past years against various paternalistic male colleagues, and instead turn my attention to the problem at hand. Did Connor not understand I'd been here for an entire week, earlier this very same month, with no chaperone … and that I had survived just fine?

My first trip to the town had begun with the horrible roach incident in my room, and continued once I met Lars downstairs in the lobby and we began to walk the dirt alleys. Coming abreast of a small café – a café which also would have girls for sale later in the evening – Lars and I had stopped to grab a bite to eat.

As we pulled up two chairs on the patio, Lars made small talk with the locals – people he'd clearly befriended on earlier trips to this region. Some hours later, at a bar-brothel down the alley to which we'd migrated after our snack, Lars began talking to a girl. She'd been fascinated by the unusual sighting of two white people, in this border town that was all brothels and Asian pedophiles. And Lars, as I came to find out, was equally interested in the situation that had caused her to be in this place. We sat down on a bench outside the brothel, facing the alley and yet more brothels across the way, and began to chat.

Like most of the girls trapped in this town, it turned out that she hailed from Savannakhet, Laos. With Lars translating, I gathered that her family had always been quite poor, but then had fallen on some truly difficult times. It seemed that her father had an accident, leaving her mother alone and with no way to feed her many children. I was completely engrossed in her story, when the madam suddenly wandered over and interrupted our conversation.

After some brief and friendly-sounding words, Lars turned to me. "Leigh, are you okay staying here awhile, and ordering drinks?"

I nodded in agreement. I had nowhere to be, and I too wanted to understand more about this town, and its girls.

And thus the three of us continued to while away the evening, with Lars chatting pleasantly with the girl and eliciting more details about her family life. Every so often, the madam would come over and deliver us more drinks – water and sodas for me and Lars – and a beer for the girl. I had started to look around and take in my surroundings while the two of them spoke rapidly in Thai, and was surprised to see what appeared to be a newer model, clean black SUV pulling up nearby.

It had a similar body style to my old Black Chevy Blazer, and as I stared at it – cars were rare in this town, as most of the inhabitants drove motorbikes or simply walked – two uniformed Thai men, holsters on their hips, alighted from the vehicle. They looked to be law enforcement. Passing by our bench, they waved and loudly greeted Lars.

"Sawadee Krap!" the men bellowed, in a hail-fellow-well-met tone, exchanging the usual greeting with Lars. After some more pleasantries were exchanged in the local dialect, with much smiling and bobbing of heads all around, the police retreated inside the building.

It was many minutes later when they emerged. I noticed a sack one of the men carried, which I'd not seen before.

"It's a good night!" one of the men called out in English to the pastor, his chest puffed out with an air of authority.

Lars inclined his head, lifting a hand in acknowledgement of their statement.

I continued to watch the two officers. They slowly ambled down the alley as if they owned the world, coming to rest briefly in front of the next brothel before walking inside. They did not stay indoors quite as long at this brothel.

But once again, when they emerged, they were all smiles.

As the night wore on, I followed with interest their progress down the alley. Down the one side, and then back up the other. And every twenty feet, as they came to another storefront, over and over again the same scene would play out. The only real difference would be the varying amounts of time they chose to spend inside: sometimes, it was just a few minutes. While other times it was the better part of an hour. And after each stop, I noted that the size of the sack they carried was bigger.

Lars stretched as the young girl excused herself to use the restroom. Leaning forward, he asked quietly, "So you noticed their bag?"

I replied that I had.

Lars continued. "Yeah, they are the police. But they are on the take. They go in and out of each brothel, and the brothel needs to pay a 'fee' to these two men in order to stay in business. It's like the mafia from last century in New York. And of course, these cops – well they can help themselves to whatever 'services' they want in addition to taking money.'"

I nodded in understanding: that explained why sometimes the trip inside only took two minutes, and while other times the men disappeared for much longer.

I felt awful for the girls. It wasn't bad enough that they were victimized by the mafia-owners involved with selling them, and by the pedophile customers buying them. They were also exploited by the police, who should have been protecting them – but instead were extorting "protection fees" from the brothels while helping themselves to free sexual services. I said as much to Lars, and he nodded sadly.

"Law enforcement here, you must understand, Leigh, is very corrupt. On scales of corruption, when foreign NGOs measure it? Thai cops come up as a four or five, on a scale of 1-5. With five being the most corrupt. It has long been a problem in this country," Lars explained.

Lars stopped talking as the madam swung by our table. He handed over more Baht, the local currency, and then exchanged some words with her, after which she beckoned us to follow her inside.

We entered the building, and sat at a little square card table with four chairs around it. "I thought this would be better. No mosquitoes ... or at least fewer mosquitoes!" Lars noted, chuckling.

I agreed, looking around at the TV monitors on the walls. It was still pretty empty inside, but Middle Eastern music was pouring from the speakers. I recognized the bouncing cursor over the Arabic-style letters roving across the screen.

"Is this a karaoke bar?" I asked Lars.

"Yes, it a brothel and a karaoke bar – with Malay music and words," Lars clarified.

Listening to the melodies, I was transported back to my youth, when my mom used to take me with her to work. She was a physical fitness instructor who'd taken up Belly Dancing with a group of her friends when I was a toddler. Finding it to be a good work out, and naturally talented at dance, my mother had begun teaching belly-dancing, while working side gigs at reunions and birthday parties.

It was quite the novelty in mid-1970's California: I remembered my father would haul her amplifiers out of the car, setting up the audio equipment, and then a bit later, my mother would come gliding out into the backyard or the living room of the family that had hired her for a birthday or some such, red scarves swirling and beaded costume jangling, as the unique wailing voices of middle-Eastern music suffused the spaces.

It had been decades since I'd heard these subtle organizations of melody and rhythm – with the vocal intonations of the singer predominating over the instrumental. But hearing again the music that had always connoted for me Arab minarets and pointy-domed mosques, I felt simultaneously very far from my home in Orange County, and somehow, like I was also three-years old again and back at my mother's knee.

A bit unnerved by it all, I turned toward Lars, who continued to translate the scenes that we were witnessing. "Even the madams, like the woman who just came over to me? They are not the problem. They are victims, too. These girls – really, they are girls – you must understand. It's not like they ever grew up wanting to run these little brothels. No one dreams of running a brothel when they are five years old and playing in the streets with their friends. No.

These women are as much the victims as the girl we've been buying drinks for…."

Lars stopped talking, his eyes looking away momentarily before he resumed.

"Let me be clear about what I'm trying to convey. The madams, Leigh? Well, they are just ***the girls who didn't die.*** Of AIDS. Or death by pimp. Or death by some violent john or customer. That's the reality: some of the girls do not die. And then? Because this is all they've ever known – since their own families sold them to the brothels to make ends meet – and now these same families will not take them back because they are 'damaged goods'? Well, here the girls remain. So when they are 'older' – which is so sad because all that means is that they are in their 20s, which course is by no means old – then these girls become babysitters of the 'new and younger' girls."

Lars stopped, sighing heavily. "But they did not want this life, Leigh. Not even the 'madams' that you see walking around tonight: keep in mind that they were really – at one time – no different than the young girl we've been talking with."

His eyes were sad, as he relayed the facts of this town to me.

"But it's not all doom and gloom, eh? We are doing much good work here. I've rented a little house, and we've got 3 or 4 folks from my ministry who are down here full time now. And they disseminate God's Word to the people of this little town. We let them know, all of them – the girls, the madams, the owners, even the buyers – we let them know there is a different way. That it doesn't have to be like this. And that God loves them. I've even started a Youth Group!"

Lars eyes twinkled with excitement at his pronouncement.

"Really?" I repeated incredulously. "A youth group – in a … in a brothel town?"

"Yes, indeed! And it sort of roves around. See one day, we'll hold youth group in our little Christian Church, which is really just the house that we rent down here. For now. And we invite all the kids – Muslim, Buddhist, and Christian."

I blinked in confusion. Noting my puzzled countenance, Lars laughed again.

"Well, there aren't so many Christian kids – yet – but we're working on it! And every week, our youth group meets in a different kids' religious building. All equal. So one week, we meet in the Mosque – because the child whose turn it is to host – is Muslim. And then, the next week, we meet at the Buddhist Temple, because the hosting boy's family is Buddhist. The next week, we meet again at my little Christian place. And each and every week? We play. AND, we learn! AND? We praise God!"

I'm sure I still had a slightly bewildered look on my face, for Lars felt the need to clarify his program. "You see, I thought about the bombers down here, the Jihadis who are blowing things up. Well, they are really all just young men, who not that long ago were just boys – many of the Jihadis are seventeen, eighteen years old. So five years ago, they were truly just… kids."

Lars shrugged, as he stopped to take a sip of his beverage. "And so I got to thinking that if the Buddhist and Muslim boys, in particular, got to know each other – play football, or soccer as you folks in America like to say – you know, if they played games, broke bread together, and could become true friends with one another, that it might change things. Minimally, I figured it would be that much harder for them to be recruited by the Jihadis and convinced to 'blow up the enemy' … when the enemy was their best friend from the last few years, eh?"

Lars chuckled again, continuing: "It's brilliant – no? But we'll have to see. And it wasn't really my idea. All glory goes to God. It was His idea – it just came to me one day while I was in prayer."

Lars stopped, as we both leaned back to make room for the young girl to rejoin our table. As she sat down, Lars signaled the waitress to bring another round of drinks for all of us. The night continued, with Lars and the girl chatting about her life, and with me, continuing to gaze wide-eyed at this world I had told myself I wanted to help.

Suddenly, the girl giggled. Tilting her head toward the ceiling, she pointed at her nose.

I turned to Lars, once again perplexed.

He translated again, for me. "So I don't think I told you earlier. But it's pretty routine for the girls here to be forced to get nose jobs and chest augmentations on the way into town, by the brothel owners. And that's because the male customers, well they want the girls to be young, but they also want them to have breasts. So the brothels will arrange for a plastic surgeon to do both the nose job and the other surgery. And our new friend here, she is showing us that she only just a few days ago had her nose job. If you look closely, you can see the remnants of bruising around her eye sockets."

I turned to the girl, and looked at her square-on. She did not mind my unflinching perusal of her face. I observed that there were, in fact, some purple and yellow shadows around her eyes and nose, which she'd covered with some makeup. But now that we were indoors and under brighter lighting, it was evident in a way that it hadn't been, when we'd been sitting outside on the benches.

"Her name is Mai," Lars continued.

Turning to Mai, he introduced me in Thai: "And this, Mai, this is Leigh."

We both smiled at each other. Mai pointed at her nose, at one nostril in particular, and excitedly said some words. I did not understand, of course, and Lars took pity on me.

"She's explaining that the surgery was so recent that her nose is still fully packed with gauze. And she's debating whether to pull that little string in her nostril, which will pull out all of the gauze."

I involuntarily flinched backward in horror, saying aloud, "No, Mai, no...."

While I knew she couldn't understand me, the meaning behind my words had transcended the language barrier. She giggled again, removing her hand from her face to grab once more for the bottle on the table. After a sip, she turned to talk to another young girl, who had come out of a back room and sauntered over to chat.

Lars leaned closer to me. "And now you know why we are sitting here. I worked a deal with the mamasan at the beginning of the evening. I saw the bruising, and figured this was the case. And I didn't want her to have to be working the floor. So I asked the mamasan if I paid for some drinks for us – and for her – if we could keep her here. With us. So she wouldn't have to work tonight ... and take customers while she is still healing."

My eyes filled with tears, as I now more fully understood why this man of God was sitting in a brothel, buying endless rounds of cola and water for us, and beer for Mai. I knew what happened in the back rooms ... and I could not imagine being made to work and perform oral sex and other such services with both nostrils completely packed with gauze.

Lars was definitely one of the kindest pastors I'd ever met. And sitting in that brothel on a dark night in 2013, I had no idea that my Christian faith would one day come under fire. And in America of all places. I had assumed that most of the danger in my future life, spiritual and otherwise, would emanate from towns like the one in which I was sitting, or other third world countries in which I might find myself. I could not foresee that I would choose to speak out on behalf of my country – and the concept of freedom – in the year of 2020 in the US, and be promptly denounced by Americans who truly had no understanding of how relatively "good" most of those living in America had things… courtesy of living in a country that was founded on the protection of civil liberties and basic human rights.

I had no idea that I would come under attack by people who decried the First Amendment – even as they ironically used the protections afforded by it to besmirch my name and the names of friends and family. No idea that there were legions of people waiting to pop out of the proverbial woodwork, after taking the polarization bait being handed out by the media. And who would then morph into haters who seemed to derive endless joy from slandering people who sought to protect the values on which our country was founded. I had no idea that I'd one day be accused of being a Satanist, a Jew, a Catholic Fascist (whatever that is!) and all manner of varying religions, sects and cults that I'd never been part of.

No, sitting in a brothel town with Lars and Mai, I'd assumed that – if I ever were to come under attack somewhere down the line – it would be for "not being Christian enough." And that my accusers would likely be some "do-gooders" who believed that following Christ meant adherence to a narrow path … and who could never conceive of a pastor who chose to mirror Christ's love for humanity by buying a young girl beverages to save her from having to go into a back room – and perhaps suffocate to death – at the hands of a pedophile who either didn't know or didn't care that she could not breathe through her gauze-packed nose.

But the passing decade has been illuminating, to say the least – the last three years even more so. And from my vantage point in the present year of 2023, I can see that there is not only much work to do on the human trafficking front in southeast Asia and elsewhere, but that there is much work to do on the *human* front – across the board.

For the root cause of the religious wars – that are tearing apart the Deep South of Thailand? And the root cause underlying a pedophile's ability to rape a little girl? And the root cause of an American citizen's ability to slander his neighbors – and argue that they should be denied medical care and "placed in camps" – because the neighbor made a different decision than he did on an experimental vaccine?

To some degree, these all stem from the same evil seed. Instead of celebrating our differences, many lost souls spend time devaluing and dehumanizing "the other" – as it is only once we have sufficiently dehumanized someone else that we can then justify the decision to treat them poorly.

And of course, that is the great lie: that there are "others" who are unworthy of our respect. Superficially different we may be, but we are equal in the eyes of God. And equal in our ability to feel both pain and love.

In my view, our job on this planet is a relatively simple one: To help. Not hurt. And to celebrate, not criticize, both the differences that make us unique – and the humanity we all share.

Chapter 29

Some weeks after we'd spent the evening buying Mai drinks so she wouldn't have to service customers, I stood in a tiny room in a larger hotel-brothel of the tiny town. I swung my gaze intently over the rearranged furnishings.

One of the girls living in the brothels had bravely agreed to be interviewed for a short documentary on the brothel trade, by the Christian film crew our NGO had flown over from Australia. Even though we'd explained we would blur the face and body in all footage that we ended up using, Noi was still the only girl courageous enough to step forward.

I'd never done filming – my experience was in courtrooms. But as my eyes took in the room, I compared it to the recollection I had from watching past 20/20 interviews with folks who'd clearly not wanted their identities known. The set-up we had arranged in this brothel room seemed similar, in my estimation.

We'd positioned a chair by the window, and pulled the curtains back, to allow some daylight to illuminate our interviewee's profile. A couch rested against the far wall, perpendicular to the chair, where we would sit, and from which we would ask questions.

The rest of the room was full to overflowing – bursting at the proverbial seams – with the two young cameramen and all their equipment. I was nervous, but could think of nothing else that was needed.

Other than Noi. It was about time to start, but she had not yet arrived to our room.

Would she show up… or get cold feet? I checked my watch anxiously.

Moments later, there was a timid knock, and one of our cameramen stood up to open the door. Noi walked quietly into our room. She looked to be about twelve or thirteen years old, but it was hard to tell. Laotian girls all seemed to look very young, at least to me. Daintily picking her way around the equipment strewn across the floor, she made her way toward the only available resting place: the lone chair we'd placed for her, next to the window.

She was dressed in a peach organza party dress, something similar to the dresses I'd worn to cotillion as a child in the early 1980's. She perched like a bird on the edge of the wooden chair, crossing her legs at the ankle. Her feet, I noticed, barely touched the ground.

A few minutes later, we started the interview. We asked background details initially, nothing too significant, and Noi responded in short and simple sentences that were being translated into English by a Laotian employee who worked in Lars' ministry. Things seemed to be going smoothly, thus far.

My London colleague's fiancée was interviewing Noi, now.

But something was upsetting my colleague. Connor leaned over to my ear, and whispered, "That can't be right – the translation must be bad. Leigh, you should ask the question again, and maybe we'll get a correct answer."

I looked at Noi, seated on her chair. She'd been asked what seemed to be, on its face, a simple question.

"Did you know, when you arrived here in this town, exactly what you would be doing?"

Prior to the meeting, my colleagues and I had discussed the types of material to be covered. For my part, I had wanted to make clear the differences between the plights of the girls that our NGO was rescuing in Europe, and the situation in Asia, which is quite different from Europe.

In Europe, the girls rescued from brothels often hail from poorer regions – they come from Roma gypsy families, or poor parts of the Ukraine or other former Soviet-bloc countries. Recruiters from big cities come to their impoverished villages, targeting girls in their mid-to-late teens, promising them better lives as waitresses or maids at large hospitality chains.

With no better prospects on the horizon, these girls will often agree to the job offers, dazzled by the notion of, e.g., going to work in Greece at an upscale restaurant or hotel and using their wages to help support their families. But once the recruiter gets the girl's agreement, and they are actually *en route* to the destination, he will then spike the girl's drink with a narcotic.

And when the girl awakens, she is typically in a "breaking house."

As its name implies, these facilities are used to emotionally and physically crush the girl: she will be repeatedly raped (as well as drugged and beaten) until she no longer has the will or desire to run away. As part of the conditioning, the girl will often also be placed in a room with a customer who appears to be a law enforcement officer, in order to see if the girl will attempt to "bend his ear" and make a plea for escape. If she does, she will then be raped and beaten all the more violently to prove to her that even the customers who appear sympathetic – and even the ones who are law enforcement – cannot be trusted.

The girl's conditioning is considered complete when she is in total apathy, and is no longer dreaming of escape (nor making any attempts to cajole would-be johns into helping her escape). At that point, she can then be transferred from the "breaking house" into a real brothel, because she is no longer a flight risk.

For the few girls in Europe who do eventually escape, and who are then routed into a shelter like the one my NGO was running, upon being interviewed, the escapee typically makes it abundantly clear that they had no idea they were going to be a sex slave. Rather it was a "bait and switch" operation: they'd been promised by the recruiter a good job as a waitress or hotel worker – and believed that such would be their reality – right up until the time they were drugged, their passport stolen, and they woke up chained to a bed.

While the above is often par for the course in Europe, I knew from my research that the situation in Asia is much different. Typically, in southeast Asia, it is the family who knowingly sells their child to a brothel. A fact that I'd had repeatedly confirmed since coming to this region, and interviewing girls like Mai. For my part, I'd wanted to highlight the difference between the European sex trafficking scene, and that which we were encountering in southeast Asia.

Hence, the question that had been posed to our interviewee Noi, before my colleague had sought my intervention.

Noi, for her part, had responded to our question by turning her head directly into the camera and stating, "Yes, I knew exactly what I'd be doing when I got to this town. But I'm not unhappy."

I looked at the profile of my very British colleague seated to my left; I was pretty sure it was Noi's last sentence that had him flummoxed. Connor leaned over again, whispering to me.

"Leigh, there's just got to be something wrong with the translation. That simply *cannot* be her answer. No one is 'happy' to be in a brothel...."

So we posed the same question for a second time. And I held my breath as our male translator's voice rang out through the room again, asking in Thai:

"Did you know what you would be doing when you got here?"

Noi looked quietly at our translator. "Yes, I knew what I would be doing." This simple statement was followed by a silence so loud that one could truly have heard a pin drop, and we all waited for her to continue.

"But I'm not unhappy."

She looked around at our quizzical expressions. Out of the corner of my eye, I saw that the first camera man's hand was now shaking on his camera, while the other camera guy was discreetly wiping a tear off his cheek. Quietly swiveling my head around the shadowed room, I noted that there was not a dry eye to be found.

Noi continued, "I'm not unhappy – because all seven of my brothers and sisters are in school. And they have food on the table."

And with that one sentence, this young girl in a brothel caused me to re-examine every single thing I thought I knew about child slavery.

Do I think it's wrong to sell a child to a brothel? Yes.

Would I ever sell my child to a brothel? As the mother of a then eight-year-old little girl living in Southern California, I could not have envisioned a scene where such a question would ever even be posed to me – so certain was I of my response.

But in that one instant, looking at a girl not many years older than my child, dressed in her frilly peach dress and sitting quietly on a chair in the corner of this brothel, I realized that I knew nothing.

Because these mothers in Laos and Cambodia who sell their eldest daughters to brothels? They are not evil – despite the temptation for us in the West to paint the world with a black-and-white brush as we look for someone to demonize in the equation.

These mothers have five, seven, sometimes ten or more children. With husbands who go missing, or get injured, or die. They live in Communist mountainous areas, impoverished regions, denied citizenship and basic necessities by even their own countries – because many of them are marginalized "hill-tribe people." These mothers have no phone, no skills, no birth control, and no way to solve their financial problems.

As I looked at Noi, smiling beautifully through her tears, running her hands nervously over her dress – truly and genuinely happy beyond belief that no one in her family was starving – I realized just how little I knew.

Is it wrong to sell a child to a brothel?

I would ask the reader, if you think you have a ready answer to that simple question, to consider the following: Is it any less wrong or more wrong to fail to sell one child to a brothel … so that the child you failed to sell – along with all of your other children – then starves to death over the next two months?

Is that a ***better*** result?

The families that we so easily demonize are trying to solve a problem – in the only way they can. And I humbly suggest that our inability to relate to girls like Noi – who are "happy" that they were sold to a brothel – is simply evidence of the fact that most reading this were raised in first-world countries.

The real enemy, I learned that day while sitting in a darkened brothel room, is the rampant poverty and lack of skills that force such families to even consider a solution that involves selling one child to save the rest.

Chapter 30

I sat in my hotel-brothel room later that night, after we concluded the interview with Noi. I had landed on a program for my nighttime attire when sleeping in brothels that I was still maintaining: a long-sleeved shirt, underneath a pair of my husband's scrubs, along with men's tube socks – into which I would shove the bottoms of my scrub pants. It was probably a pointless exercise, and I debated the wisdom of continuing to wrap myself in saran wrap over the top of my scrubs.

I knew many of the brothels had not just a roach problem, as I'd discovered on my first night, but also a bed-bug problem. And it was bad enough I was spending two out of every four weeks in such places in Asia – I did not want to bring any unwanted visitors home to my third-grade child and physician husband. I was already on thin-ice with my family, and I figured I would be promptly divorced if I were to inadvertently bring home any hitchhiking critters.

My musings about how much nighttime attire to swath myself in were harshly interrupted by an unusually loud sound coming from the hallway. I was still in Jihadi country, where bombs went off all the time. While I'd been fortunate enough this trip to avoid being in the direct path of any overly-near explosions during my stays in the Deep South, two bombs had been detonated the day after I'd left the region previously. For my part, I'd studiously avoided any mention of this to my family, figuring it would not further enamor them of my work.

But the fact remained that I was always on high-alert when in the region. While I'd thought I'd left the constant-vigilance of my youth behind, I'd since come to understand that old habits die hard.

Hearing another wall-rattling noise, I figured it was better to suss out the source of the sound before I attempted to fall asleep. Opening the door to my room and sticking my head into the hallway, I eyed the usual assortment of grown men with young girls tucked into their armpits as they stood in the door jambs of their rooms, half-naked.

Gazing to my left to check out the rest of the hallway, I was startled to see something slithering along the floor, just where the wall met the carpet. It was bigger than a roach. Much bigger. In fact, it looked to be the size of a small cat.

But how had a cat gotten up to this floor?

As it trundled closer to me, in no particular hurry, a wave of horror washed over me as my mind finally made sense of what I was seeing. It was a rat – a rat that was the size of a small American cat! Holy heck! I yanked my head back into my room and slammed the door shut before he got any closer.

Sitting down gingerly on my bed sheets, I contemplated again my conclusion that everything seemed super-sized in these tropical regions. Roaches were the size of rodents, while rodents were the size of fuzzy felines. In fact, earlier that night, while walking down a dark alley on my way back to my "brothel-hotel," I'd seen two animals running in front of me. As they passed into a circle of light that was spilling into the alleyway from one of the nearby brothels, I noted with alarm that it was a rat that seemed to be chasing an emaciated cat. I'd never seen the likes!

In California, it was a strictly one-way street: cats hunted rats. Not the other way around. But in Thailand, the street cats were uniformly skeletal – obviously starving – and very, very small. While the rats, on the other hand, appeared to be able to grow to truly stupendous proportions.

Briefly pondering the rat who had been hunting the cat earlier that evening, as well as the super-sized rat now residing in my hallway, I decided the smart money was on adding layers to my night-time pajama routine. Thus resigned, I began the charming ritual of swathing my limbs and torso in layers of saran wrap.

A few days later, I was set to fly home. The flight from Narathiwat to Bangkok was just under 2 hours, but I had a significant layover in Bangkok. Most flights to LAX from Bangkok departed between 11 p.m. and midnight, and from there it was a good 25 hours, assuming I could catch a short layover in Seoul or Hong Kong. If I caught a longer one, the flight from Bangkok back to California could be upward of thirty hours. With my 90+ minute flight from the Deep South back to Bangkok, as well as a six-hour layover in Bangkok until my midnight flight home departed – along with its requisite stop in Hong Kong – my all-in flight time was going to be close to 35 hours this trip.

De-planing in LAX, I noticed that I felt like I'd been flying for days. Only to realize, with some amusement, that I had. Just then, I spied my husband and daughter in the terminal. Giving a little yelp of excitement, I ran over to them.

"Mama, mama – how was your trip?" my daughter exclaimed.

"Oh honey, it was... well, a little bit of everything: scary, exciting, sad. But also? Amazing and wonderful."

"Well, mama, you know what daddy always says?" she chirped brightly. I was sure I did know – we'd been married for close to fifteen years – but then again I hadn't slept in three days.

"Remind me, baby, what does daddy say?" I cooed as I endeavored to not rub my fatigued eyes like an over-tired infant.

"He says," my child replied, dropping her voice into a very studious pitch "that fear and excitement are the exact same physiological response. Your hands sweat, your breathing gets rapid, your heart feels funny. Both things happen with both emotions."

She looked up, her voice getting much louder now, "So it's really just the emotion we decide to call it – and when in doubt – it's better to not call it 'fear' and to instead call it 'excitement!'" Proudly beaming up at me with this lesson she had recycled from my husband's grad school days, I leaned over to kiss her on the forehead.

"You are sooo spot-on, my love. I'm gonna have to do a better job of remembering that! And here, I got you a little something!" I said, digging a tissue-wrapped gift out of my large purse.

"Ooh, a souvenir!" my daughter shrieked, tearing the tissue paper from the gift. She got down to the items and started jumping up and down. "Oh mama, THANK you! You know how I just *love* little elephants!"

I'd purchased a white and pink-patterned little elephant from a souvenir shop for my daughter, which was small enough to fit in the palm of her hand, and which also had a key ring on it so she could attach it to her school backpack.

My daughter yelled again, "I just LOVE it!"

I smiled as my husband picked up my big tote bag, and grabbed the handle on my large suitcase, while my daughter attempted to tow my carry-on luggage back to our car in the parking garage. I let them wrestle the luggage on my behalf, too tired to protest.

Ensconced in the car, we hopped on the 405 freeway and started heading toward Orange County. Watching the suburban city scenery whizzing by our vehicle as I fought to stay awake, I was reminded of the Sunday cartoons of my youth where characters would prop their tired eyelids open with toothpicks. I was just about to doze off when we rolled into our driveway, my husband hitting the remote button on the visor to lift the garage doors.

"I'm just gonna leave your suitcases right here to air out," said my husband, who'd exited the SUV and was now busily toting my luggage into our covered patio. "And I think we should take your clothes directly out of the suitcases and throw them straight into the washer," he added.

I moved to pass by him, *en route* to the back door. "Um, yeah, honey, whatever," I replied sleepily, "that sounds fine."

"Um, and hold up, babe," my husband lifted a hand as I turned toward him. "Before you go in the house, well, umm, when was the last time you had a shower – did you get a room in Bangkok?"

I thought back to the blur of my last few days. No, I had not gotten a hotel room in Bangkok. Or on my layover in Hong Kong. In fact, I was pretty sure that the last room I'd had was in the brothel town.

"No, love, I didn't – I've been flying nonstop for days. I think my last room and shower was actually in the brothel town."

"Oh." He stared at me. "Well, I, uhh, I just think it would be a good idea if maybe you showered out here."

"You – wait – you want me to do WHAT??" I retorted, beginning to look a bit wildly around our little patio and the backyard. We did not have a pool, or a pool house, or an outdoor shower last I checked. And it appeared – from my cursory review – that my husband had not installed any such items in my absence.

"You want me to shower OUTSIDE? With what, exactly?" I retorted a bit querulously.

My husband threw a quick and apologetic look over at the garden hose, as a nascent understanding began to unfold in my mind. Apparently, my daughter – clearly not sleep-deprived in the least – had reached the same conclusion but a bit quicker than me, for she yelped out loud, and started laughing.

"Oh, OOH, Daddy, you want Mommy to take a shower OUT HERE?" she practically screamed. "With the little green hose that we use for ***the yard??!!"***

Well, this was just great. It was midday, and now the neighbors were probably going to tune in to this bit of joy. Luckily, there was enough tall foliage around that folks couldn't exactly see into our back yard, but still, voices carried.

"Well," my husband shrugged his shoulders, again rather apologetically, "you know ... I just think it's a good idea and all. I mean, if you haven't showered since the brothel town, well… we just don't want to be inviting any… uhh… well you know, babe… any little FRIENDS into the house."

He looked at me sheepishly, while my mind flitted back to the saran-wrapped evenings. And the roaches… and the rats.

My hubby knew I was tired, and he also knew he was making sense. Deciding to press the point, he said: "I'll just turn the water on while you get undressed, okay? And it'll go fast, I promise!" he said brightly.

I quickly stripped down to my undies and bra, cursing my desire to work in this charming industry, as I realized with fresh horror that it was actually winter here in Orange County. And that my husband had now done just what my daughter had anticipated: He'd trained the green garden hose on me.

My mind slipped back to the 1983 film *Silkwood* where Meryl Streep ended up in a decontamination shower after being exposed to radiation. I gritted my teeth, and heard myself scream as the freezing water connected with my bare stomach. While I'd not been exposed to radiation like the *Silkwood* movie portrayed, the rational part of my brain noted that I was still doing a fair approximation of Streep's performance from a few decades earlier.

My logical brain began to quietly catalog the craziness: of my own voice – screaming like a bloodcurdling banshee. Of the fifty-degree water, as it fell over my goose-pimpled flesh.

And of my daughter, who – for her part – had never known such joy to explode into an otherwise boring winter afternoon. I couldn't really hear her anymore, not over the rushing sound of the water, but I could see her little mouth moving – it appeared to be wide open and cackling loudly.

Yes, the neighbors were definitely overhearing at least some of this debacle.

"Turn around!" yelled my husband.

"WHAT???!!!" I cried, number and colder than I could ever recall having been.

"I said," my husband yelled out loudly, "TURN AROUND – YOU KNOW – SO I CAN GET YOUR BACK!!"

I glanced at my daughter who had now also decided to join the crazy train.

"YOU KNOW MOMMY – LIKE THIS!!" my child yelled, while gleefully doing her best Charades imitation of a ballerina twirling.

At least, I think that's what she was saying – I still couldn't really hear either of them over the hose that was going full blast. And not for the first time, I took in my husband's satisfied smile.

"This," he seemed to be thinking to himself, "will keep my family safe from any bedbugs!"

Vehemently cursing our water pressure which I'd always been so fond of – but which was also now causing the garden hose to have approximately the same volume of water escape from its mouth as a large fire hose – I began to turn my body 180 degrees. I felt like a chicken on a Rotisserie, but colder. A LOT colder.

My daughter, by this point, had given herself over quite unabashedly to the role of interpretive dance-Charades girl. Swirling around and around in circles, like a Rhythmic Gymnast on crystal meth, she was clearly hoping I would eventually mimic her … so that I could more fully experience the benefits of the freezing impromptu hose-shower.

"AHH, AHH, AHH, it's so FLIPPING – C-C-C-CCOLD!" I screamed, starting to dance around in a fair imitation of my eight-year-old. "Yup," the rational half of my brain catalogued dryly, "FOR SURE the neighbors are hearing every word now!"

After what felt like an epoch had passed, my husband finally turned off the hose, which had begun to assume mortal enemy status in my mind. Eyeing the now floppy green hose that posed no further risk to my goose-pimpled flesh, I shiveringly made a mental note to never again fly straight back home from a brothel town. Fifty degree showers in the middle of winter – even in the rather temperate regions of sunny Southern California – simply could not be good for one's health.

Chapter 31

Two weeks later, I was back in Asia. But this time, I was sitting in a high-end private dining club in Hong Kong, meeting with the head of in-house counsel for one of the world's largest banks. We were discussing a plan to attack the human trafficking problem on a macro level.

"Well, the wrong thing to do is nothing," David said. I agreed, but I wasn't used to people in traditional industries, inhabiting positions of power, being so committed to addressing the problem. David worked for a bank that was a veritable Goliath. And he knew that I had also represented large banks while litigating at major law firms.

The waiter refreshed our water glasses, as the conversation moved to a discussion of money-laundering. And how the laws and rules against such crimes might be able to be put to good use in the fight against trafficking.

Reduced to its essence, when a criminal profits from a crime, and then attempts to put the "dirty" money that was generated from his actions into a legitimate institution like a bank, that transaction is known as "money laundering." Phrased alternatively, money laundering is the concealment of the origins of illegally-obtained money, typically by means of transfers involving foreign banks or legitimate businesses. And of course, as most know, it is a crime to launder dirty money through banks.

But what many people don't understand – if they don't work in legal or banking circles – is that there is also a broad set of regulations to which banks must adhere that prohibit *the bank* from knowingly allowing money laundering to occur in their branches. And if the financial institution intentionally turns a blind eye to the practice, the bank can then become subjected to various criminal and financial penalties. My new friend David asked if I'd seen the case involving HSBC from the year prior.

I grabbed a sip of water. "Yeah, I saw it. I think it made the front page of the New York Times, or one of those papers," I replied. "And as I recall, our Department of Justice hit HSBC with an almost $2 billion fine for knowingly allowing the Mexican drug cartels to run dirty money through the American branches."

"Exactly," David paused, slathering some more butter onto his roll. "As a bank, we have a duty to do our due diligence, and to ensure our customers are not criminals who are putting the proceeds from their crimes into our bank. And if we fail in that process, well then the Justice Department in America can slap the bank's hands, for turning a blind eye to it."

I nodded, "So what you're thinking is that if the Justice Department can sanction banks like they did with HSBC – for allowing dirty drug money into the bank – then DOJ could equally sanction banks for turning a blind eye to profits made from sex trafficking transactions that were being routed into their institutions?"

"That's right. And I think all we'd have to do is figure out a way to put the names of the bad guys' into some sort of system that would alert the banks," David replied. "Because obviously, the banks cannot be expected to ferret this out themselves. But if the bank were to come into possession of credible evidence showing that bad guys are putting dirty money into their institution, and the bank then chooses to ignore it? Well, that's a problem – for the bank. Potentially, a billion dollar problem, if they get caught and sanctioned by DOJ."

I nodded again. "Yeah, with as much press as HSBC received when the Justice Department fined them for knowingly allowing dirty money from simple drug trafficking into their branches – well, imagine how much worse the press would be if the source of that money were known to be mamasans depositing proceeds from the rapes of seven-year-old children?"

"Right," David concurred, lifting his hand to flag down a nearby waiter. "So I think if we can systematize this plan, we can get the banks to do the right thing. Because they can't afford the monetary hit from DOJ, nor can they afford the bad press. The banks will essentially become an enforcement arm – by being favored with credible information we provide to them – which will in turn cause them to suspend the bad guys' accounts. Or minimally, take action against the accounts of the bad guys that are running these human trafficking types of operations."

I scooped some more salmon from my plate onto my fork, as we proceeded to hammer out the finer points of such a plan. To my mind, hamstringing the money lines of a $150 billion per year industry sounded like a decent workaround to the problem of dirty cops being unwilling to arrest the bad guys ... due to the fact that said dirty cops were typically moonlighting for – and on the payrolls of – the bad guys.

A decade after that transformative brainstorming session with my colleague in Hong Kong, I'm proud to say that the anti-money laundering initiative, which was just a theory that first day, went on to become a reality – with information on nefarious actors collated, and then routed to intelligence-profiling organizations to generate reports that made their way to 7,500 world banks, in turn enabling such financial institutions to do their due diligence and take appropriate steps against any accountholders that may have been running dirty money into their banks.

Chapter 32

Using anti-money laundering regulations to encourage banks to push back against the human trafficking industry was a clever concept. And it was with such concepts in mind that I contemplated my latest conundrum. The year was 2021, and America, along with most of the world, had been rocked by a series of orders in the wake of Covid-19.

The orders had initially been to lockdown. And then, to mask. And now, in Orange County, California? To adopt vaccine passports.

For my part, I had been quite outspoken about my views on social media, and in county board meetings, and in school oversight committees, and in front of state capitols and courthouses. While I'd researched the actual science on masking and vaccines and obviously had my own opinions, at the root of my concern was the fact that this was a personal liberty issue.

If one was immuno-compromised and wanted to stay home, that was fine. Just don't force me and my family to stay indoors. Ditto for the vaccines and masks: I had no problem with others availing themselves of these items. What I did – and still do – have a problem with is others forcing their "solutions" on me, and attempting to restrict the rights and freedoms granted to all of us in a misguided and unlawful effort to facilitate compliance with such mandates.

In Orange County, California, our Board of Supervisors was almost entirely Republican. And yet, in Spring of 2021, our Board was proffering an agenda item that would mandate that all OC businesses adopt digital vaccine passports, which would make second-class citizens out of any who could not flash such a passport. Apparently, having abandoned all logic, our County Board had also failed to realize that large proportions of minority and elderly groups did not own smart phones and that – by proposing such a ridiculous measure – they were thus excluding even these vaccinated individuals from participation in society (in a way that was disproportionately discriminatory against these groups).

By this point of my career, I was no stranger to totalitarian regimes. I'd spent a good portion of the preceding decade working in southeast Asia, amongst Cambodians who had lived through a Communist overthrow, and with families from Laos and Vietnam that were still living under communist regimes. I'd also studied the Holocaust and the Cambodian Genocide at length.

Throughout my research, I'd tended to gravitate toward first-person accounts, more than the dry facts and figures so often recited by history books. For it was in these personal recitations that I could find the flavor, and begin to sense the climate – the early red flags – that had heralded the impending doom.

While I understood that not everyone shared my work trajectory and personal reading predilections, I was still pretty shocked that so many of my colleagues in America in 2020 seemed to be rather oblivious to the parallels between the totalitarian takeovers of our history books, and what was now occurring in our country – particularly in places like New York, California, and Hawaii (which latter state had arrested – arrested! – the U.S. Surgeon General for walking on the beach without a mask).[71]

[71] Kim, A. (Oct. 8, 2020). *US Surgeon General Cited in Hawaii for Taking Pictures in a Park That Was Closed to Stop COVID-19*, CNN. https://www.cnn.com/ 2020/10/08/politics /jerome-adams-hawaii-citation-trnd/index.html

The last Orange County Board meeting, in particular, had been a flashpoint – especially for those of us who did not sleep through our high school and college history classes. To a person, all of us in attendance were gravely concerned about "passport" systems – for we understood that such systems were how Nazi Germany began.

I'm ashamed to say that – prior to March of 2020 – I'd never attended my County's Board or Education meetings. I'm not proud of that lack of involvement, and in hindsight, I can definitely see the error of my earlier conduct. But the rash of tyrannical and runaway diktats emanating from state and local governments in 2020 had quickly reformed my ways, and like many of my concerned neighbors, I was now spending many Tuesday mornings and Wednesday evenings in county board and county educational meetings.

As I stepped up to the microphone for my turn during public comment in the Spring of 2021, I blasted the Board in a fiery, two-minute spiel with everything I had, reproduced in part below:

> There is a reason our health officer shied away from calling it a "passport system" on air the other night, stating that the term was "controversial." HELL YES – it's controversial!! It is the beginning and the end of Nazi Germany. It is: "Show me your papers please – before you pass!"
>
> It is an ELECTRONIC DOG COLLAR.
>
> And since when did Orange County, California, become the People's Republic of China? You won't need Warsaw Ghettos! I won't be able to leave my house – because no one will service me.
>
> And are you really okay with Big Tech knowing everywhere you've been? From Chipotle to the Post Office to

> Disneyland to your kids' school – because you had to flash your cell phone passport and scan it at every single business you visited after leaving your house??
>
> And do not, for one second, attempt to absolve yourselves, and transition blame to the marketplace – saying: "Oh, the marketplace, not us, are the ones who are going to do this! The businesses will implement this – it's on THEM to do this passport system – it's the fault of Costco or Disneyland for implementing – not OUR fault." That's like the guy who drove the cattle car to Auschwitz saying "Well, there's no blood on my hands – because all I did was drive the train." Unlike you, I'll call this exactly what it is: **This is a NAZI PLAN – and YOU are the new FOURTH REICH if you vote for it....**[72]

By the point in time that I'd laid into my county board over their proposed vaccine passport system, I'd been litigating for nearly 30 years. That board meeting was not my first rodeo. Far from it.

Early in my career, I had actually represented boards just like the Board of Supervisors, because my law firm had litigated on behalf of local cities and municipalities. I had thus sat through more municipal board meetings than I could count – having been the lawyer retained to give advice to such boards when it had questions or when things got dicey during the bi-monthly public board meetings.

To say that my past career had left me with an intuitive knowledge of exactly how hard to hit – and where to find the proverbial Achilles Heel that would typically cause a Board to re-think its position – would be an understatement. And even without that knowledge, I

---

[72] To see the video of that speech, visit: https://rumble.com/v132lb7-leigh-dundas-rips-into-county-board-over-vax-passport-plan-60-seconds-51121.html

knew that with enough venom and logic and soundbytes flying off my tongue, I could often get opposing parties to just stand down.

Walking away from the vaccine passport Board Meeting, I instinctively knew – well before the clip went viral – that I'd delivered one hell of a blow. As had dozens of folks who had also spoken up that day.

But our board had not even blinked. They hadn't seen fit to pull the plan, table it, or kill it. In fact, in the days after their meeting, all that our Board members appeared to have done was activate their friends at the newspapers, who then released some hit pieces on me. Which hit piece included one of the papers quoting a spokesperson for the Anti-Defamation League, who had essentially called me a Nazi for my pointed comparisons between Orange County's actions and that of the Third Reich in the late 1930's.

I pondered this turn of affairs. It was clear to me that big money was coming into our county, to effectuate what was likely a worldwide passport scheme. And I was virtually certain we were one of the first counties to be hit with such nonsense. I was equally certain that – once the bad guys had "taken" our little conservative enclave and forced vaccine passports into place – their poisonous plan would spread to the other counties in California.

We already had many folks in our county who were devoting themselves to researching exactly what people and organizations were funding this totalitarian nightmare. And I knew, given same, that repeating their research efforts was not my highest and best use. A lawyer friend once told me: "Do NOT what you can do – do what ONLY you can do." It was spot-on advice.

And that said, I felt that I had a duty to give my all to defeating this page out of the Nazi Germany playbook. While my family were

Romani and Hungarian on my mother's side, and had escaped Eastern Europe for the safety of America, many of their relatives and friends had been left behind (including my grandfather's oldest brother). Those left in Europe had no doubt faced the Third Reich some twenty years hence, in what became the lesser known Romani Holocaust – a holocaust that, like the Jewish genocide, had claimed the lives of many.

I reflected back on what I had learned about the Romani Holocaust over the years. It was known by a variety of names: the "Porajmos" which literally translated means "The Devouring." And the "Pharrajimos" which meant the "Cutting Up," or the "Destruction." Finally, it was also referred to as the "Samudaripen" – which is simply the term used to denote a "mass killing." Regardless of the name given it, virtually all experts now agree that the Romani Holocaust was the effort by Nazi Germany and its World War II confederates to commit an ethnic cleansing that morphed quickly into an outright genocide against Europe's Romani people.

In November of 1935, Hitler issued a decree parallel to the Nuremberg Laws, which classified all Romani as "enemies of the race-based state." The friends and relatives of my maternal grandfather's family who had not escaped Europe were thereby placed on similar footing to the Jews, and suffered a similar fate: Historians now estimate that between 250,000 and 500,000 Romani and Sinti were killed by the Third Reich. All told, somewhere between 25% and 50% of the estimated fewer than 1 million Roma living in Europe at the time were exterminated at the hands of Hitler and his Nazi party.

So it was with no small amount of irony that I – of all people – should be castigated in the newspapers by the Anti-Defamation League, whose stated mission is to "secure justice and fair treatment" to those persecuted by Hitler. But if 2020 and the ensuing months had made anything clear, it was the fact that logic had long since left the building.

I contemplated my next steps after the Board of Supervisor's meeting, where so many of us had called out the injustice of the proposed passport plan, and where the Board had taken literally zero heed of our concerns. I was a decent communicator, particularly on a microphone. And I'd made fair points. As had many. But the Board of Supervisors had managed once again, through their press connections, to reverse reality: magically painting themselves as victims of the concerned citizens who'd shown up. To quote my child, it seemed like "upside down day" – where the bad guys had accused those who dared to hold them accountable of their own misdeeds.

Well, I decided, resolutely, they could call me an anti-Semite, but I figured they'd have a hard time slapping that label on someone who had actually lived through Nazi Germany's concentration camps. Suddenly, I had a new plan.

Chapter 33

I sat down at my desk – intent on burning through my Rolodex until I found someone who knew a Holocaust Survivor that was still alive and spoke English – in order to poll them and determine their take on this "vaccine passport" system. Even if some of my neighbors in Orange County seemed to not know the role of IBM in Hitler's regime, and how IBM's passport technology was the *sine qua non* by which Hitler had been able to catalog and then erase millions of people's lives, I figured those who had actually lived through Hitler's camps would not be so ignorant.[73]

It took me a good week of non-stop "pounding the pavement" before I finally secured such a phone number. It belonged to a woman by the name of Vera Sharav. I dialed her New York area code and number, holding my breath in the hopes that she would pick up.

She did not disappoint: a polished older woman's voice came on the line. "Hello?" she queried.

I launched into my mini-speech. "Oh, hello. My name is Leigh Dundas – you don't know me. I'm an attorney from California, and a mutual friend was kind enough to share your number." I paused, filling my lungs with oxygen and praying that my supposition was not wrong, before hurriedly continuing my spiel.

---

[73] *Sine qua non* refers to "an essential condition; a thing that is absolutely necessary."

For a thorough discussion of IBM's role in the Holocaust, check out Edwin Black's incredible read: ***IBM and the Holocaust: The Strategic Alliance Between Nazi Germany and America's Most Powerful Corporation.*** (New York, Crown Publishers, 2001).

"If I may ask, Vera: what is your opinion of these digital vaccine passport systems that New York and now California are toying with adopting?"

There was a slight pause, before a voice that brooked no fools started to speak. Her tone was much lower, now, than her greeting had been. I felt the hair on my arms begin to rise.

"Oh… ***that.*** Yes, that plan is a Nazi plan. ***THAT*** is how Hitler started hunting my people down. That – ***THAT*** – is the beginning of the end."

I released my breath in a quiet rush. "I agree. I don't suppose you would mind saying something like you just said, in a 30-second sound byte, that I could lay to a video track, so that we could make a TV commercial and air it here in Orange County next week? In an attempt to get the powers-that-be to NOT adopt this bad plan?"

Again, the pointed and gravelly reply came back over the phone line: "I don't mind at all, my dear. You call me back at six a.m. your time, tomorrow. And here's my email, for the zoom link." Hanging up the phone, I squealed aloud – and ran downstairs to tell my husband that I'd finally succeeded in reaching Vera Sharav.

At 6:00 a.m. the next morning, Vera's face came on the zoom call. She was prompt, and blunt. "I took a look at the sample script you sent me. It's okay. But I would much prefer to use my own."

I shouldn't have been surprised: anyone who had survived from age three to age eight in a concentration camp clearly had a spine of steel, and equally formidable views. I told her I had no objection, and hit the "record" button. Chills once again washed over me as she read her own script – a script that was countless times better than any that I or anyone could have authored. Because it was hers.

Her story. Her words. Her passion.

Her unflinching blue eyes bore into the camera from her well-appointed study in New York City, and she began:

> I'm a child survivor of the Holocaust. One of the discriminatory actions against Jews was special 'Passports' to identify, discriminate and persecute us. I shudder to think that places like Orange County, California, are considering special digital vaccine passports. If enacted, those passports will create a two-tiered society, and deny citizens equal access.
>
> Those who disregard history's lesson? Are doomed to repeat it.

She proceeded to give me three, 30-second takes of the above script. Word perfect, each time. And then? She told me she had a "charity gala to attend," and that accordingly, she must be signing off.

Thanking her for her time, we parted ways. Then I raced downstairs to my husband, handing him the link to the audio-file so he could clean it up.

Looking at me with raised eyebrows, he said: "Let me guess: We're making another TV commercial?"

I nodded. By training, my husband was a physician, and we owned what had been – prior to our governor closing down our state – a profitable stem cell company. Neither of us had ever been to film school.

But I'd come to learn that I possessed a decent eye for scripts and ideas. And my hubby didn't lack for skills in the creative arena either:

In addition to his day job, he'd been employed in high school as a photographer, had taught himself video-editing, and was a drummer. Plus, we'd had the earlier go-rounds making the TV ads in the context of fighting the bad vaccine bill years earlier.

As I showed him the link from Vera, my husband – somewhat grudgingly – agreed to begin working on it. With the stated caveat that I not "breathe down his neck and ask him to make the music crescendo 1/100th of a second earlier" ... lest the new project pave the way to divorce court.

And while I cannot say that my husband was thrilled at the notion of putting our marriage to the test by once again doing a joint-video project featuring a Holocaust Survivor, he was the least resistant I'd ever seen him.

He knew what was at stake. Though he had not studied global genocides to the degree I had, at least he had not slept through his World History classes like some of our (former) friends. Handing him the notes of which video clips I wanted to run, and what music should play during the various parts of Vera's statement, I left him alone to begin working on the first draft of the ad.

A few minutes later, I was ensconced back at my desk upstairs, where I picked up the phone to call my friend, Sandra Brown, who owned the Orange County-based Marketing and PR firm named Brown & Berrey. I asked her to gather quotes for what it would cost to run a 30-second ad, once per hour, during prime-time (from 4 p.m. to midnight) – in all of the Orange County zip codes – and across CNN, MSNBC and FOX, in the seven days leading up to the next Board of Supervisors' meeting.

Sandra called back later that day. "It's just under a quarter million dollars, Leigh." Then, she uttered words that turned my bone marrow to ice. "And the networks are going to need a credit card to hold the slots – assuming you still want the ads to start running next week."

Realizing I had no choice – as the next Board meeting was rapidly approaching – I gave her my credit card information. And then, I went downstairs to tell my husband what I'd done.

"Oh my gosh, Leigh – ***are you high??!"*** my shocked husband nearly shouted.

My "Pookie Bear" – as I fondly called him – was typically the "Type B" person in our marriage. It was I who was normally the dramatic one. But not today.

"Well…" I said quietly, "we needed to pay now in order to reserve the advertising slots…" I trailed off again, shrugging apologetically.

My husband looked me in the eye. "Leigh, the Governor has had our business shuttered for a year. How – exactly – do you expect to be able to pay an almost quarter-million dollar credit card bill in two weeks??!"

My husband had a point.

"Well, I'm just going to go raise the money. I'll – I'll do some fundraisers, or something…." I petered out, once again.

"And you really think the good people of Orange County will backfill the amount of money you just fronted – so that we'll be able to pay off our credit card, in full??" he queried, his face still a mask of shock and horror.

"I do, honey," I said, keeping my voice calm. "I have faith. I don't think most people living in this uber-conservative county are going to want to return to some Warsaw Ghetto era. It's simple. They either help us with this plan, or they're going to have to spend thousands of dollars – or millions of dollars, in many cases – relocating their established businesses entirely out of state. Because if this program gets passed in Orange County, you and I both know Newsom will mandate it for the whole darn state. And of course, that is what the enemy is banking on. Because as goes California, so goes the nation."

I paused briefly, stopping to inhale a ragged breath before continuing.

"Babe, even the *vaccinated* folks I know are horrified by this plan. It's *such* an invasion of privacy – everyone knows that Big Tech will be tracking us even more. Because we'll be forced to leave a digital bread crumb trail like some… like some… modern-day Hansel and Gretel! Trust me – NO ONE wants this thing enacted. It's the worst episodes from history all rolled into one – like the Warsaw Ghetto meets George Orwell meets, I dunno, Rosa Parks. And gosh-darn-it, there's no place for second class citizens in 2023 in the USA! But make no mistake – that is ***exactly*** where we're headed … if we don't stomp these plans out once and for all."

I stuttered to an abrupt stop, shrugging and looking down at my eternally tolerant spouse sitting in his desk chair.

Looking back at me, his calm blue eyes met mine. Then, he nodded, just once, in quiet agreement with my plan. And – not for the first time – I realized just how much love and patience it probably took to be married to the Type-A tornado that was me.

His voice was solemn now. "So you're willing to bet the farm, Leigh? Or, in this case, our literal house – and indeed our entire life as we know it? On the fact that other folks in Orange County will see it your way… and will then decide to help fund a quarter-million-dollar ad buy for one little TV commercial?"

I stared back at him, fire beginning to burn in my eyes.

"Yes," I replied, "I am willing to bet it all. In fact, I just did."

Chapter 34

Back upstairs at my desk, I put my head in my hands. I had talked a good game, but my husband had a point. I had to get cracking, immediately. Or I was going to crash our family's credit rating, among other things.

All told, it took about six fundraisers to raise the money – not the two or three I'd first envisioned. (I'm an optimist – habitually underestimating the amount of time it will take to get things done). But it turned out just like I had told my husband it would: the people of Orange County felt as we did. And they donated to the cause.

And they, in turn, also knew others who were equally horrified that Orange County was flirting with re-enacting a page from the Third Reich's playbook. So six fundraisers and one week later, the ads launched.[74]

And, for the last two days the ads were on air, I'd put a banner along the bottom of the video – asking anyone on our side of the Mississippi River to show up at Orange County's next board meeting ... regardless of whether they lived or worked in Orange County.

As we pulled up on the street adjacent to the County Hall building at 7 a.m. the following Tuesday, my jaw hit the floor. My husband, who

---

[74] To see the ad featuring the Holocaust Survivor that was run on TV, visit: https://rumble.com/v132m75-tv-ad-against-vaccine-passports-featuring-holocaust-survivor-spr-2021-orang.html.

We also ran an ad addressing the digital vaccine passport's discriminatory impact on elderly and minorities, visit: https://rumble.com/v132ndn-tv-ad-digital-vax-passports-are-a-bad-plan-40-of-elderly-do-not-own-smart-p.html.

was driving, could not even navigate our car anywhere close to the building.

"Why don't you hop out here, honey," my husband encouraged as he pulled alongside the curb, "and don't forget to grab the signs and the bullhorn – while I will go and park the car." Pushing the button to open the back of the SUV, he idled in the slow lane while I exited the vehicle.

And no sooner than I opened the door to the vehicle was I inundated with offers of help from people I did not know.

"Here, Leigh, I got that!" some man cried. Another lady approached. "Here, give me that bag – I'll help!"

I was stunned at the turn out, speechless at the offers of help.

Together, we walked through the quad area toward the back of the county hall building. Santa Ana Police and OC Sheriff's officers were already out in force. As was Orange County itself. There were probably close to one-thousand concerned citizens already spilling over the sidewalks and cement pathways. Above us, news choppers were circling – and it wasn't even show time yet. I grabbed a bullhorn.

"Listen up, folks. Thank you for coming. If you've never been to one of these meetings before, this is what you do. Go to the front, grab a speaker card, and put your name down. You fill in the agenda item you want to speak about – which I'm going to assume is the vaccine passport plan...." I paused as the crowd laughed aloud, knowing darn well they'd responded to the TV ad I'd been running.

"Anyway, you put that agenda number down on your card, and then just turn your card in up front. Thank you." Setting the bullhorn down, I proceeded to mill about the outdoor area, talking to reporters and friends who had turned out, in force, as we waited for the meeting to commence. A couple of hours later, I heard from someone that the Board had cut off public comment on the passport item after having had close to 800 people sign up to speak about it. There were now well over 2,000 people in attendance outside the County building. Pissed that the Board had cut off comments, I grabbed my bullhorn for a second time.

"Hey folks, here's the deal. They just cut off comments to our agenda item, meaning you can't sign up to speak on the vaccine passport plan unless you've already turned in your card. So this is what you're going to do instead. If you've not yet submitted a speaker card, you're going to sign up for the 'catch-all' category at the end of the meeting – that is, the 'public comment' section that is NOT specific to any one thing. And then, you voice your opinions about the Vaccine Passport Plan during *that* part of the meeting."

Pulling my finger off the bullhorn mic, I once again thanked God that I had worked at a large law firm. While I'd hated almost every minute of it, it certainly had been a great training ground. Representing a local southern California city during their bi-monthly board meetings, I had spent my fair share of evenings watching the clock hands tick past midnight, then past one a.m., then past even two a.m. – on the evenings when the public had gotten a burr under their proverbial saddle about some issue on our agenda.

Having been on the inside of these meetings, I knew that there was nothing – absolutely nothing – that a board hated quite as much as looking at a mile-long line of upset residents… knowing full well they had to keep the meeting going until every last person had spoken.

My past knowledge ended up proving spot-on, because halfway through the afternoon – and still nowhere close to wrapping up the end of comments on the "vaccine passport plan" – the chairman of Orange County's Board of Supervisors suddenly announced that the Board "could not afford this kind of disruption to their meetings." (Ah the irony: didn't the Board understand that this "disruption" was actually a constitutional republic at work?) As a result, the Chairman announced, the Board had decided to "table the vaccine passport plan" and not implement it.

Hearing that last, I laughed out loud. I didn't particularly care why the Board had tabled its plan – I cared only *that* they had tabled it. We were unlikely to get even the Republicans on the Board who were busy shoveling CARES Act money into the pockets of their friends to agree to do the right thing for the right reason.[75] But we could darn well make them consider doing the right thing for a different reason.

If impatience at the workings of a constitutional republic, combined with the specter of all-day long meetings replete with angry citizens chanting outside, and not least, the knowledge that TV ads were playing during primetime every evening announcing to the Board member's professional colleagues how the Board was flirting with a Nazi-Germany-style passport plan – as detailed by a Holocaust Survivor who survived a concentration camp – if *that* is what it took to get the ball over the finish line? So be it.

I had learned well, from my time in Asia fighting the most hardened criminal syndicates, that you must do what is necessary to handle injustice, so long as it's not illegal or immoral. Now, as of the time of this book's writing, it's been three long years since the COVID

[75] The CARES Act is a short-hand reference to the Coronavirus Aid, Relief, and Economic Security Act, which was a $2.2 trillion economic stimulus bill passed by the 116th U.S. Congress and signed into law by President Donald Trump on March 27, 2020, to partially address the economic fallout from the COVID-19 virus.

lockdowns began, which lockdowns in turn sparked all manner of unlawful and unconstitutional edicts from the executive branches of our federal and state governments.

For my part, and in response, I've largely chosen to NOT file lawsuits: I knew, early-on, that lawsuits in liberal states were more often than not going to be non-starters given the climate we were facing. And I've personally never been a fan of throwing time or money down the toilet. If litigation strategies work? Great – I'll be first in line to push them forward. But if they were going to be 95% or more ineffective in liberal states, as I'd predicted in the Spring of 2020, then why would I undertake them?

The question is not whether I can do a lawsuit, but whether I should. At the end of the day, what sets the great law firms and lawyers apart – i.e., the ones who represent Fortune 100 clientele and are paid $1,000+ per hour for their services – is their ability to get a product. And to create lawful and clever strategies that will get the clients the results they desire.

My first year at a large law firm, I realized that my lawyering skills actually came second fiddle to my ability to provide value to a client. Not only that, but my legal skills were actually less important than my gut instincts, which were rarely if ever wrong. My legal skills also took a back seat to my business sense – which was predicated on the simple concept that you ***do what works,*** and ***only*** what works, and that you ***cease any actions that do <u>not</u> work.***

So while lawyers everywhere from California to the east coast were gearing up in the middle of 2020 to file lawsuits, I was referring them plaintiffs, brainstorming with them about their strategies over lunch … and then? Letting them run with the ball to file their suits. While I remained focused, for once in my life, on doing NOT the things that I can do, but rather on doing the things that ONLY I can do.

And what I do – and do well – is play chess, in real life. I'm highly creative, and I have zero compunction about changing lanes as many times as necessary in order to get the job done.

Persistence is an underrated ability. Persistence pays off. Virtually always. People don't see this as readily as they should, because sometimes, it takes a really long time for a certain path to gain momentum: indeed sometimes, an effort takes even longer than one's lifetime before it succeeds.

And we as humans tend to be myopic. But when one looks at history, I mean really looks, I believe what can be seen is that eventually good people begin to win their battles against injustice – sometimes infinitesimally slowly – but nonetheless in a manner that pushes the dial closer to liberty and freedom.

And so for the last 36 months, I've done leverage moves – not law firm moves. I've out-bullied the bullies. I've named and shamed: trying the tyrants not in courts of law, but in courts of public opinion. Making their bad plans known until they – duly embarrassed by the outing of their moral, legal, or other ethical failings and transgressions – decide to pull their punches (or they are otherwise de-throned from their positions of power, or of their own accord choose to resign their roles due to the pressure of the campaign exerted against them).

I've forwarded one such plan every 30-60 days for three years now. And I've been a 100% hitter – they were all effective. The campaigns I've spearheaded will be recapped in a future tome, but suffice to say, there was not one such plan that was not novel and creative, and which did not capitalize on the power of the masses to ensure victory.

In a word, I've brought to America the lessons I learned on the streets of Asia, fighting a rape-for-profit industry. And as well, I've incorporated the lessons I learned fighting the adult bullies of my childhood.

Too true it is that, in America, we should not have to combat injustices so cleverly and lawfully – and outside the three main branches of government envisioned by our forefathers – in order to ensure our evildoers' plans do not carry the day. But when one is living in a state whose executive and legislative branches are runaway freight trains, what options remain? Leverage moves that capitalize on the grass roots power embodied by the masses are virtually incapable of defeat, when done lawfully and when done well.

Looking back at history, we can see that Hitler changed 400 laws in the first six years of his takeover of Germany – ostensibly to protect the German people from a communist threat – but in reality, to usher in his ulterior plan which was to rid the world of the Jews. And the Romani. And Jehovah's Witnesses. And the disabled, the elderly, the political dissidents – and so many others.

But my Governor? Well, he changed 400 laws in the *first six months* of his lockdown. And in response to the newspaper that took me to task for calling out the parallels between Hitler and Newsom – by stating that Newsom's *modus operandi* was not identical to Hitler's operating basis? My response is that, technically speaking, the newspaper was correct in noting that my analogy was not perfect: Because – by the numbers – my governor is moving 12 times faster than Hitler did during his totalitarian takeover.

And to those who claim that I'm being hyperbolic because unlike Hitler, Newsom did not kill anyone?

First, such an assertion is not an apples-to-apples comparison. Hitler was not a mass murderer in the early days of his rise to power. Second, such assertion assumes Newsom has not killed anyone with his lockdown measures. As to that point, a Mercury News article from September 5, 2020 bears review.[76]

That article correctly notes that Newsom "recklessly pushed to place more coronavirus patients in nursing homes and assisted living facilities – while COVID-19 cases and deaths were mounting rapidly in California's care residences for the elderly."

Put simply: if one truly believed that COVID was highly contagious (as Newsom was fond of stating), and if one also understood that folks in old age homes typically had compromised immune systems (as every adult with a decent IQ knows), then forcing highly contagious individuals into said homes amounted to a reckless act that a prosecutor could well argue was constitutive of manslaughter. Phrased somewhat differently, it's not clear that our governor did NOT kill people in California. And indeed, based on the Mercury News article's reasoning and facts, it would appear that his policies may have been responsible for foreseeable deaths from nursing home residents who fatally contracted the virus from other COVID-positive patients that were ordered to be transferred into such facilities.

More broadly, folks who think that it's inappropriate to draw parallels between the rise of the Third Reich and what went on during the last three years in our country are, in my book, simply unaware of their history. Almost daily, my critics contend it's inappropriate to talk about the Holocaust or make comparisons to it. To me this is nothing short of astounding, as the only thing, in my book, that is

---

[76] The Mercury News (Sept 5, 2020). *Newsom's Failed Response to COVID-19 Nursing Home Deaths.* https://www.mercurynews.com/2020/05/06/editorial-newsom-falters-as-covid-19-nursing-home-cases-soar/

"wrong" with "talking about the Holocaust" is NOT talking about it … such that we ignorantly and accidentally wander into a second one.

In short, there are many parallels between the Holocaust and the events of the last three years, and between Hitler and Newsom. Parallels that we must speak about, if we are to avoid a repeat of history. The chart on the following page gives voice to just a few of them.

Hitler
False Flag Event: Reichstag Fire[77]
Induced fear to change 400 laws in 6 years
Closed all non-essential businesses
Hitler targeted children – not allowing Jewish youth to go to school
Targeted Berlin Police Chief
Used race to polarize, and bait cops to provoke crackdowns on Jewish people that could then be exploited
Deprived Jews of oxygen in gas chambers
Rolled out experimental programs to inject into targeted population toxic chemicals that produced fatal reactions
Hitler forced highly contagious sick people into densely populated camps
Supported programs that caused the "weaker races" to die

[77] The burning of the Reichstag building is a well-known example of a False Flag Event, defined as "an attack … that obscures the identity of the participants carrying out the action while implicating another group or nation as the perpetrator…." Dictionary.com.

The US Holocaust Museum describes the Reichstag event as follows: "On February 27, 1933, the German parliament (Reichstag) building burned down. The Nazi leadership and its coalition partners used the fire to claim that Communists were planning a violent uprising. They claimed that emergency legislation was needed to prevent this. The resulting act, commonly known as the Reichstag Fire Decree, abolished a number of constitutional protections and paved the way for Nazi dictatorship."

United States Holocaust Museum, Holocaust Encyclopedia, *The Reichstag Fire.* Washington DC, https://encyclopedia.ushmm.org/content/en/article/the-reichstag-fire.

Newsom
Virus that is 99.9% survivable
Induced fear to change 400 laws in 6 MONTHS
Closed all non-essential businesses
Newsom did not allow millions of public school youth to go to school
Defunded police & released felons
Used race to polarize: okay for BLM to protest Floyd incident, but not okay for patriots to protest at Sacramento Capitol holding signs that said, "Let us work!"
Deprived 40 million citizens of oxygen over time via mask mandates
Rolled out programs to inject into targeted population experimental MRNA vaccines that were fatal for many
Newsom "recklessly push[ed] to place more coronavirus patients in nursing homes and assisted living facilities" when deaths were already "mounting rapidly in California's care residences for the elderly." *~Mercury News, Sept 5, 2020*
Supported programs – such as transferring COVID positive patients into old age homes – that caused certain populations to be more likely to contract the virus and die

And all these diktats have occurred while our courts have been dismissing justiciable cases out of hand – unwilling to even hear them on the merits. And the state legislatures? They are equally out of control in some of the states. To wit, in California, the Legislature just passed Assembly Bill 2098, which essentially criminalizes free speech of doctors on the topic of COVID.[78]

After the California legislature passed the above monstrosity, Governor Newsom then immediately signed said bill into law, further gutting the principle of free speech in our state. While legal

[78] Legal challenges are currently being brought against AB 2098.

challenges are being brought as of the date of this writing, it remains to be seen whether the appellate courts will rise to the task of putting the brakes on this evisceration of our First Amendment.

All of which beggars the question: What are we, as citizens, to do – when the three branches of government set in place by our forefathers to protect us appear to be failing? I believe that at least part of the answer lies in us, as citizens, putting to use what is left of our First Amendment rights – to gather, to speak, to peacefully protest.

While I never in a million years envisioned that standing on raised brick planter beds at County Hall meetings – and making TV ads with Holocaust Survivors – would be the crowning achievement of my legal career when I exited law school nearly three decades ago, neither do I regret my choices over the last three years to use what is left of our freedoms to mobilize the masses in an attempt to save Freedom.

And while my father was a complex and flawed individual, whose child-rearing skills left a lot to be desired, he was indisputably a great Games Theory thinker, a patriot, and a Navy Man who believed that the best defense was always a good offense. He bowed his head in church, and he and my mom sang their lungs out whenever the National Anthem was played.

In my family, sitting through the Pledge of Allegiance was never an option. Indeed, simply failing to put one's hand over one's heart with alacrity during the Pledge, or failing to remove one's hat, was on par with a mortal sin. Looking back at my upbringing, I can see that both of my parents did their utmost to ensure that I had a good grounding in what freedom meant. And an understanding, as well, that I was descended from people who were prepared to defend that freedom with everything they had.

Chapter 35

Even though many decades have now come and gone, I can still remember my mother taking out the newspaper clippings that had been written about her father-in-law who passed away before I was born.

I was probably around twelve years old the day she first showed me the yellowed and faded article from the 1940's about my paternal grandfather's role in World War II.

"This is your dad's father. He was a Navy man like your Dad. He first tried to join the service at the age of sixteen, which of course was not allowed. I think he eventually either lied about his age, or got his parents to sign a permission slip, but it didn't matter because when they weighed him he didn't make the weight cut-off – he was too skinny. So he went home and ate as many bananas as possible ... and didn't use the bathroom. And after three days of such nonsense," she stopped, looking at me indulgently, as I giggled at the notion of someone ballooning their weight by consuming only bananas, "after three days, he went back to the Navy Recruiter's office. And apparently, he'd gained enough weight to be let in."

I blinked in surprise that the banana plan had worked. I was tall and skinny too, at age twelve. But I still couldn't imagine seriously entertaining a decision to gain weight by eating only fruit for three days.

My mother continued, "So they let your grandfather in, and he was put on a ship called the *U.S.S. West Virginia.* It was docked in Pearl Harbor, Hawaii. And on the morning of December 7, 1941, your grandpa walked out onto the decks from the washroom to see, as he told this reporter in the news article I have here, 'a head, rolling around looking for a body.'"

"Ohmigosh, mom, yikes! So it was like – a headless body?" I shrieked.

"Yes, it was. Gory, I know. As you can see here in the article, two torpedoes had struck his ship. The men, including your granddad, thought it was a drill, until the boatswain's mate – that's the guy in charge of maintenance on the hull of the boat – until that guy screamed, 'The Japs are attacking!' as it notes right here in the article. And then that guy pointed overhead, to where the Imperial Sun image was painted on the wings and underbelly of the planes that were diving toward them from the skies. The Japanese had invaded us, and were bombing the heck out of our Pacific Naval fleet."

I looked at the article in front of her, shocked that people from my family had been so intricately involved in the events I'd studied in school. She continued again with the story.

"So your granddad manned some guns that were trying to take out some enemy planes, until the ammo ran out. Then, the surviving men picked up potatoes and threw them at the bombers overhead – that gives you some idea of how unprepared the US was for this attack. All we had left to fight off the enemy once the munitions on the ship ran out... were potatoes."

I tried to comprehend what that must have been like for the men aboard the *Virginia*. "What happened next?" I inquired timidly.

"Well, the ship your grandfather was on had been fatally wounded. It ended up sinking. And its life boats were being used to transport the men who were severely wounded. Any man who was still upright and ambulatory – even if injured – was expected to help himself survive, or else, go down with the ship. So some of the men threw a cable from the *U.S.S. West Virginia* to the *U.S.S. Tennessee,* which was a neighboring ship. And the men on your granddad's ship started hand-over-hand rapelling themselves over the ocean, which was on fire."

My eyes opened wider at this last. I leaned in, urging my mother with my eyes to continue with her gripping saga.

"You see, there was so much oil on the surface of the water, from the ships that were sinking, that it had created an oil slick, which then ignited from the bombings and gunfire. And that resulted in a burning inferno. It was a literal fire – on top of the water."

I sat in my chair, transfixed, as my nimble imagination filled in the horror of such a scene as best I could.

My mother carried on: "So your grandpa was getting ready to get off the ship, when his buddy was wounded. So your grandfather and another officer instead started belaying the injured off their sinking ship, into the life rafts, when all of a sudden another plane came by. And dropped a bomb directly onto the deck on which your grandfather was standing."

"But he lived, didn't he?" I asked.

"Yes," my mother replied, "through the grace of God, somehow your granddad survived. You can see here in this last full paragraph on the left side of the page – where he told the reporter that interviewed him after the War – that his 'last conscious memory was one of legs, arms and other parts of bodies flying in all directions.' It's truly a miracle he survived. He was put in the hospital for a few days. And then, not even a week later, he ended up on a cruiser bound for

Australia. He spent some months there, when the Navy put him on a transport boat bound for Fiji, which was again bombed –"

"Wait, he was bombed a *second* time, right after the first time in Pearl Harbor??" I interrupted, incredulous.

"Yes," my mother replied. "But that's not the half of it. Because then he had to swim through – look here, up on the top right hand column in this news clipping – it says 'the transport was torpedoed three miles out' and then it says that he 'swam back to Australia.' That's a really long way, Leigh. Three miles might seem like nothing when you're driving or even walking it, but it's a darned long distance in the water, especially in a rough ocean with sharks circling, which is what this was."

My father loved the ocean. And apparently, so had my grandfather, notwithstanding all the sharks and other near misses.

For my part, I liked body-surfing, but I was always cognizant of the size and power of the ocean. I couldn't imagine being bombed off your ship, on the other side of the world, and then having to swim back to a rocky coast with sharks hunting nearby.

"Wow, mom, that's just … crazy – I had no idea!" I leaned back from the table, about to stand up.

"I'm not done." She looked at me. "He got bombed a third time."

"He did??" I queried, sitting back down. It sounded impossible – like something that should be on an after-school television special.

"Yes, he did – look here." And my mom began to quote more from the faded news clipping which had quoted my grandfather:

> We were only 3 days out when we got hit again. This time, from a dive bomber. We spent four and a half days on a life raft with no food of any kind – and no water – only a little Australian Rum. Then a patrol plane spotted us, and a destroyer carried us [back] to the *U.S.S. Boise.*

My mother looked up from her reading of my grandfather's direct words, noting, "And then, if you can believe it, the *USS Boise* hit a reef – but at least it didn't sink!"

"Wow, mom! Like ... just, WOW!" I said, my mind at a loss for words.

My mother smiled. "You know I'm not a fan of the word 'like' as a verbal crutch. Let's try to eliminate that word. But your point is well taken – you are descended from folks who truly do seem to have nine lives. And also descended from people who give a good gosh darn about Freedom. My family did, and your dad's family did. They were willing to flee their homes and everything they knew in search of it – that's how I ended up being born here – and they were willing to fight and die for it, if need be."

She paused, and I felt the house settle. It seemed like even our home wanted to quietly lean in and bear witness to the lesson she was about to deliver.

My mother picked up again, quite solemnly this time.

"Leigh, there are some things that are worth everything, as you'll learn when you grow up. Family. Integrity. Freedom. Family is the support system: without it, we are nothing. Integrity is the exchange with which you walk through life. Don't alloy it, and don't lose it. Because without your integrity? No one can trust you, and you will have nothing."

She paused to take a breath before continuing. "And freedom? Well, sweetheart: that's the most important piece of all."

I looked up again, at this woman who I'd always known was wiser than all my friend's parents with all their degrees.

"How so, mom? How is freedom the most important piece?"

"Well, think about it, my love," she said, bending over to kiss me on the forehead. "Freedom is what allows you to travel. To meet other like-minded souls. To gather with them. To work. To brainstorm. To hatch ideas that will elevate this planet we call our home. Freedom allows us the space to experiment, to try and to fail, to love and to learn."

She tilted her head to one side, and smiled again. "Without freedom, you wouldn't even be able to have a family. Freedom is the foundational bedrock on which everything we know and love is formed. And without it? Why, we are nothing. So don't you ever forget it – and don't ever let it be sold out on your watch, okay? You are its guardian – we all are. And as the heirs to this country's freedom? It's our job to protect it."

I nodded my head soberly, as she leaned over and gave my hairline a final quick kiss. I could not imagine a time where I – a girl raised in 1970's and '80's in "Valley Girl" America – would be called upon to protect freedom. But I understood, intrinsically, in that moment while sitting in my mother's kitchen, what exactly I would be expected to do should that time ever come to pass.

And now, nearly forty years later?

I reflect not infrequently on these conversations, and my roots.

So much of what I believe in, what I've learned, what I've urged others to do since March of 2020 – so very, very much of my passion, my words, my speeches, my knowledge – it came from the first fifteen years of my life. Not from the last thirty.

With perhaps, one big exception.

Chapter 36

It was the Fall of 2013, and my first trip back to Thailand, working in my new position as General Counsel for the NGO. I'd arrived with clear marching orders – to open a physical office for our non-profit – and to train undercover former law enforcement officers to gather intelligence on the child brothel scene in the region.

In the interim, and until such time as our new office was opened, I was working in a high-rise building in the heart of Bangkok, a building not unlike the high-rise in Los Angeles where I'd last rated a corner office, *of counsel* to one of the biggest firms in the country, back in the early aughts.

But now, everyone spoke Thai. Except me. Our in-country liaison, an older gentleman who told me to call him Ben, showed me to the office in his headquarters that I would be using during the weeks I was in town.

"So this is the office. I expect it will be sufficient for your needs?" he inquired graciously. The Thai people were nothing if not polite, I'd learned, and he was quite fluent in English.

"Yes," I responded kindly back.

"Well that's good. And one other thing. I hope you don't think me too forward, but well… we assumed you would need some secretarial assistance. So there's a girl we hired, Jenny, and she'll be starting tomorrow to assist you. She will also help you, undercover."

I was about to smile and nod my head in acquiescence to his plan, but his last sentence threw me for a loop. I was used to undercover law enforcement assets looking like former Navy Seal guys. Largely because they *were* retired Seals, or Special Forces – or minimally, highly trained former municipal law enforcement guys who'd worked SWAT. And I was also used to my secretaries looking like, well, secretaries. Young, and female, generally speaking. My mind tried – and promptly failed – to wrap itself around the image of a tiny Thai female secretary and Navy Seal dude… all merged into one.

"Umm, I'm sorry. Maybe I misunderstood you, Ben. This new gal – she's going to be my secretary, but we're also going to deploy her undercover… like, into the brothels?"

"Well, not exactly. But yes, she's an intelligence asset. She has a lot of data about the child brothel scene, especially along the Thai-Burmese border, and also down toward Rayong and Chon Buri."

I must have stayed blinking in surprise for one second too long, because Ben finally said, "I know, it's confusing, but you'll see. I'll let her tell you her story."

I nodded, and returned to work. I had plenty to do before my plane ride back to the U.S. in ten days' time.

The next morning Jenny arrived, promptly at nine a.m., and introduced herself to me. I scrutinized her closely. She was shorter than me, and much thinner. Which was par for the course in Thailand. I did not think of myself as a particularly tall woman in America – I'm only 5'8" – but in Thailand, I'd learned I was a veritable Amazon. And Jenny was quite young. Seventeen, she'd said?

I stared at her surreptitiously as she worked on some computer cables in the corner of my office. She seemed like a typical Thai woman, except for the slightly younger age. I refrained from asking her about her "undercover" skills – thinking perhaps I had misunderstood Ben. The last thing I needed was for my new secretary to think I was a raving idiot due to some cultural or linguistic misunderstanding.

It was a few days later when Jenny casually wandered into my office and informed me she'd managed to get my laptop communicating with the printer. I thanked her, expecting her to leave.

But she did not. Instead, she hovered around my desk, idly running her hands over the stapler and pens, and then quietly taking a seat in one of the guest chairs on the far side of my desk.

I stopped what I was doing, leaning back in my own chair, and waited.

She began quietly.

"So the reason I speak English fluently? It's because I'm one of those kids that happens when Western men come over and marry local Thai women. My dad is Australian, and he married my mom, who's from northern Thailand. But my parents… yeah, they fought all the time, when I was growing up." She paused, and stared through my floor-to-ceiling windows at the bustling metropolis.

I nodded slowly – I could certainly relate to what that was like.

Jenny continued. "So one day, when I was about twelve years old, they had a really bad argument. I left the house to clear my mind, and walked down the dirt road that our house was on, and took a seat on a bus bench. I went there for some peace and quiet…."

She trailed off, as I could feel the air in my office somehow get heavier, more oppressive. I stilled my body, and nodded once more – afraid that any abrupt movements on my part would give her a reason to flee from whatever burden she was about to share.

"So I'm sitting on this bench when a pick-up truck comes barreling to a stop in front of me. Three guys jump out and – before I could even stand up to run – they grab me, and force me to the ground, sticking a needle in my arm. Whatever was in the needle knocked me out completely."

Jenny's eyes shifted around my office, but they studiously avoided landing on me. Like a scared rabbit, she hovered at the edge of my guest chair, and then resumed.

"When I wake up, I'm a long way away, in an isolated camp in the jungle, literally miles from anyhere. The camp is full of girls – girls from about my age at the time, which was 12 or 13, down to toddlers and babies. What had woken me up was the sound of a gunshot – one of the guards had executed a toddler that was next to me. He killed her simply because she was crying."

Her voice was dead, as were her eyes. There was no emotion at all emanating from Jenny, except a palpable feeling of fear that found resonance somewhere in my solar plexus. It felt as though we were no longer in a high-rise office in Bangkok. Certainly, I was no longer under the illusion that this girl was simply my new secretary.

"The camp was basically a place where brothel owners from other countries would come and scope out new purchases, and they could buy whatever struck their fancy. But the guards? Yeah, they were a whole new kind of evil. And we were just an expendable commodity. So, if one of us upset a guard, we would just be shot."

My gaze did not waver from her face. Jenny was still not daring to look at me directly, but for my part, I couldn't tear my eyes away as she quietly continued.

"One day, the guards just lined us up, like a firing line, and just went down the line, shooting girls one after another, for no reason. And all the girls, you know, when the guard would level the gun at their heads, they'd cry and scream and fall to their knees, begging for their lives."

She paused briefly, and blinked. "So eventually, it's my turn. The guard is making his way down the line, and he comes to me."

At this point, Jenny stops her story and finally drags her eyes to meet mine. I raise my eyebrows in silent question, but Jenny stays mute, turning toward the window again, as a thousand-yard stare overtakes her.

"Jenny," I say softly, "what did you do… when the guards got to you?"

She snaps her head back to me, the room suddenly alive with an undercurrent of electricity. And when she opens her mouth, there is pure venom in her voice, and fire burning in her eyes.

"I did not kneel. And I did not beg. Instead, I stood up."

"I. Stood. Up."

"And I said to that guard: 'To hell with you. I don't want to live like this anymore. Just give me the gun: I'll shoot myself….'"

You could have heard a pin drop. The air conditioning had clicked off, and there was a discernable chill now in the air, but Jenny was still on fire, and her words began to tumble out, one after the next.

"So the owner of the camp, he – he – he happened to be walking by, and he'd overheard me. So he orders me to follow him, and to go back into his hut. And we get in there. And he tells me, 'I've been doing this for years. And everyone – when a gun is pointed at their head – ***every one will eventually beg for their life***. But you did not. And I want to know – why?'"

Jenny stopped speaking again, almost as if seeking permission to continue. I gently reiterated: "Yes, why?"

She picked up the thread again, quiet. And resolute.

"Well, I listened to that voice inside, and I told the owner of that camp what I told the guard: 'I don't want to live like this anymore – give me your gun, and I'll shoot myself, if only to escape.' And the owner? Well he leaned back in his chair, flicked his hand at me, and said: 'Get out of here. You're free to go.'"

With that last, Jenny paused for a moment, and then silently stood up from her chair. As she made to leave, I stopped her.

"Jenny?"

"Yeah?" she inquired solemnly, as she turned her head back over her shoulder to catch my gaze.

"You did good." I said it gently, firmly, and without hesitation.

She lit up. "Really?"

I looked into her eyes, holding back my tears. "Yes Jenny. Really. You did good. So very, *very* good. You made decisions that kept you alive. In a place that very few ever survive."

I smiled, blinking back tears. "And I'm happy you're here. Thank you for telling me your story."

And then – like any child who's been told they've done well – Jenny flashed a thousand-watt smile in my direction, and walked out my door.

For my part, I sat in my office stunned, tears filling my eyes. Reflecting once again on the fact that the path most frequently taken is not always the right path. Contemplating further how, in life, sometimes just when you think you've gotten the important lessons nailed down, there's a new one.

I mulled over what I thought I knew about injustice, and courage. What I thought I knew about "standing up" to bullies, to opposing counsel, to out-of-line bosses and family members. Didn't I know about standing up? Wasn't I drilled in that topic, courtesy of my parents? Courtesy of my law school professors?

Indeed, I had been.

So then what, pray tell, was the missing link that forced my mind to keep repeating Jenny's story at intervals throughout the day?

Was it the realization that courage is always a choice? Even when most people would say they "had no choice" – or when exercising that choice meant to risk certain death?

I'd never had cause to view courage from this perspective, and it was a lesson. One that I knew would not soon be forgotten.

That when you are looking at a locked-and-loaded weapon, full of hate and anger and unfairness that is ready to do you in?

You stand up.

You. Stand. Up.

Always.

For – to quote the famous adage – it is better to die on your feet than live a life on your knees.

I'd always known, deep inside, that courage was an action word. And that we do, indeed, always have a choice – even when we think we don't.

From the vantage point of this writing in 2023, and looking back at all of my business associates and attorney friends – many of whom I've heard moaning and groaning and justifying their obedience to mandates over the last few years with the reasoning that they "didn't have a choice?" That, e.g., they "had to vaccinate," or "had to mask," or "had to keep their kids in online learning platforms….???"

Well, the ugly truth is that we *always* have a choice.

Whether we like the options presented is a separate matter.

In Bangkok, the day Jenny came into my life, and after she'd softly retreated from my space, I slipped out of my office and hit the ladies' room. In the quiet of a restroom stall, I finally let myself cry for this child that God had put in my universe. I did not think that she had ever before heard anyone tell her that she had done a good job. Acknowledgements were so important – why were we as humans so parsimonious with our praise?

I flicked on my cell phone, and looked up the Churchill quote that her story had brought to my mind.

"When in Hell, keep going."

That was a good one, no doubt, but not the one I was thinking of. I kept scrolling. And then, it came into view:

> If you will not fight for right when you can easily win without blood shed;
>
> If you will not fight when your victory is sure and not too costly;
>
> You may come to the moment when you will have to fight with all the odds against you and only a precarious chance of survival.
>
> There may even be a worse case.
>
> You may have to fight when there is no hope of victory, because it is better to perish than to live as slaves.

Yes, that was it. Churchill had a way with words. But I'd never before met anyone who had actually chosen to fight and risk perishing, instead of continuing to live enslaved.

Until Jenny.

A decade has now elapsed since Jenny first told me her story. And in looking back at our pivotal conversation, I can see how, in the final analysis, there are moments in our lives that present as forks in the road, sometimes buried beneath proverbial hard knocks, and less frequently, manifesting as life-and-death choices.

And it is in these moments, if we can find the wherewithal to be still and listen to our own internal voice, we will come to recognize these places for what they are: a wake-up call. A place where the road diverges. A place where one door is shutting, even while another opens.

A place where courage can supplant fear, if only we let it. And frequently, a place where we get to make decisions that will define not only us, but others in our future.

For Jenny, that moment came early in life, as she stared down a firing line and looked evil square in the face. For me, that moment came later, at age forty, in a tiny canoe in Cambodia, when a mother offered me her little girl for sale and I realized that – there but for the grace of God – went I and my child.

The only reason I was so certain I would never sell my child is because I'd had the good fortune to be born in a place where I would never have to confront selling her versus watching her starve.

My work in the brothel towns of Cambodia and Thailand over the last decade have also revealed other, more subtle truths: that while America is overrun with lawyers, vast sections of this planet are enslaved – and literally crying out for someone to help end their servitude and poverty. That entire genders in certain areas of the world have no understanding of the fact that they are people, not chattel.

It was a decade ago that I began to understand, as I approached the halfway point of my life, that I could either pretend that the safe road, the road well traveled – the road that kept me so neatly insulated from the echoes of my own childhood – was the right road.

Or I could have the courage to begin to take the roads less traveled.

In the years that have followed my decision to begin fighting child sex slavery in southeast Asia, I have had many scary, heartwarming, crazy, gut-wrenching experiences.

I would not trade a single one.

For it is in experiencing what it is like to bring real help to a girl in need, or in communicating the stark realities of child slavery through writings and the spoken word, or in talking to the brothel owners that perpetrate these crimes and then fleeing a *coup d'etat* in Thailand as the airports are shutting down – or more recently, in taking on state and municipal governments in the U.S. which seem hell-bent on destroying the fabric of this great country – it is in these moments that I know that I am truly living the life that I was put here to lead.

And truth be told?

It is only in these moments of standing up to injustices that I get to appreciate the beauty of what Nelson Mandela once said:

"Courage is not the absence of fear, but rather the triumph over it."

The End

Post-Scripts

Post Script 1: A good friend once said that a slave cannot free another slave. Regardless of your political viewpoints or background, there are certain truths that have emerged in the last few years which are undeniable: (1) Human slavery is the fastest-growing criminal economy in the world – it is a $150 billion dollar a year industry, with 40 million people currently enslaved. (2) Big Tech-Pharma-Media-and-Big-Government are executing programs – lockstep and globally – that are eviscerating our rights to work, travel freely, and maintain personal decision-making control over our bodies. (3) The above programs are gutting the civil liberties and freedoms found in most first-world countries – which liberties, in America, were enshrined by our Founding Fathers in the U.S. Constitution and the Declaration of Independence. (4) If we are to address this threat before it succeeds in rolling countries back to a less-free existence, and also address the threat posed by human trafficking, we need to ***not*** funnel 100% of our dollars into only the campaigns which are betting that massively-broken executive, legislative and judicial branches are going to become knights-in-shining armor that will ride in and save us all. It's never good to have all of one's proverbial eggs in one basket: we must understand that other paths to victory exist, and start researching and funding those.

Post Script 2: It's just my two cents, but I humbly believe that we are facing the above threats for the simple reason that we did not fully learn the lessons presented by previous historical atrocities. Here are the lessons of our era: We are the heroes we've been waiting for, and no one wins against the power of a people united. So think creatively, think big – and learn more about uniting to win and funding *successful* campaigns at: **FreedomFighterNation.org**

Nobleus

What is Nobleus? Quite simply, it is the answer to some of the largest problems facing this country.

In the autumn of 2021, just after I'd met Jason Sisneros on a Freedom stage, we were having a telephone chat. Toward the end of the call, I remember belly-aching that it was absolutely ludicrous that every person in attendance at the Re-Awaken events ***knew*** we needed to stop patronizing the large shopping platforms that were taking our money and using it to harm us ... and yet? There were virtually no viable alternatives.

"Literally, Jason, I go to these awesome events, and we are all of the same mind: to a person, we agree we need to stop using our dollars to fund entities that are putting their profits to no good use – and everyone knows that whenever we shop like this, all we are doing is the functional equivalent of handing bullets to Hitler. But there's just not a lot of alternatives ... and I'm so darned tired of waiting on someone else to solve this problem. After my last event, I came back with a business card for 'Cousin Eddie's Patriot Super Store' or some such. I was all excited and ended up handing my husband the guy's card while telling my hubs to place our next online order from Cousin Eddie."

Jason chuckled. "How'd that work out?"

"About like you'd imagine, oy. My hubby yelled down the hallway a whopping two minutes after I gave him Cousin Eddie's card and said he was 'on the guy's website' – and that Cousin Eddie was apparently selling '*only* basketballs and hand lotion.' And then, never one to miss an opportunity for a joke, my hubby added that he was 'having a hard time figuring out if he should buy our cats some hand lotion – or a basketball – for the kitties to use in their litter box!'"

The sound of Jason abandoning himself to a few moments of unbridled mirth came back down phone line. "Yeah," Jason finally replied, "that's probably not gonna work so well. Frankly, I was having misgivings from the point in your story where you said that the guy's business name was 'Cousin Eddie....'"

"I know," I retorted, "it's just impossible, and I'm so tired of waiting. So I'm seriously thinking about just opening my own online store, for the good people of this country that actually give a darn about freedom and want to use their buying power accordingly."

"Hmm. You don't say," Jason replied, followed by a moment of silence. "Well, I guess I should mention – before you go off to the proverbial races – that I've been having the exact same thoughts. And I think it would be absurd for us to both waste our time developing the exact same business model in separate silos."

I laughed. And in the next minute, on a handshake and a promise – and a prayer backstopped by the certain knowledge that this country was born on the concept of freedom and capitalism, and that such notions were overdue for a revival – Nobleus was born.

Nobleus is all that Cousin Eddie's store had hoped to be, and a whole lot more. It is an online, inclusive e-commerce platform – selling WAYYYY more items than Eddie ever envisioned – primarily the items the average American family needs and wants (including kitty litter)! Better yet, Nobleus is NOT an online store owned by just Jason and me to run profits into our own pockets. Rather, it is a platform that allows anyone to ***own their own Nobleus store*** – and instantly begin selling goods to their families and friends and work colleagues

– while further allowing that store owner to keep 70% of the net profit generated from their own store's sales.

For the reader who is interested, it only takes a few minutes to sign up, after which you will be provided with your customizable online store – named with whatever name you choose – that is fully-loaded with a million products (and more coming daily)! And the best part is that you do not need to worry about handling all the nightmarish details that give new business owners endless headaches: the payment processing, shipping, receiving, customer communications, and data reports. All of that stuff is handled by Nobleus. All you are responsible for is: (1) signing up for your store, and (2) telling people to quit supporting the enemy and instead start buying their needed items from YOUR store.

That's it. After you do that, you simply sit back and collect 70% of the net profit from items sold through your store. And while this is not an MLM system, folks who refer other store owners do get a tiny referral bonus in the form of an additional 5% of the net profit generated from any stores for which they were the referring entity.[79] As a business model, we have already discovered that this has been a huge hit with non-profit, religious, scholastic and sports institutions – many of which are setting up their own stores to generate what is essentially passive income from the online purchases their existing parishioners and clientele are already habitually making on a monthly basis.

From my perspective, one of the best parts of our whole concept is that folks who care about freedom now have an opportunity to make money in a way that is actually reinforcing the concept itself. I view

---

[79] There is also a one-time sign up fee (that during discount promotional time periods is sometimes waived), and a small monthly fee to cover Nobleus' overhead costs. That said, the fees are minimal, particularly given the 70% upside net profit that exists once your store is open for business. Note: the 5% referral bonus only goes "one level deep" and does not attach to stores signed up under the level of the first store referred.

this as a crucial piece of rebuilding America's future: the ability to give regular Americans – whose financial health has taken a beating over the last three years courtesy of the Executive Branch's policies, and a further beating in many cases courtesy of the mass terminations of jobs held by many people who refused to bow down to the unconstitutionally-mandated experimental injection – the freedom to reinstate their family's financial well-being (and to do so outside the "matrix" of the old institutions that kept us all in an indentured servitude status to some degree).

And for those who do not ever want to procure their own Nobleus store? These individuals can still "hit a homerun for Freedom" by *buying* their family's necessities each month from another Freedom Fighter's store that they want to support.

I believe the combination of the above measures – the selling of items by freedom-lovers, and the purchasing of goods by freedom-lovers – will over time start to erode and eventually topple the monopolistic chokehold which large companies have had for so many centuries over the common, liberty-loving man, woman and child.

Finally, as a nation, it is now evident to me that this is an idea whose time has more than come. To wit, when I first announced Nobleus' soft launch at the Re-Awaken America Missouri event in November of 2022, I think there were only about 1,000 people in the audience. And yet, by the next morning, we had more than 1,100 sign-ups, culminating in 2,000 by the end of the weekend. (To see my speech launching our company, go to: https://rumble.com/v1ugsf2-leigh-dundas-launches-e-commerce-giant-nobleus-at-re-awaken-tour-nov-2022.html).

While I'm aware that I'm a pretty decent spokesperson for the things I believe in, even the best salesman on a great day doesn't close

100% of the people 100% of the time. And they certainly don't close ***more*** than 100% of the people sitting in front of them.

And yet? That's what happened here. Which indicates to me that our launch day in Branson was basically a litmus test designed to elucidate whether Americans were truly fed up with the systems of old. And guess what? It turns out our countrymen had, indeed, "had enough" – and moreover, it seemed that they were ready to start changing their habits, and begin building new ones.

The weekend of our soft launch we experienced what was essentially a ***200%*** sign up ratio. Nobleus had ***double*** the amount of people sign up for stores as were in the audience – which is unheard of no matter *what* one is selling – particularly given that there had been no opportunity for one-on-one follow up conversations or any sort of Q&A afterward.

And that, my friends? Was a beautiful thing.

That was America, batting for Freedom.

That was mothers and fathers and veterans and grandparents, standing up and essentially saying: "I will re-build – from the ashes of these imploding leftist structures – a new and beautiful parallel economy and society." That was family member after family member basically saying: "I will do better by my children – and I in turn will encourage my fellow citizens to do better by *all* of our children – than has been done to date." That was every red-blooded American in the room and then some telling our elite power-broker overlords in no uncertain terms: "We will use the power of a people united – and the power of our dollars – to break the back of the crazy companies that are pushing frightening agendas which endanger our children, and indeed our very nation."

At base? It was the descendants of the great men who founded this country saying on November 5, 2022: "We're not going to take it anymore – and do not even *think* of betting against us – because today marks the day that we become the heroes on which we've too long waited."

Join us, won't you? So that, together, we can hurdle the present challenge – and walk arm-in-arm with our spouse, children, parents and other patriots – toward the *true* Freedom that awaits us on the other side of this defining moment in time.

To make your own mark on history, sign up at: www.nobleus.com/partners/liberty

Or scan this QR code: 

And for qualified investors who would like to get in on the ground floor of this company – or for influencers and/or podcasters interested in owning a store – please email me directly at: Leigh.Esq@gmail.com

Questions for Discussion

1. Leigh discusses the Stanley Milgram experiment on obedience as a lesson in why we must be wary of blindly "following authority" or "following the masses." What are your views on obedience? Is it ever okay to be obedient, and if so, to what, to whom, and in what types of settings? Conversely, are there times during which you believe one should never be obedient – and if so, under what types of circumstances?

2. Leigh speaks of how her mother explained that their ancestors left Eastern Europe in the early 1900's due to the Red Terror death squads that would terrorize the Romani people and e.g., arrest them for "not supporting the government," or detain them for "being of a different political view than those in power." How important is it to be able to hold and speak a different viewpoint from that of the government, without persecution? Is it ever acceptable for a government to detain or arrest people for their views without due process? Is it ever okay for a government to isolate people because they allegedly pose a threat to greater society – as our government did with the Japanese in internment camps in World War 2, or as Australia did in 2021 by forcing people – some of whom were not even Covid-positive – into quarantine camps? How are each of these situations both similar to and different from each other?

3. Leigh notes in later chapters that many girls trapped in southeast Asian brothels were sold there by their families. Why were these families forced (or tempted) to take such actions? Is it ever acceptable for a family to sell a family member – and if not, why not? Can you conceive of any life conditions under which selling a family member might be a less bad alternative than not? And on the note

of trafficking: why are so many communist/formerly communist countries beset with severe human slavery issues?

4. Leigh touches on governmental responses to Covid during the last three years in various chapters. Did the COVID executive orders in your state seem constitutional to you? If not, why not? Were any lawsuits or legislative actions successful in your state at curtailing any Covid mandates that were *not* constitutional? And if lawsuits and legislation were *not* successful in curtailing unconstitutional executive actions, why do you believe that was?

5. Why did Leigh decide to make a TV ad featuring a Holocaust Survivor instead of filing a lawsuit, or pursuing other actions? Was her ad successful? Why do you think more groups are not using the educational power of television ads to leverage the power of the people to defeat tyrannical schemes?

6. Leigh says that she believes in the concept that people who "know more, do better." Do you also believe this? If so, how can you be an agent of change and education in your community?

Extra Credit:

(1) Make a list of the top three topics about which you believe you could help educate others.

(2) Make a list of the top three venues in your region at which you could hold a group educational meeting.

(3) Call the venues and secure a date.

(4) Make a list of whom you would want to invite to such a meeting (students, senior citizens, church members, mothers, businessmen and women…).

(5) Invite people.

(6) HOLD THE MEETING!!!☺

PS: Remember whenever you might be tempted to NOT do the foregoing that: (1) you ***do*** have the ability to make change – it's never too late – all you have to do is start; and that (2) I love you for being willing to try your hand at this extra credit – as do many whose lives you are touching and will touch, and (3) YOU are the HERO that YOU have been waiting for.

Today is YOUR time to shine and make a difference.

With lots and lots and lots of love,

Leigh

Acknowledgments

~~TLDR~~ – Too long and DO READ. Because if one likes the work that people like me do, it needs to be understood that there are a ton of people who help and without whom our work would not be even remotely possible. (And acknowledging them here is the least I could do: they deserve these words of praise and gratitude – and I dare say, much more than this – for the help they've rendered through the years).

At the outset of this round of thanks, it bears stating that even lone wolves don't ride entirely alone. As a child, I detested most groups. To this day, I still have a horrid memory from junior high of being assigned to a group for a project that was worth half of our final grade, only to discover – after the kids in my group had assured everyone they'd "done their part" – that they had not. Unwilling to blow my straight-A track record, the night before the project was due I ended up running around like the proverbial chicken with its head off, frantically doing "everyone else's piece of the project." It's fair to say that encountering a number of such similar experiences during my youth did not exactly endear me to "group activities."

Of course, after the above instances, I then attended college with a group of child geniuses way smarter than me, who actually did do their homework, but who were wired like I was: lone rangers, all. Probably courtesy of the fact that – by the point in time we crossed paths – we'd been trained to work solo or risk being burned by slackers.

Then came the lawyer season of my life. And suffice to say there actually *is* a reason for the plethora of lawyer jokes involving sharks ... which is another way of saying that law school and law firms did not exactly become the antidote to my earlier established fear/hatred of groups.

Indeed, it was only after I met my husband and began working in his office, and after the birth of our child, that I discovered there could be such a thing as a "normal" group (and, even, a "good group"). Where people were actually sane, and supportive, and kind, and – shock of shockers – actually pulled their weight to produce great things. And at the same time that I was discovering on the career-front that such groups could exist, I was also uncovering the same truth on the home front: I and my husband had created our own little group with the birth of our daughter. (Who was and still is an unmitigated joy, and who from the git-go, has always pulled her weight, and more than contributed to the fun times and challenging goals we set for ourselves as a family).

Courtesy of the foregoing, by the time 2020 hit, I knew that if I were left to my own devices to create groups at work or in the personal realm, I could in fact attract and engineer, through intentional design mixed with some good luck, teams of dynamic people who would work well together. But it wasn't until 2020 unleashed itself on the planet that I can honestly say I found "my group." The actual group I believe I was born to be a part of. The group that has already changed history, and will keep changing it for the better. The group that is my ride-or-die. Our group has lots of lone wolves, and black sheep, but dang if we don't make an effective pack.☺

I know who's in this group even when I don't actually know them. Because the people in this group value freedom, above all else. Above even life itself – for without freedom, no one truly has a life … at least, not one worth living. And we are all connected, town to town, throughout this great nation, and indeed around the world. By our commitment to freedom, to liberty, to human rights. By our decision to daily take a stand against injustice and tyranny, in ways both big and small – because it *all* matters. And heads up – if you've read this far? You're in the group – and thank you for being part of this important tribe that I can call home.☺

While this group is big, it is also in some respects small – for there are always subgroups within the larger whole. And as the reader likely surmised at some earlier point in this tome, the first person I came to know in my little "sub-group of people who cared about freedom" was my mother. Now that I am a mother myself, I truly cannot imagine the patience, tenacity, endurance, and love it took to raise … me. I certainly wouldn't have wanted the job! I was high energy, always talking, always questioning, always wanting to know more, and forever begging to squeeze one more minute of action, fun, learning, running, doing…out of every hour of every day.

Indeed, I can remember my mother telling me, as a child during car rides, to "see how long" I could "sit on my hands for." I never understood the point of the activity. Much later in life, it occurred to me that I should ask my mother about her fondness for this strange game.

She replied: "Well, I'd learned early, honey, that you cannot seem to talk without flapping your hands around. You would always talk with your body, gesturing wildly as the words exited your mouth at a mile a minute. So when I had you 'sit on your hands,' that was because as soon as your hands came to rest, your mouth would stop moving as well ... which would buy me sixty seconds of pure peace to hear myself think!"

We both doubled over with laughter. Me, with a dawning understanding, finally, of *why* she had liked the game so much ... and my mother, in shocked amazement that I had not earlier divined the real reason for the game. I've no doubt that now, as she watches me pacing around Freedom Stages far and wide – refusing to stand still for more than about two seconds in front of a podium – she sympathizes from a distance with the poor cameramen whose lives are likely sheer misery as they dutifully try to keep me in the frame for the fifteen minutes I'm on stage.

So while this is a long acknowledgement to my mother (which I will not apologize for, since mothers are rarely thanked enough, methinks): officially, thank you, mom, for putting up with my verbosity ... which I finally found an outlet for in 2020, lol! And for not taming too much the little lion with which God gifted you. I never did well in a cage, and you did your level best to keep me far away from the enclosures both big and small that life can sometimes toss into people's universes. And my gratitude as well for grounding me in freedom, in liberty, in truth, in righteousness, in justice – and for always supporting my efforts to stand up for the little guy (even when it landed me in hot water with the school principal). And not least, for being the first to tell me I would be a writer, and a speaker! While it's definitely taken me a bit o' time to "come around" to that notion, a mere fifty short years into this journey called life, I think I've finally seen the light, and now I'm a-gonna print these words in ink: ***You were right.*** And in case you never noticed, it is your passion, your cadence – and the rhythm of your storytelling and righteous upset at injustices – that I invoke in all that I now do. I wouldn't be me, without you. Love you bunches.

To my husband, what can I say? Nothing I do would be possible but for you. You are, truly, the unseen wind beneath the wings of my efforts. Never refusing to turn a hand to jobs well outside your chosen profession and far below your actual pay grade, so long as they will advance the cause for freedom. You knew long before I did that God had gifted me with "too many words" and that I should find channels to deploy them. I finally found my lane, with your help – and it's way more fun and productive with you riding beside me in that lane. And for the readers who don't yet know? My hubs is my video editor, my typesetter and cover artist for this book, my photographer, my AV guy, my physician, the one with whom I brainstorm, the creative spark that brings our ideas to the next level, and (along with my mom and daughter) my biggest fan. I know I'm not easy to live with, but your patience and love knows no bounds, and I'm a better person for it. Thank you, pookie.

And for my daughter … where do I even start? Other than to begin by stating a simple truth – that, like most parents, I love you endlessly, and that to some degree everything I do is with you in mind. And that's never been more the case than the last 1,000 days.

I know these last three years have not been easy.

I still remember the month before Covid hit, when you came home upset that a history teacher had not given you credit for a question that asked you to describe the Holocaust. As I recall, you'd responded to the Holocaust test question along the lines that it "was an era in history when Hitler and the SS persecuted Jews, deprived them of rights, and placed them in ovens to die" – and the teacher marked you wrong. I remember distinctly your conversation with me after this occurrence – your upset over the fact that you didn't understand what you'd done wrong, and your sense of unfairness about the whole thing given that a classmate had responded nearly identically … but received full credit. I told you that you were *not* wrong and that it was indeed unfair, and listened to your reply which involved wondering aloud if the "issue was worth challenging."

I'll never forget my response to your musings, which was perhaps more strident than it needed to have been for that point in time, but in hindsight, perhaps not impassioned enough … given what I now know was headed our way.

"It may be, honey, that your life is just an endless bowl of cherries. That certainly is what most parents wish for their children: good long lives without much heartache. But it is far more probable that life will be… life. And at some point, you will more likely than not be faced with a big injustice. Maybe someone falsely accuses your husband or you of wrongdoing at work, or your kid of wrongdoing at school. Maybe a government or some other group is out of line, and persecuting you. I don't know what it might be, but at some point, my love, ***the odds are that there will be an injustice.*** And it will be far easier for you to stand up to that injustice and argue for a correct result in that moment if – earlier in life – you've 'cut your teeth' on the littler injustices. You do not want to wait to learn to stand up for yourself until late in life, and have the first time you do it be when everything you know and love and value in the world is hanging in the balance. Far better for you to have some experience fighting the tinier injustices. And frankly, it's often less about the outcome and more about the fact that you chose to go to bat for the truth. So promise me, tomorrow, that you will point out this incorrectly-graded question to your teacher and ask her how in the heck she didn't give you full credit for answering the question the way you did."

And I remember, as well, your pride the next afternoon in relaying that you had challenged the teacher's incorrect marking, and received credit.

Two weeks later, COVID hit.

And there hasn't been a day since that I've *not* thought about that incident – and wished that I could have held back the tide to give you and your friends a longer lead time before the "*not* a bowl of cherries" part of life jumped out of the shadows. You and your friends are now facing far worse than I'd foreshadowed in my little sermon: unprecedented erosions of constitutional rights, changing of languages to accommodate false new narratives, censorship at levels unseen since the rise of the Nazis (or the CCP, or the Khmer Rouge), and endless amounts of psy-op-false-advertising campaigns that are being hurled with relentless vigor from all quarters, at every person in your generation. And which ironically are emanating from the very the people who are supposed to be protecting you: the educational boards, your schools, your own government.

I know as well that my decision to take a bold and outspoken stand against these things has cost you much social capital across-the-board: friends, invitations to high school events, and many other things that I'm sure you've never spoken about to me, because you didn't want to "clip my wings" or "add to my plate." In that, you are a far more mature person than I was at your age (and even than I sometimes am now). Your father and I have no idea how we lucked out: we can take no credit, as you came into our world that way. I understand as well that my work in Asia that began when you were in third grade left a hole in your life, as did my decision to ride on the Arise Freedom Tour, away from you and our home, for one entire summer before your senior year, and that my decision to forward the Nationwide Walkout and spearhead the People's Convoy and so many other campaigns has left me similarly missing-in-action during some of the important times in your life.

And yet, through it all, you have been singularly kind and compassionate about my departures (and I've been aided immensely when I'm out of town by a great husband and the grandmothers – who have never failed to step in and fill the vacancy created by my absence). I recognize that I cannot now undo these decisions I made, anymore than I could have cloned myself at the time I made them. So instead, I pray each night for a continued forgiveness of that which you've already once forgiven me for, and as well for an understanding that I believe you already possess: that in the times that I left you, I did so because I honestly believed that the world would be a safer place for my leaving and fighting … than it would have been had I remained near your side. Perhaps this is merely the retroactive justification of a mother's guilty conscience, but be that as it may, the undeniable truth is that you are an amazing, kind, bright and warm beacon of light, who possesses a wisdom beyond your years and who is wired to stand up for all beings (animals and humans) less fortunate… and I simply could not bear to ***not*** take up the cause of trying to make this planet worthy of the incredible gifts which you and the others in your generation bring.

Know that my love for you knows no bounds and will never die, and that there is literally nothing I would not do to try and protect you. Indeed, all that I've done to date, be it at your side or geographically removed, has been done with the certain knowledge that if the good people of this planet do not stand shoulder-to-shoulder against the enemy at our door, that you and your peers will not inherit the world that by all rights you deserve. In point of fact, you and your friends deserve so much – *so very, very much more* than this planet is currently bestowing – and I won't stop pursuing sanity and justice until things have been righted. I love you, 'Lil Pookie, to the moon and back – most, moster, mostest, mosterestestest, forever and ever. Never be afraid to stand strong, but also do not fear to fly high ... for it is only in flight that the beauty of your wings becomes evident.♥♥♥

And to the girlfriends from the 80's who are still in my posse? You rock. We always had each other's backs, and the fact that this has not changed over the decades warms my heart no end.

To Jason, we know why we fight, *n'est-ce pas?* You're one of a kind: I don't know any donors so distraught by the reality of sex slavery that they actually went out and joined the Navy Seal teams busting down doors to save little girls *after* they'd already donated to the cause. But you did – and my hat's off to you for seeing the need, and filling the void. You are brilliant, kind, well-read, humorous, and fearless when it comes to being the change you want to see in the world. On a different note, my undying apologies for all things blue tarp-related and for stealing you from your 50th birthday party – but that said, we did good work when Freedom urgently called, and I've no doubt we will continue to do more good with Nobleus & other projects. Still don't know just how you found me in 2021 – but grateful you did.☺

To Eric M. and Pastor Dave and my friends up north: you lead by example. You work ceaselessly, love much, and strive always to make your corner of the universe a better place. When you know, you know: what we did moved mountains and changed history. I'm grateful for the opportunity to call you friends, and help freedom ring (or should I say, blow its horn loudly).

To my favorite Thailand pastor: much of this book was a nod to your shining example. Your love for Jesus and heart for spreading his Word is moving beyond description, and the lives you have touched – too many to count – are the better for it. Cannot wait until we see each other again to do more good work. Ditto to all my friends who showed me the ropes on combating slavery – you're a blessing to the children you encounter, and were a blessing to me as well.♥

As the reader can likely discern by this point, I've been graced with great friends, and my luck in this regard extends to my great in-laws. My mother-in-law is never far away: joy-filled, God-loving, always up for babysitting the menagerie of pets my daughter has diligently collected over the years, and for doing that final load of laundry or pile of dishes in my sink. Again, I don't know what I did to deserve you, but my life is saner and infinitely more livable because of your generous heart and hands. And this paragraph of appreciation would not be complete without a special sentence thanking you for being willing to use your printing presses to publish these pages, and get my book out in time for all the exciting events in my future. You rock, and I owe you one.

There are a number of folks I've come to know in the Freedom Fight that I never in a million years would've connected with but for this crazy time period. You are the silver lining of the last three years. Clay and Vanessa Clark: you put me on the map, and helped me find my purpose. Words alone can never repay the debt of gratitude I owe you for that. And not only did you help me out, you've done our country – and indeed the entire world – a huge service by kicking your own behinds every day of the week on a killer schedule to put on the Re-Awaken America events. Never doubt that you are doing God's work, and that you are collectively making one heck of a difference in waking folks up and helping them learn to stand up. And of course, this book would never have gotten written but for Clay's constant encouragement for the better part of the last two years: "Leigh, you need a book." "Leigh, speakers have BOOKS – you need to write a book!" "Leigh, people really like you – and want to know more about how you do what you do – can you just write the darned book already?!" Witty and persistent as all get-out, I have you to thank – Clay – for this book finally exiting my head and finding its way into print.

As regards my book, in addition to Clay and my mother-in-law, I owe a debt of gratitude to my agent, Robert Abrams of Big Ideas Speakers Bureau. I'd written the 350-page manuscript the first week in October when I caught a cold, but thereafter it remained languishing on my hard drive, buried beneath the constant flow of urgent emergencies that hasn't stopped in three straight years. But then – Robert – you found me. And offered to rep me. And discovered my little piece of written work. And convinced me it should see the light of day… and that my stories might just resonate. Thank you greatly, my new friend: for believing in me, advocating for me, and helping these words find a home beyond my hard drive.☺

General Michael Flynn: your courageousness in the face of opposition, your continued bold stand for freedom and justice, your down-to-earth kindness and generosity of spirit – they are each in their own right the true hallmarks of a great leader, and you possess them all. I've never doubted that the world is a better place with you in it, and it's been a joy and an honor to get to know you more as the Re-Awaken events proceed. May the future see you and me and others finding novel ways to combat human trafficking and continuing to advance freedom in the name of bringing more sanity to this planet.

To my fearless female freedom-fighting colleagues, Mel K and Ann Vandersteel: thanks for showing me the ropes and for always sharing a warm shoulder and a kind ear. Thank you as well for being willing to stop everything, down tools, and listen to the people oppressed in this country… and then? To take what they said, formulate a plan, and step up and actually *do something* about it. You are unique, and the world is safer because of your brilliance and tenacity and relentless pursuit of truth.

And to all the friends I've met on Clay's stage and in the Green Room? Charlie Ward, Pastors Artur Pawlowski, Jackson Lahmeyer, Dave Scarlett, Amanda Grace, Leon Benjamin, and Greg Locke, Drs. Christiane Northrup, Bryan Ardis, Eric Nepute, Cordie Williams, Mark Sherwood, Stella Immanuel, Rob Marsh and his wife Amy, Judy Mikovits, and Sherri Tenpenny, fellow attorneys Joey Gilbert and Tom Renz, and Patrick Byrne, Eric Trump, Gene Ho, Dave, Stacey & Colton Whited, Pete Santilli, John Michael Chambers, James Grundvig, the Jacos, Scott McKay, and Tracy Slepcevic, General Flynn and Jackson and Gabby, Mel K, Ann Vandersteel and so many others? You are an amazing tribe. The conversations we've shared over dinner, drinks, campfires, and in media and green rooms have given me hope, renewed my spirit, elevated my game, and left me on fire to do more for freedom. It's truly an honor to know you.

To Florida Surgeon General Ladapo: you are an amazing unicorn (and I mean that in the best sense of the word)! Enough degrees to choke a horse, humble beyond description, with a warmth of spirit and kindness that knows no bounds. You are willing to take decisive action with the gifts bestowed upon you, and you have made thousands of children and people safer, happier, and more free. May God Bless you, your lovely wife, and your children with abundance and more years… because you are one of the honorable ones …

who takes his blessings and spreads them exponentially out into the universe.

To Robert Kennedy: not just I, but the planet, owes you. I've watched you work tirelessly and genuinely on behalf of the oppressed, to make the truth about vaccine injury known, to redress the harms wrought by the pharmaceutical giants in court, to make the world a cleaner and safer place. Because of your birthright, you had no need to do any of this ... and yet? You did. You're a credit to your father and mother, and the legacy of a family that is known for having the best interests of this country at heart. And if I've never said it before today, my gratitude to you, as well, for your kind support four years ago – when we first met, and you encouraged me (an absolute unknown) to say my piece on a microphone to Senator Pan as regarded SB 276. I did not fall in love with Sacramento's politicians that day, but I did fall in love at that Senate hearing with what it felt like to publicly work for freedom, which you have modeled so long and so well for so many. You are one-of-a-kind, and your leadership has inspired countless souls around the world to step up and fight for a better existence. Not least, me. Thank you.

And for all the ladies – Kristina, Ida, AJ, Maureen – who came alongside me over the years, initially in a professional capacity to assist my company in some way, but who underneath the boring corporate labels were actually harboring fellow freedom-fighting inner spirit animals? Thank you for believing in me... even when I didn't. For encouraging me to make that call, stand my ground, agree to make a bold move, and level up to the next season of my life. Couldn't have done the last ten years without you.

And to my OG California Freedom Fighters: Tara and Denise of Freedom Angels, Amy Bohn and the PERK crew and Nicole Pearson, Stefanie Fetzer, the CHD crew, Amy Debby, Lauren, Angela, Kristen, Morton and Marianne and Elaine and Jennifer and Maudi and Patty and Kristen and Laura and Tony and Kim and Louise and Monica and Elsa and Kristi and Vickie and Ashley and Allison and Dianne and Rick and Dr. G. and Linda and Suely and Janette and Shannon and Marisa and Lindi and so many others, and to my pastors Robert & Donna Schuller who stayed open, and to Pastors Rob McCoy and Jack Hibbs who also kept your churches open: ***You are warriors***. I've learned and loved and cried and rejoiced at your knee, on my knees, and by your side. I love you because you never say die, and never stop fighting. We will get there, I've no doubt, because of folks like you.

To Kevin and Josh: You know who you are, you know what you've done, and you've done good. No words can ever convey my thanks… so I'll just try to pay it forward, as you always have and are still doing.

And to the people who worked themselves to the bone – Brittany and Anthony and Matt and Lori – through rain and shine and heat and hell and dust and dirt and broken bones and being left on mountaintops and crawling through trailers and persisting through dead roadies and bugs of *all* kinds and being hit by lightning … through the crazy and the sad and the mad, and all for no pay – or certainly not enough pay – save that which comes from knowing WE DONE GOOD? Yeah, I think it's fair to say WE DID GOOD! I don't know that I'd do it twice, but I wouldn't trade the first time for the world! (And please know that you will be making frequent appearances in the stories I one day tell my great-grandkids from the rocking chair).☺☺☺

And for the other folks over the last 3 years that made heavy lifts possible? The ladies I met in Troncones whose names start with I and L and C, the gentleman whose last name rhymes with "riddle" and who kept me sane and fed and laughing as he rolled down the road, the men like Christopher and Ray who made trucks closing long distances possible and Daryl and crew who gave them a launch point, and the two colonels who had the brains and guts to blow that whistle and the senator who gave them a forum in which to do so? You had my back, kept me sane, and in many cases, chose courses of action that literally risked everything for which you've worked so hard this lifetime. And you did it gladly, steadfastly, without doubt, and honorably – because it was the right thing to do, consequences be-damned … and because your conscience did not allow for anything less. The world is a better place for your brave actions (and it could stand to learn a thing or two from the courage you displayed).

And for the people who have their own jobs and own lives but who drop everything to come hold my bags … and find me water … and keep track of my speech … and hold cameras for photos … and rock locked Suburbans out of the way so attendees can get their cars out …. and who just generally help events go smoothly – to Dhawk, and

Sandra Brown and Lori – my life would be a shambles without you. The cute vision that folks likely have of me of being a collected, well-spoken, professional attorney is directly correlated to me being fed, watered, and having my speech in hand … which I seem constitutionally unable to do for myself on the big event weekends. I'm pretty certain when y'all were in kindergarten that your life goals did not include growing up to help a crazy attorney called Leigh… and yet, you've made time to do just that, repeatedly. I owe you one… make that, a million, lol.

To the sound guys – Avery, my hubs, Mark, Pags and the Devin-Devyns: I'm a nightmare and I know it. I talk loud, I pace and rant on stage, I blow out batteries on wireless mics – heck, I blow out the whole darned microphone itself, more often than not, from screaming into it – I move around way too much, I trip in your cords and yank them out of your amps, and I drag you and your equipment to places that no one in their right and sane mind should ever go. Chased by cops, wild animals, haters, Antifa, and Stasi CHP running riot lines off the Sac Capitol, all I can say is you must like the adrenaline rush and the rodeos, because God Bless You Boys… you just keep showing up, ensuring I'm plugged in and sounding amazing … even when you have to put your amp in a little red wagon, or on a truck bed, or on the back end of my power boat as it sits beside the west steps of the Capitol. As Jackson Browne said in the *Load Out*:

> You "pack it up and tear it down" [and you're] "the first to come and the last to leave… [you] roll them cases out and lift them amps, haul them trusses down and get 'em up them ramps – cuz when it comes to moving me? You know, you guys are the champs!"

What the world likely doesn't understand is that my message is ***only ever as good as my voice carries***: you are integral, valued, and frankly – without you – there would be no message, no show, no victories. I owe you many thanks, and more than a few beers. And the same is true for the security teams that have kept me safe at various events (along with the folks who donated said teams to keep us safe): I will not name you since that would be functionally incompatible with you continuing to do a good job. But a good job – nay, great job – you have done. And not only I, but my hubby, daughter and mother are eternally grateful to you.♥

And to the donors who've funded some of the campaigns? Again, without you we wouldn't have been able to do the good we did, and the world deserves to know that. Thank you.☺

Finally, I owe an extra round of love and gratitude to Holocaust Survivor Vera Sharav and my marketing guru Sandra Brown, without whom there would have been no TV ad – explaining that digital passports were the devil's work and a fast-track to Warsaw Ghetto status. There would have been no airtime for said ad – and it never would've appeared hourly during primetime on CNN, MSNBC and Fox. There would have been no truth being told to 3 million people and firing them up. And without the foregoing? Make no mistake: Orange County would've fallen to a Warsaw Ghetto passport regime in the Spring of '21, after which I've no doubt California would have followed suit … and I equally know that it is unlikely we would have ever pulled back from that brink. Thank you as well to the donors who made this specific TV ad possible.

The history books will remember your work, if not your names.

Because your efforts? Held off tyranny for another day, and prevented a slide into the atrocities of yesteryear.

You did God's work – don't ever forget it. I know I won't.

Yours in Freedom,

Leigh

Remarks From The Virginia Convention

This is no time for ceremony. The question before the House is one of awful moment to this country. For my own part, I consider it as nothing less than a question of freedom or slavery ....

They tell us ... that we are weak; unable to cope with so formidable an adversary. But when shall we be stronger? Will it be the next week, or the next year? Will it be when we are totally disarmed?....

Shall we gather strength by irresolution and inaction? Shall we acquire the means of effectual resistance by lying supinely on our backs and hugging the delusive phantom of hope, until our enemies shall have bound us hand and foot?....

The millions of people, armed in the holy cause of liberty, and in such a country as that which we possess, are invincible by any force which our enemy can send against us. Besides, sir, we shall not fight our battles alone. There is a just God who presides over the destinies of nations, and who will raise up friends to fight our battles with us.

The battle, sir, is not to the strong alone. It is to the vigilant, the active, the brave....

Gentlemen may cry, Peace, Peace! But there is no peace. Our brethren are already in the field! Why stand we here idle? What is it that gentlemen wish? What would they have?

Is life so dear, or peace so sweet, as to be purchased at the price of chains and slavery?

Forbid it, Almighty God! I know NOT what course others may take; but as for me ...

Give Me Liberty ... or Give Me Death!

~ My ancestor, Patrick Henry. March 23, 1775. Richmond, Virginia.

About the Author

Known the world over for her blazing & fiery speeches in defense of freedom and liberty, Leigh Dundas, Esq. is a human rights attorney and abolitionist dedicated to preserving basic freedoms, while also combating global injustices like child slavery and the peddling of medical tyranny disguised as progress. She began her career nearly thirty years ago, representing Fortune 500 companies in state and federal court, before she was offered the dual role in 2013 of working for an anti-slavery NGO as their General Counsel and Prosecutions Director.

In 2020, Leigh took the lessons she learned – fighting Asian criminal syndicates that were hell-bent on destroying children – to the streets of America, where she joined with others to defeat an even greater threat: a second Holocaust designed to eradicate our very humanity, and crush any who would speak against it.

To which Leigh resolutely believes: *Fiat Justitia, Ruat Caelum* ... Let Justice Be Done, Though the Heavens May Fall.

To book Leigh as the Keynote Speaker at your event, please contact Robert Abrams at Big Idea Speakers – Robert@BigIdeaSpeakers.com – or phone (647) 308-7704.

To host a fundraiser in your town benefitting Leigh's anti-slavery or freedom work – or to directly reach out to Leigh on other matters – please contact her at: Leigh.Esq@gmail.com.

Check her out at FreedomFighterNation.org or LeighDundas.com – or on Facebook, Insta, Twitter, Truth Social and Rumble under either of the above handles. And be sure to check out www.nobleus.com/partners/liberty

Or scan this QR code for Nobleus: